J. B. FIRTH

* *

DAILY TELEGRAPH
SECOND
MISCELLANY

HUTCHINSON & CO. (Publishers) LTD.
LONDON : NEW YORK : MELBOURNE

To

LADY CAMROSE

Made and Printed in Great Britain at St. Albans by
The Mayflower Press (of Plymouth).   William Brendon & Son, Ltd.

CONTENTS

		AGE
ACKNOWLEDGMENTS		7
INTRODUCTION		13
1. THE BANNER OF ENGLAND . .		19
2. THIS CARDINAL TIME . . .		37
3. A MUSTER OF BRAVE MEN . .		51
4. LADIES' ASSEMBLY		85
5. THE TIDE OF THE SPIRIT . .		115
6. A COMPANY OF WORTHIES . .		151
7. THE COUNTRY SCENE . . .		199
8. WINGED WORDS		233
9. THE PHILOSOPHY OF LIFE . .		263
10. AUTHORS AND THEIR WAYS . .		299
11. LONDON PRIDE AND PREJUDICE .		335
12. MAN PROPOSES		369
13. TREASURE TROVE		397
INDEX TO FIRST LINES . . .		451
INDEX OF SUBJECTS		459

ACKNOWLEDGMENTS

*

FOR permission to use copyright material the following acknowledgments are made:

To Sir Edward Grigg for an extract from *The Faith of an Englishman* and to the publishers, Messrs. Macmillan.

To the Master of Trinity, Cambridge, for a passage from Sir George Otto Trevelyan's *Life and Letters of Lord Macaulay* and to the publishers, Messrs. Longmans Green.

To Mrs. Wilhelmina Stirling for extracts from *William de Morgan and his Wife*, and to the publishers, Messrs. Thornton Butterworth.

To Mr. Edmund Blunden for a poem, *Forefathers*, and to the publishers, Messrs. Macmillan.

To Mr. E. C. Bentley for passages from *Those Days* and to the publishers, Messrs. Constable.

To the Trustees of the late Earl of Beaconsfield and to the proprietors of *The Times* for an extract from *The Life of Disraeli*.

7

ACKNOWLEDGMENTS

To the Countess of Oxford and Asquith for an extract from *The Autobiography of Margot Asquith* and to the publishers, Messrs Thornton Butterworth.

To Mrs. Alfred Lyttelton for a passage from her account of the Life of Alfred Lyttelton and to the publishers, Messrs. Longmans Green.

To Mr. R. H. Bruce Lockhart for a passage from *Retreat from Glory* and to the publishers, Messrs. Putnam & Co.

To Sir Richard Livingstone for an extract from *The Future in Education* and to the Cambridge University Press.

To the Hon. Lady Winifred Fortescue for an extract from Sir John Fortescue's *History of the British Army* and to the publishers, Messrs. Macmillan.

To Mrs. J. W. Mackail for extracts from Lady Burne-Jones' *Life of Sir Edward Burne-Jones* and to the publishers, Messrs. Macmillan.

To Sir Ronald Storrs for an extract from *Orientations* and to the publishers, Messrs. Nicholson & Watson.

To Dr. Bell, Bishop of Chichester, for extracts from his *Life of Randall Davidson, Archbishop of Canterbury*, and to the publishers, The Oxford University Press.

ACKNOWLEDGMENTS

To Mr. Walter de la Mare for four poems and to Messrs Faber & Faber, the publishers of his *Collected Poems,* in which they appeared.

To Mrs. Montague for a passage from C. E. Montague's *Disenchantment* and to the publishers, Messrs. Chatto & Windus.

To Mr. Herbert Asquith for two poems from *Youth in the Skies* and to the publishers, Messrs. Sidgwick & Jackson.

To Mrs. Edward Thomas for permission to use certain poems by Edward Thomas from the *Collected Poems* and to the publishers, Messrs. Faber & Faber.

To the Executrix of the late Mr. Rudyard Kipling for *The Reeds of Runnymede,* from *A History of England* and to the publishers, The Oxford University Press.

To Mr. Maurice Healy, K.C., for an extract from *Stay me with Flagons* and to its publisher, Mr. Michael Joseph.

To Messrs. Macmillan and to the Trustees of the Hardy Estate for poems by Thomas Hardy; for extracts from Sir James Frazer's *The Golden Bough* and *Introduction to Pausanias* and to the author's representative; for an extract from Frederic Harrison's *Memories and Thoughts* and to Mr. Godfrey Harrison; for extracts from Canon Ainger's *Life,* from Ernest Myers' *Gathered Poems,* from F. W. H. Myers' *St. Paul;*

and Edward Fitzgerald's *Letters*; for extracts from Lord Acton's *Historical Essays* and to the author's representatives; for extracts from Hallam Lord Tennyson's *Life of Lord Tennyson*, and for a passage by Dr. James Martineau.

To Messrs. Longmans Green for poems from William Morris' *Jason* and *Poems by the Way*, and for extracts from Professor Sully's *An Essay on Laughter*; from E. E. Bowen's *Harrow Songs;* from Francis Paget, Bishop of Oxford's *Spirit of Discipline*; from Dean Inge's *Speculum Animae*; from Mrs. Creighton's *The Life and Letters of Mandell Creighton, Bishop of London;* from Col. Henderson's *Stonewall Jackson.*

To Messrs. Constable for extracts from Mr. Logan Pearsall Smith's *Unforgotten Years;* from Mr. Irwin Edman's *Philosopher's Holiday*, and from George Meredith's *Letters.*

To Messrs. Cassell and the author's representatives for extracts from G. A. Sala's *Life and Adventures.*

To Messrs. Methuen for an extract from W. H. Hudson's *Shepherd's Life* and to the author's representatives.

To Messrs. Gerald Duckworth for an extract from W. H. Hudson's *Birds and Man* and to the author's representatives.

INTRODUCTION

THE favourable reception given to the *The Daily Telegraph Miscellany* on its appearance a year ago has encouraged the preparation of a second volume on similar but by no means identical lines. The material is practically inexhaustible.

It is like entering a large garden—formal, landscape, rose and wilderness—to gather a mixed bouquet acceptable to the public taste. One cannot expect each flower to be the particular choice of all; enough if the general eye of the beholder is taken with the beauty and harmony of the whole. Often in the old flower pictures some of the blooms seem somewhat crude in colour and ragged in form compared with their more sophisticated descendants, yet the pictures themselves are still masterpieces of anthology.

Since anthologies naturally reflect at least in part the conditions in which they appear, in war-time they must needs re-echo the clash of opposing principles and arms. Who would have it otherwise? The few who pride themselves on their complete detachment from a war in which all that makes life worth living for free men is cast like a stake upon the table and may be lost in a final throw, are selfish, contemptible and odious. We have watched breathlessly during this autumn the grapple of vast armies continuously locked in desperate encounter at the bidding of a cold-blooded aggressor to whom a daily toll of fifty thousand lives is no more than the sudden swirl of dead leaves in a gale.

Yet, though the war claims all our best energies, there are moments when we must relax and seek refreshment and renewal in occupations and thoughts which for a while keep the combatants at a far distance. It is then, if we cannot escape into the open fields or the woods, that we have resort to books—blessed books in which an east wind loses its bite, the sun warms without scorching and the dragging feet cease to tire. The best literature is generous with its furloughs and relaxes; it rarely fails to supply the vitalising word, the verse or the phrase which will sustain in the darkest hours. It provides, in fact, what the wise king called "the spirit which sustains a man in his infirmities".

Other generations have had their Great Wars, their "decisive battles", their rivers running blood, their fields piled high with dead, their villages and towns scorched into blackened ruins, their people trampled under the heel of the conqueror or carried away into distant servitude. If it is the lot of our age to suffer most, ours is also the distinction of enduring best. Nor, happily, are we under any temptation to compromise. "In England is one breath—'tis Victory or Death."

"To deride patriotism," John Morley once wrote, "augurs impoverished blood." We had our school of pacifist teachers and writers after the last war who, in their zeal for Disarmament and Peace, were lured into "deriding patriotism" as part of the process of "debunking" some wholly imaginary persons whom they accused of glorifying **war** because, having been caught disastrously unprepared so often, they feared to be taken unprepared again by an enemy ostentatiously bent on a war of revenge. These idealists, alas! merely smoothed the path of the aggressor.

I make no apology, therefore, for drawing freely once more from the noble eulogies pronounced in days gone by upon the principles of Freedom, Liberty and Patriotism, and upon the primordial and permanent virtue of Courage in the Council Chamber and in the field. They inspire fortitude: they confirm the faith within us that we do not fight in vain or for a cause unworthy of the fearful price which must be paid for victory.

I have, therefore, been proud to add a special Section consisting of extracts from the speeches and broadcasts of the British Prime Minister, Mr. Churchill, and of the President of the United States, Mr. Roosevelt. The quality of their speeches has never been surpassed in any age: they have the rare authentic touch of immortality about them. We were privileged, so to speak, to attend the *première* of new "Classics" as we listened to a second Lincoln in President Roosevelt and in Mr. Churchill to a third Pitt.

I have not looked abroad for many of my illustrations. Most of the characters in the Muster of Brave Men or in the "Company of Worthies" are British born: they are of stubborn temper: they reveal the strength of fibre which goes to the production of the character that we would fain believe part of the true British birthright. Soft fibres in a world once more ringing with eulogies of force and swinging violently towards reaction have been proved a delusion and a snare.

The passages selected for the Section on "The Philosophy of Life" mainly illustrate the peculiarly British outlook in small things and in great—an outlook free from the special tyranny of logic— and I hope the passages dealing with spiritual matters are no less characteristically British. I have not considered their orthodoxy—that lies outside my province—but I have admitted the widest differences of opinion on matters where the last word has not been—and never will be—said.

The colour of the Country Scene is predominantly English. That is the scene I know best and love most. The Section "Man Proposes" is by way of a lighter interlude on a theme of universal interest.

To the longest Section I have given the title of "Treasure Trove". This collection is as miscellaneous as I could make it. It hides no propagandist design. The Ludicrous and Serious are thrown together at random as in life. The authors, if they could only come together, would make a most remarkable "literary swarry", and the fun would grow uproarious before the party broke up. Each piece has its own individuality. There are good gold nuggets, much fine silver and many precious and semi-precious stones in "Treasure Trove".

J. B. FIRTH.

November, 1941.

I

The Banner of England

*

All that the world can give without Liberty hath no taste.—GEORGE SAVILE, 1st Marquis of Halifax.

O give me liberty! for even were paradise my prison, still I should long to leap the crystal walls.—JOHN DRYDEN.

Liberty is not a means to a higher political end. It is itself the highest political end.—LORD ACTON.

The people never give up their liberties but under some delusion.—BURKE.

Arbitrary power has seldom or never been introduced into any country at once. It must be introduced by slow degrees, and as it were step by step, lest the people should see its approach.—LORD CHESTERFIELD.

No people have true common sense but those who are born in England.—MONTESQUIEU.

I find the Englishman to be him of all men who stands firmest in his shoes.—EMERSON.

I contend that we are the first race in the world and that the more of the world we inhabit the better it is for the human race.—CECIL RHODES.

As for Buonaparte, forget him,
　He's not like to land—But let him!
Those strike with aim who strike for wives and sons;
And the evil boats built to float him
'Twere but wanted to upset him,
　A slat from Nelson's guns.

T. HARDY.

You have accounted yourselves happy in being environed by a great ditch from all the world besides. Truly, you will not be able to keep your ditch nor your shipping unless you turn your ships and shipping into troops of horse and companies of foot, and fight to defend yourselves on *terra firma.*—CROMWELL.

Instinctively the Englishman is no conqueror. He carries his English weather in his heart wherever he goes, and it becomes a cool spot in the desert and a steady and sane oracle amongst all the deliriums of mankind. Never since the heroic days of Greece has the world had such a just, sweet, boyish master. It will be a black day for the human race when scientific blackguards, conspirators, churls and fanatics manage to supplant him.—SANTAYANA.

The only freedom which deserves the name is that of pursuing our own good in our own way, so long as we do not attempt to deprive others of theirs, or impede their efforts to obtain it. Each is the proper guardian of his own health, whether bodily or mental and spiritual. Mankind are greater gainers by suffering each other to live as seems good to themselves than by compelling each to live as seems good to the rest.—JOHN STUART MILL.

> We sailed wherever ship could sail,
> We founded many a mighty state;
> Pray God our greatness may not fail
> Thro' craven fears of being great.
>
> TENNYSON.

THE DAUNTLESS SPIRIT OF RESOLUTION

Be great in act as you have been in thought;
Let not the world see fear and sad distrust
Govern the motion of a kingly eye:
Be stirring as the time; be fire with fire;

20

Threaten the threatener, and outface the brow
Of bragging horror: so shall inferior eyes,
That borrow their behaviours from the great,
Grow great by your example, and put on
The dauntless spirit of resolution.

WILLIAM SHAKESPEARE (1564–1616).
"King John," Act V, Scene I.

*

A PEOPLE BLESSED BY GOD

I look at the people of these nations as the blessing of the Lord: and they are a people blessed by God. They have been so and they will be so, by reason of that immortal seed which hath been and is among them—those regimented ones who are all the flock of Christ and lambs of Christ.

OLIVER CROMWELL (1599–1658).

*

WHEN FREE PEOPLES CROUCH

If King Charles had found the nation plunged in corruption: the people choosing their representatives for money, without any other regard: and these representatives of the people, as well as the nobility, reduced by luxury to beg the unhallowed alms of a Court, or to receive, like miserable hirelings, the wages of iniquity from a Minister; if he had found the nation, I say, in

21

this condition he might have dishonoured her abroad, and impoverished and oppressed her at home, though he had been the weakest prince on earth and his Ministers the most odious and contemptible men that ever presumed to be ambitious. Our fathers might have fallen into circumstances which compose the very quintessence of political misery. They might have sold their birthright for porridge, which was their own. They might have been bubbled by the foolish, bullied by the fearful, and insulted by those whom they despised. They would have deserved to be slaves and they might have been treated as such. When a free people crouch, like camels, to be loaded, the next at hand—no matter who—mounts them, and they soon feel the whip and the spur of their tyrant; for a tyrant, whether Prince or Minister, resembles the devil in many respects, particularly in this: He is often both the tempter and tormentor. He makes the criminal and punishes the crime.

VISCOUNT BOLINGBROKE (1678–1751).
From "Dissertation on Parties".

*

NOT ONE JOT OF ENGLAND'S HONOUR

My Lords, I have in different countries seen much of the miseries of War. I am, therefore, in my inmost soul a man of peace. Yet would I not for any peace, however fortunate, consent to sacri-

fice one jot of England's honour. Our honour is
inseparably combined with our genuine interest.
Hitherto, there has been nothing greater known
on the Continent than the faith, the untarnished
honour, the generous public sympathies, the high
diplomatic influence, the commerce, the power,
the valour of the British nation.

LORD NELSON.

From a speech in the House of Lords,
Nov. 2, 1802.

*

ENGLAND COMPARED TO A SHIP OF WAR

The resources created by peace are means of
war. In cherishing those resources, we but
accumulate those means. Our present repose is
no more a proof of inability to act, than the state
of inertness and inactivity in which I have seen
those mighty masses that float in the waters
above your town (Plymouth) is a proof that they
are devoid of strength and incapable of being
fitted out for action. You well know, gentlemen,
how soon one of those stupendous masses now
reposing on their shadows in perfect stillness—
how soon upon any call of patriotism it would
assume the likeness of an animated thing, instinct
with life and motion—how soon it would ruffle,
as it were, its swelling plumage, how quickly it
would put forth all its beauty and its bravery,
collect its scattered elements of strength and

awaken its dormant thunder. Such is one of those magnificent machines when springing from inaction into a display of its might—such is England herself—while apparently passive and motionless, she silently concentrates the power to be put forth on an adequate occasion.

GEORGE CANNING (1770–1827).

From a speech at Plymouth.

*

NO REFUGE IN LITTLENESS

"We have nothing to dread from France but a rivalry in commerce," says the honourable gentleman opposite to me (Mr. Fox). Look round, Sir, on the state of the world; and can such an argument, even from such a man, need further refutation? "We may be safe and happy if we will but keep to ourselves," says an honourable friend of mine (Mr. Wilberforce), "if we will abjure the continent; if shut up in our own island, safe within the surrounding impassable barrier of the sea, we confine our attentions to objects immediately concerning our own comfort and happiness and cultivate the arts of peace, unmolesting and unmolested."

True, if unmolested: but these pictures of flowing felicity, these exhortations to unoffensive quiet, do they suit the times to which they are applied? Happy times, indeed, if ever they shall come, when we can realise these dreams of independent and unconnected security, when we can do without any intercourse with the corrupt nations of the continent, whose territories are separated from each other by no other barriers but mountains and rivers, and who are consequently unfit for any intercourse with a pure insulated people like ourselves. Then shall the din of war never reach our tranquil shores. Then, instead of traversing the boisterous ocean, at the imminent hazard of our lives, our sailors shall be raised for peaceful purposes on the margins of duck ponds and the towing paths of canals.

But till this millennium does arrive, in God's name, Sir, let us look about us! Let us not seek to hide from our own eyes or diminish in the eyes of those who look to our deliberations for information the real, imminent and awful dangers which threatens us, from the overgrown power, the insolent spirit and still more the implacable hatred of our natural rivals and enemies. Let us not amuse ourselves with vain notions that our greatness and our happiness, as a nation, are capable of being separated. It is no such thing. The choice is not in our power. We have, as my hon. friend (Mr. Sheridan) has well observed, no refuge in littleness. We must maintain ourselves as we are or cease to have a political existence worth preserving.

GEORGE CANNING (1802).

*

THE BEACON LIGHT

Had'st thou but liv'd, though stripp'd of
    power,
A watchman on the lonely tower,
The thrilling trump had rous'd the land,
When fraud or danger were at hand;
By thee, as by the beacon-light,
Our pilots had kept course aright;
As some proud column, though alone,
Thy strength had propp'd the tottering throne:
Now is the stately column broke,
The beacon-light is quench'd in smoke,
The trumpet's silver sound is still,
The warder silent on the hill!

Oh think, how to his latest day,
When Death, just hovering, claim'd his prey,
With Palinure's unalter'd mood,
Firm at his dangerous post he stood;
Each call for needful rest repell'd,
With dying hand the rudder held,
Till, in his fall, with fateful sway,
The steerage of the realm gave way!
Then, while on Britain's thousand plains,
One unpolluted church remains,
Whose peaceful bells ne'er sent around
The bloody tocsin's maddening sound,
But still, upon the hallow'd day,
Convoke the swains to praise and pray;
While faith and civil peace are dear,

Grace this cold marble with a tear—
He, who preserved them, PITT, lies here!

SIR WALTER SCOTT (1771–1832).
From "Marmion".

*

TO THE LAST MAN AND THE LAST GUINEA

I detest croaking: if true, it is unpatriotic, and if false, worse. As to my simple self, I would, were it in my power, blow up the ruins of Melrose Abbey and burn all the nonsensical rhymes I ever wrote, if I thought either the one or the other could survive the honour or independence of my country. My only ambition is to be remembered, if remembered at all, as one who knew and valued national independence, and would maintain it in the present struggle to the last man and the last guinea, though the last guinea were my own property and the last man my own son.

SIR WALTER SCOTT. Oct. 1812.

[From a letter to Joanna Baillie on certain opinions expressed by her after Mrs. Barbauld had presaged the decadence of Great Britain and a flow of American pilgrims crossing the Atlantic to contemplate the desolate ruins of London, while Melrose Abbey was preserved from further decay by the Genius of Sir Walter Scott.]

27

UNDER A DESPOTISM

If the souls of the citizens are debased, who cares whether a city's walls and houses be still upright or thrown down? When free men become the property of one, when they are brought to believe that their interests repose on his alms and must arise from him, their best energies are broken irreparably. They consider his will as the rule of their conduct, leading to emolument and dignity, securing from spoliation, from scorn, from contumely, from chains; and they seize this compendious blessing (such they think it) without exertion and without reflection.

W. S. LANDOR (1775–1864).
From "Solon and Pisistratus".

*

A PULSE LIKE A CANNON

I was given to understand in my childhood that the British Island from which my forefathers came was no lotus garden, no paradise of serene sky and roses and music and merriment all the year round; no, but a cold, foggy, mournful country where nothing grew well in the open air but robust men and virtuous women, and these of a wonderful fibre and endurance; that their best points were slowly revealed; their virtues did not come out till they quarrelled; they did not strike twelve the first time; good lovers, good haters and you

28

could know little about them till you had seen them long and little good of them till you had seen them in action: that in prosperity they were moody and dumpish, but in adversity they were grand. Is it not true that the wise ancients did not praise the ship parting with flying colours from the port, but only that brave sailer which came back with torn sheets and battered sides, stript of her canvases but having ridden out the storm? And so I feel in regard to this aged England, with her possessions, honours and trophies, and also with the infirmities of a thousand years gathering around her, irretrievably committed as she is now to so many old customs which cannot suddenly be changed—I see her not dispirited, not weak, but well remembering that she has seen dark days before; indeed, with a kind of instinct that she sees a little better on a cloudy day, and that in storm of battle and calamity she has a secret vigour and a pulse like a cannon. I see her in her old age, not decrepit but young, and still daring to believe in her power of endurance and expansion. Seeing this, I cry, All Hail! mother of nations, mother of heroes, with strength still equal to the time; still wise to entertain and swift to execute the policy which the mind and heart of mankind require in the present hour.

R. W. EMERSON.

(Replying to a speech of Welcome in Manchester in 1847).

THE CESSION OF GIBRALTAR

Yes and keep it still:
Lean on it safely.

MILTON. "Comus."

Britain belted by the sea
Island of the fair and free,
Thou hast ever gloriously
    Held thine own.

Once the sea was thy domain,
Yea and must be thine again:
Kings who cede can never reign:
    Hold thine own.

Wouldst thou shut the Midland Sea,
Though all Europe hustled thee?
Keep in Tarik's will the key
    At thy belt.

Quote to me no right of Spain,
Right with her was ever gain:
What the Moor took we have ta'en,
    And we keep.

Is it Justice east and west
Rules so widely that 't were best
We should cede our tall Rooke's nest
    By the sea?

What we bought with blood and bone,
We will set our face as stone
To maintain and keep our own,
    Though we die.

English mastiff is our breed,
Free to let blood as to bleed:
But our nature's not to cede
    Though we die.

Christmas Day, 1868.   C. A. W.

*

INTERVENTION OFTEN NECESSARY

Look abroad over the face of the world, and you will find that few are the nations which have, in recent times at least, established their own liberties without foreign aid. Liberty was established for Spain by England in the Peninsular War. The same was done for Belgium by France and England in 1830. The liberties of Greece and Italy were established by the aid of foreign arms; in the case of Italy by the arms, first of France and then of Germany. The liberties of Portugal were, if not established, yet preserved by Mr. Canning in 1826, and by the use of foreign arms. The liberties of the United States themselves were only established, at the date when their emancipation took effect, by the powerful aid they received from foreign arms. So much, therefore, for the twin propositions—that coercion by Europe means war with Turkey, and that the liberties of a country cannot be established by the aid of a foreign force.

W. E. GLADSTONE.

[From a speech in the House of Commons, May 14, 1877.]

31

NEW YEAR, BE GOOD TO ENGLAND

New Year, be good to England! Bid her name
Shine sunlike as of old on all the sea;
Make strong her soul; set all her spirit free;
Bind fast her home-born foes with links of
    shame
More strong than iron and more keen than flame;
Seal up their lips for shame's sake; so shall she,
Who was the light that lightened freedom, be,
For all false tongues, in all men's eyes the same.

ALGERNON CHARLES SWINBURNE.
(1837–1909).

*

WRITTEN AS WITH A SUNBEAM

The sacred rights of Mankind are not to be
rummaged for among old parchments or musty
records. They are written as with a sunbeam
in the whole volume of human nature by the hand
of the Divinity itself and can never be erased or
obscured by mortal power. I consider civil
liberty in a genuine unadulterated sense as the
greatest of terrestrial blessings. I am convinced
that the whole human race is entitled to it
and that it can be wrested from no part of
them without the blackest and most aggravated
guilt.

LORD ACTON (1834–1902).

*

32

BETWEEN MIDNIGHT AND MORNING

You that have faith to look with fearless eyes
    Beyond the tragedy of a world at strife
And trust that out of night and death shall rise
    The dawn of ampler life:

Rejoice, whatever anguish rend your heart,
    That God has given you, for a priceless dower,
To live in these great times and have your part
    In Freedom's crowning hour:

That you may tell your sons who see the light
    High in the heavens, their heritage take:
"I saw the powers of darkness put to flight;
    I saw the morning break."

SIR OWEN SEAMAN.

(Written during the Great War.)

[*Reprinted by permission of the proprietors of* "Punch".]

*

THE REEDS AT RUNNYMEDE

Magna Charta, June 15, 1215.

At Runnymede, at Runnymede,
    What say the reeds at Runnymede?
The lissom reeds that give and take,
That bend so far but never break,
They keep the sleepy Thames awake
    With tales of John at Runnymede.

At Runnymede, at Runnymede
    Oh! hear the reeds at Runnymede:

"You mustn't sell, delay, deny,
A freeman's right or liberty,
It wakes the stubborn Englishry,
    We saw 'em roused at Runnymede.

"When through our ranks the Barons came,
With little thought of praise or blame,
But resolute to play the game,
    They lumbered up to Runnymede:

And there they launched in solid line,
The first attack on Right Divine—
The curt, uncompromising 'Sign!'
    That settled John at Runnymede.

At Runnymede, at Runnymede,
Your rights were won at Runnymede!
No freeman shall be fined or bound,
    Or dispossessed of freehold ground
Except by lawful judgment found
And passed upon him by his peers!
Forget not, after all these years,
    The Charter signed at Runnymede."

And still when Mob or Monarch lays
Too rude a hand on English ways,
The whisper wakes, the shudder plays
    Across the reeds at Runnymede,
And Thames, that knows the moods of kings,
And crowds and priests and suchlike things,
Rolls deep and dreadful as he brings
    Their warning down from Runnymede!

        RUDYARD KIPLING (1865–1936).

TWO NAKED ALTERNATIVES

The war of 1914 was unquestionably a war of liberation. But the democracies threw away their opportunity by their selfishness and lack of vision. For that none of them can claim an alibi.

When the menace of dictatorship raised its head once more, we and all the democracies tried to evade the responsibility of decision. We in Britain can now see clearly enough the consequences for ourselves of our inability to break through uncertainty and indecision until it was almost too late. But in the end, after no one can tell what suffering, we, because we are free men and women, will do what is necessary, not only for victory but to prevent such a catastrophe from overtaking mankind again.

Freedom creates a resisting power greater than authority and in the end adversity may drive the free peoples to see that the application of the principles of constitutional unity and government which were worked out in your great Constitution a hundred and fifty years ago, in some novel form, are the only means whereby mankind can assure themselves of lasting liberty and peace.

We live in the greatest era of history. There stand before us two naked alternatives. On the one side Western civilisation may for a time take a plunge back into a darker age than we have ever known before. On the other we may rise to levels of national unselfishness and vision and

35

dedication which may give mankind the greatest new birth of freedom it has ever known.

LORD LOTHIAN (1882–1940).
From a Speech to the English Speaking Union at New York, May 11, 1940.

NEAR DOVER
(*September*, 1802)

Inland, within a hollow vale, I stood;
And saw, while sea was calm and air was clear,
The coast of France—the coast of France, how
    near!
Drawn almost into frightful neighbourhood.
I shrank; for verily the barrier flood
Was like a lake, or river bright and fair,
A span of waters; yet what power is there!
What mightiness for evil and for good!
Even so doth God protect us if we be
Virtuous and wise. Winds blow and waters roll,
Strength to the brave, and Power, and Deity;
Yet in themselves are nothing! One decree
Spake laws to *them*, and said that by the soul
Only, the nations shall be great and free.

W. WORDSWORTH (1770–1850).

*

II

This Cardinal Time

*

No parleying now!   In Britain is one breath;
We are all with you now from shore to shore:
Ye men of Kent, 'tis victory or death.
                                    WORDSWORTH (1803).

The success of the superb British morale is in the masses
of the British people, who are completely clear in their
minds about the one central fact that they would rather
die as free men than live as slaves.
                                    PRESIDENT ROOSEVELT.
                                    March 15, 1941.

Our aid to the resisting nations is not the mere crusading
of a world benefactor.   It is based on the definite knowledge
that every free nation everywhere is a bastion of strength
to all remaining free peoples everywhere.
                CORDELL HULL, U.S. Secretary of State.
                                    April 25, 1941.

Give me leave to tell you that I do not believe that in
any war that ever was in former times, nor in any engage-
ments that you have had with others, this Nation had
more obligations upon them to look to itself—to forbear
waste of time, precious time!—OLIVER CROWMELL (1656).

You have become a leading nation. . . .   In the great
battle which is fought throughout the world between right
and wrong, justice and arbitrary rule, equality and privilege,
duty and egotism, republic and monarchy, truth and lies,
God and idols, your part is marked.   You must accept
it.—MAZZINI.
[From an open letter to the American people.]

THIS CARDINAL TIME

When an extreme case calls for a remedy which is in its own nature most violent, and which, in such cases, is a remedy only because it is violent, it is idle to think of mitigating and diluting. Languid war can do nothing which negotiation or submission will not do better; and to act on any other principle is not to save blood and money, but to squander them.—MACAULAY.

> Stick to your aim; the mongrel's hold will slip,
> But only crow-bars loose the bull-dog's lip;
> Small as he looks, the jaw that never yields
> Drags down the bellowing monarch of the fields.
>   O. W. HOLMES.

It is always better to lose a thing by force than from the fear of force: for if you give up a thing through fear you do it to avoid a war, and most times you do not so avoid it. For the man to whom you have granted this by an act of open cowardice will not stop at this one thing, but will desire to take others from you also, and will be all the bolder against you in that he respects you less.—MACHIAVELLI.

My outstanding impression of England to-day is that of the courage, the action, the endurance of her women. Wherever I go I see them, and I marvel.
                        THE RIGHT HON. ROBERT G. MENZIES.
                        (Prime Minister of Australia.)

> Another Athens shall arise,
>   And to remoter time
> Bequeath, like sunset to the skies,
>   The splendour of its prime;
> And leave, if naught so bright may live,
> All earth can take or Heaven can give.
>   SHELLEY.

*

38

"LET IT ROLL!"

Undoubtedly this process of Anglo-American co-operation means that these two great organizations of the English-speaking democracies, the British Empire and the United States, will have to be somewhat mixed up together in some of their affairs for mutual and general advantage. For my own part, looking out upon the future, I do not view the process with any misgivings. I could not stop it if I wished; no one can stop it. Like the Mississippi, it just keeps rolling along. Let it roll! Let it roll on full flood, inexorable, irresistible, benignant, to broader lands and better days!

RT. HON. WINSTON CHURCHILL.
Aug. 20, 1940.

*

THE STARS PROCLAIM MANKIND'S DELIVERANCE

The destiny of mankind is not decided by material computation. When great causes are on the move in the world, stirring all men's souls, drawing them from their firesides, casting aside comfort, wealth and the pursuit of happiness in response to impulses at once awestriking and irresistible, we learn that we are spirits, not animals, and that something is going on in space and time, which, whether we like it or not, spells Duty.

A wonderful story is unfolding before our eyes.

39

How it will end, we are not allowed to know. But on both sides of the Atlantic we all feel, I repeat all, that we are a part of it, that our future and that of many generations is at stake. We are sure that the character of human society will be shaped by the resolves we take and the deeds we do.

We need not bewail the fact that we have been called upon to face such solemn responsibilities. We may be proud, and even rejoice amid our tribulations, that we have been born at this cardinal time for so great an age and so splendid an opportunity of service here below.

Wickedness, enormous, panoplied, embattled, seemingly triumphant, casts its shadow over Europe and Asia. Laws, customs and traditions are broken up. Justice is cast from her seat. The rights of the weak are trampled down. The grand freedoms of which the President of the United States has spoken so movingly, are spurned and chained. The whole stature of man, his genius, his initiative and his nobility, is ground down under systems of mechanical barbarism and of organised and scheduled terror.

For more than a year we British have stood alone, uplifted by your sympathy and respect and sustained by our own unconquerable will-power, and by the increasing growth and hopes of your massive aid. In these British islands, that look so small upon the map, we stand, the faithful guardians of the rights and dearest hopes of a dozen States and nations now gripped and tormented in a base and cruel servitude. Whatever happens we shall endure to the end.

But what is the explanation of the enslavement of Europe by the German Nazi régime? How did they do it? It is but a few years ago since one united gesture by the peoples, great and small, who are now broken in the dust, would have warded off from mankind the fearful ordeal it has had to undergo. But there was no unity. There was no vision. The nations were pulled down one by one while the others gaped and chattered. One by one, each in his turn, they let themselves be caught. One after another they were felled by brutal violence or poisoned from within by subtle intrigue.

And now the old lion with her lion cubs at her side stands alone against hunters who are armed with deadly weapons and impelled by desperate and destructive rage. Is the tragedy to repeat itself once more? Ah no! This is not the end of the tale. The stars in their courses proclaim the deliverance of mankind. Not so easily shall the onward progress of the peoples be barred. Not so easily shall the lights of freedom die.

But time is short. Every month that passes adds to the length and to the perils of the journey that will have to be made. United we stand, divided we fall. Divided, the dark age returns. United, we can save and guide the world.

RT. HON. WINSTON CHURCHILL.

[From his broadcast on receiving the Doctorate of Laws of Rochester University, U.S.A., June, 1941.]

"OUR SOLID STUBBORN STRENGTH"

A year ago his Majesty's Government was left alone to face the storm, and to many of our friends and enemies alike it may have seemed that our days, too, were numbered and that Britain and its institutions would sink for ever beneath the verge. But even in that dark hour, when our Army was disorganised and almost weaponless, when scarcely a gun or a tank remained in Britain, when almost all our stores and ammunition had been lost in France, never for one moment did the British people dream of making peace with the conqueror and never for a moment did they despair of the common cause.

On the contrary, we proclaimed to all men, not only to ourselves, our determination not to make peace until every one of the ravaged and enslaved countries was liberated, and until the Nazi domination was broken and destroyed.

See how far we have travelled since those breathless days of June a year ago. Our solid, stubborn strength has stood the awful test. We are masters of our own air, and now reach out in ever-growing retribution upon the enemy. The Royal Navy holds the seas. The Italian fleet cowers, diminished, in harbour; the German navy is largely crippled or sunk. The murderous raids upon our ports, cities and factories have been powerless to quench the spirit of the British nation, to stop our national life or check the immense expansion of our war industry. The food and arms from across the oceans are coming safely in. Full provision to replace all sunken tonnage is being made here, and still more by our friends in the United States. We are becoming an armed community. Our land forces are being perfected in equipment and training.

Hitler may turn and trample this way and that through tortured Europe. He may spread his course far and wide, and carry his curse with him; he may break into Africa or into Asia. But, it is here, in this island fortress, that he will have to reckon in the end.

We shall strive to resist by land and sea. We shall be on his track wherever he goes. Our air power will continue to teach the German homeland that war is not all loot and triumph. We shall aid and stir the people of every conquered country to resistance and revolt.

We shall break up and derange every effort which Hitler makes to systematise and consolidate his subjugations. He will find no peace, no rest, no halting place, no parley. And if, driven to desperate hazards, he attempts the invasion of the British Isles, as well he may, we shall not flinch from the supreme trial. With the help of God, of which we must all feel daily conscious, we shall continue steadfast in faith and duty till our task is done.

RT. HON. WINSTON CHURCHILL.

[From a Speech to Representatives of the Dominion and Allied Governments at St. James's Palace, June 12, 1941.]

THE ATLANTIC MEETING OF PRESIDENT ROOSEVELT AND MR. CHURCHILL

The meeting was symbolic. That is its prime importance. It symbolised in a form and manner which everyone can understand in every land and in every clime, the deep underlying unities which stir and at decisive moments rule the English-speaking peoples throughout the world.

Would it be presumptuous for me to say that it symbolises something even more majestic, namely, the marshalling of the good forces of the world against the evil forces which are now so formidable and triumphant, and have cast their cruel spell over the whole of Europe and a large part of Asia?

This was a meeting which marks for ever in the pages of history the taking up by the English-speaking nations amid all this peril, tumult and confusion, of the guidance of the fortunes of the broad, toiling masses in all the continents, and our loyal effort, without any clog of selfish interest, to lead them forward out of the miseries into which they have been plunged, back to the broad high-road of freedom and justice.

This is the highest honour and the most glorious opportunity which could ever have come to any branch of the human race.

When one beholds how many currents of extraordinary and terrible events have flowed together to make this harmony, even the most

44

sceptical person must have the feeling that we all have the chance to play our part and do our duty in some great design, the end of which no mortal can foresee.

RT. HON. WINSTON CHURCHILL.

From a Broadcast, Aug. 27, 1941.

*

THE PHILOSOPHY OF FORCE

We see to-day in stark reality some of the consequences of what we call the Machine Age. Where control of machines has been retained in the hands of mankind as a whole untold benefits have accrued to mankind. For mankind was then a master and the machine was the servant. But in this new system of force the mastery of the machine is not in the hands of mankind; it is in the control of infinitely small groups of individuals who are without a single one of the democratic sanctions that we have known. The machine in the hands of irresponsible conquerors becomes the master; mankind is not only the servant, it is the victim, too.

Surely the new philosophy proves from month to month that it has no possible conception of the will of life, of way, of thought, of a nation whose origins go back to Jamestown and Plymouth Rock; and, conversely, neither those who sprang from that ancient stock nor those who have come hither in later years can be indifferent to the destruction

45

of freedom in their ancestral lands across the sea.

Some indeed still hold to the now somewhat obvious delusion that we of the United States can safely permit the United States to become a lone island—a lone island in a world dominated by the philosophy of force. Such an island may be the dream of those who have still thought and voted as Isolationists. Such an island represents to me and to the overwhelming majority of Americans to-day a helpless nightmare—the helpless nightmare of a people without friends. Yes, the nightmare of a people lodged in prison, handcuffed, hungry and fed through the bars from day to day by the contemptuous, unpitying masters of other continents.

PRESIDENT ROOSEVELT
June, 1940.

*

FOUR ESSENTIAL FREEDOMS

In the future days that we seek to make secure, we look forward to a world founded upon four essential freedoms.

The first is freedom of speech and expression—everywhere in the world.

The second is freedom for every person to worship God in his own way—everywhere in the world.

The third is freedom from want which, translated into world terms, means economic understandings which will secure to every nation a healthy peace-time life for its inhabitants—everywhere in the world.

The fourth is freedom from fear which, translated into world terms, means a world-wide reduction of armaments to such a point and in such a thorough fashion that no nation will be in a position to commit an act of physical aggression against any neighbour—anywhere in the world.

This is no basis of a distant millennium. It is a definite basis for a kind of world attainable in our own time and generation. That kind of world is the very antithesis of the so-called "new order" of tyranny which the dictators seek to create with the crash of bombs.

PRESIDENT ROOSEVELT.

Jan. 6, 1941.

*

OF ONE MIND ON GREAT ISSUES

It is really desirable to establish a saner view of Anglo-American relations. The first step is for all sections of British opinion to realise that neither our diplomacy nor our Press nor anything else that is ours exercises the slightest influence upon the main stream of American opinion. Whatever we say or do, the great American democracy will continue to deal with its problems by its own lights and to pursue its own immediate objectives.

The second point is to understand that the American democracy is, broadly speaking, moved by ideals very similar to ours and is marching in the same direction. If we both remain true to ourselves and to our traditions, we shall always find ourselves of one mind on really great issues, though the American democracy will always be slower than ours to react to world events which affect its interests. There is, indeed, an even stronger similarity in standpoint between the United States and the Dominions than between the United States and Britain, because all the Dominions (except the Irish Free State) are equally remote from Europe and shy of "European entanglements".

Co-operation between us, if that is to be called co-operation which springs not from reasoned policy but from similar instincts, aims and traditions, resembles the natural and inevitable but quite unconscious co-operation of the Mississippi and the Missouri, which cannot help flowing towards the same point at St. Louis despite détours and divagations. I do not say that the two political streams, like the two great rivers, must ultimately blend and flow to the sea together. If that time comes, the world will be much nearer attainment of the League ideal than seems possible to our short vision. I say only that they are flowing towards the same objectives and cannot by their very nature, if they are true to it, escape from doing so. The only alternative is flood and devastation, and even so the main streams will keep the course which Providence has assigned to them. *Natura obstat,* said Edmund Burke in an earlier age. It did. On the main issue of human progress, however, *Natura imperat:* and she requires no artificial stimulus.

SIR EDWARD GRIGG.

From "The Faith of an Englishman" (1936).

*

THE ONLY NUCLEUS FOR DEMOCRACY

Some people are spreading a legend that democracy is disappearing from Britain and that she will come out at the end of the war as a Fascist or Communist State. Nothing could be further from the truth. I have never known Britain more truly democratic. The British are not going to change their essential character. It has shewn itself in this war. They will move forward of course with the times, but without revolutionary violence.

But the more people think about the future the more they are drawn to the conclusion that all real hope depends on some form of co-operation between the United States and the British Commonwealth of Nations. Even if we win total victory there will be no chance of immediately creating an effective new League of Nations. There will be nothing in Europe from which to

49

make it. A majority of the younger generation consists of people who have been educated in such brutish doctrines as blood and earth, that might is right, that Jews are social poison or that business men are hyenas only fit for destruction. No man can even say what France to-morrow will be like.

The plain truth is that peace and order always depend not on disarming the police but on there being an overwhelming power behind just law. The only places where that power can be found behind the laws of the liberal and democratic world are the United States and Great Britain supported by the Dominions and some other free nations. The only nucleus round which a stable, peaceful, democratic world can be built after this war is if the United States and Great Britain possess between them more aeroplanes, ships of war and key positions of world power than any possible totalitarian rival.

LORD LOTHIAN.
British Ambassador to the U.S.

From his last speech (Dec. 11, 1940).

*

III
A Muster of Brave Men.

*

Surely, Sir, this is nothing but the hand of God.
                              CROMWELL after a victory.

"Were I to die at this moment *want of frigates* would
be found stamped on my heart."
        NELSON to the Admiralty after the Battle of the Nile.

"Please, Duke, did you really say at the Battle of
Waterloo, 'Up Guards and at 'em' ? "
        "No, I didn't, my boy. I'll be damned if I did."
[The Duke of Wellington to a young boy, afterwards
Canon Meade, when a visitor at Walmer.]

I heard once from an eye-witness the account of a poor
sailor whose legs were shattered by a ball in the action off
Algiers in 1816 and who was taken below for an operation.
The surgeon and the chaplain persuaded him to have a
leg off: it was done and the tourniquet applied to the
wound. Then they broke it to him that he must have
the other off too. The poor fellow said, "You should have
told me that, gentlemen," and deliberately unscrewed the
instrument and bled to death.—CARDINAL NEWMAN.

THERMOPYLÆ
Of those that died in Thermopylæ,
    Glorious is the fortune, fair is the fate;
For a tomb they have an altar,
For lamentation, memory,
    And for pity, praise.
A grave like this shall neither rust corrupt,
    Nor Time, that conquers all.
                              A. BURRELL.
        From the Greek epigram by Simonides.

KING ARTHUR'S LAST FIGHT

And never was there seen a more dolefuller battle in no Christian land: for there was but rushing and riding, *foining and striking, and many a grim word was there spoken either to other, and many a deadly stroke. But ever King Arthur rode throughout the battle of Sir Mordred many times and did full nobly as a noble King should, and at all times he fainted never: and Sir Mordred that day put him in devoir and in great peril. And thus they fought all the long day and never stinted till the noble knights were laid to the cold earth: and ever they fought still till it was near night and by that time was there a hundred thousand laid dead upon the down. Then was Arthur †wood wroth out of measure, when he saw his people so slain from him.

Then the King looked about him and then was he ware of all his host and of all his good knights were left no more alive but two knights: that one was Sir Lucan the Butler and his brother, Sir Bedivere, and they were full sore wounded. Jesu mercy! said the King, where are all my noble knights become? Alas that ever I should see this doleful day, for now, said Arthur, I am come to mine end. But would to God I wist where were that traitor Sir Mordred, that hath caused all this mischief!

Then was King Arthur ware where Sir Mordred leaned upon his sword among a great heap of

* Foining, *i.e.* thrusting. † Wood, *i.e.* mad;

52

dead men. Now give me my spear, said Arthur unto Sir Lucan, for yonder I have espied the traitor that all this woe hath wrought. . . . Then the king got his spear in both his hands and ran towards Sir Mordred, crying, Traitor, now is thy death-day come. And when Sir Mordred heard Sir Arthur he ran unto him with his sword drawn in his hand. And there King Arthur smote Sir Mordred under the shield, with a foin of the spear, throughout the body, more than a fathom.

And when Sir Mordred felt that he had his death wound he thrust himself with the might that he had up to the *bur of King Arthur's spear. And right so he smote his father Arthur, with his sword holden in both his hands, on the side of the head, that the sword pierced the helmet and the brain pan and therewithal Sir Mordred fell stark dead to the earth: and the noble Arthur fell in a swoon to the earth, and there he swooned oft-times. And Sir Lucan the Butler and Sir Bedivere oft-times heaved him up.

And so weakly they led him betwixt them both, to a little chapel not far from the sea side. And when the King was there he thought him well eased.

SIR THOMAS MALORY (1470).
From "Le Morte D'Arthur".

*bur, *i.e.* hand-guard.

*

THE DEATH OF KING HAROLD

From nine o'clock in the morning, when the combat began, till three o'clock came the battle was up and down, this way and that, and no one knew who would conquer and win the land. Both sides stood so firm and fought so well that no one could guess which would prevail. The Norman archers with their bows shot thickly upon the English: but they covered themselves with their shields, so that the arrows could not touch their bodies, nor do any mischief, how true so ever was their aim, or however well they shot. Then the Normans determined to shoot their arrows up into the air, so that they might fall on their enemies' heads and strike their faces. The archers adopted this scheme and shot up into the air against the English: and the arrows in falling struck their heads and faces and put out the eyes of many, and all feared to open their eyes or leave their faces unguarded.

The arrows now flew thicker than rain before the wind: fast sped the shafts that the English called "wibetes". Then it was that an arrow that had been thus shot upwards, struck Harold above the right eye, and put it out. In his agony he seized the arrow and threw it away, breaking it with his hands: and the pain to his head was so great that he leaned upon his shield. So the English were wont to say and still say to the French that the arrow was well shot which was so sent up against their King, and that the archer

won them great glory who thus put out Harold's
eye.

ROBERT WACE, the Norman (1170).

*

THE FIRST GREAT ENGLISH SOLDIER

At length, in 1376, the Prince came up to
Westminster to attend, even in his sick bed, the
deliberations of Parliament. This was his last
effort. Two months later, on the 8th of June, he
summoned his faithful Crusaders to his chamber
to bid them farewell, and as they filed past he
thanked them for their good service and asked
their pardon for that he could not reward them as
they wished. Then he entreated them to be
faithful to his son as they had been to himself,
and they swore it, weeping like women, with all
their hearts.

The end came with a flash of the imperial
soldier's spirit. Observing that a knight, who
had offended him, had come in with the rest, the
Prince instantly bade him begone and see his
face no more; and then the noble heart cracked
and with a last ejaculation that he forgave all
men as he hoped to be forgiven, the Black Prince,
the hope and pride and treasure of England, sank
back and died. Two months later he was buried
with military pomp in the cathedral at Canterbury,
and over his tomb were hung, and still hang, his
helmet, his surcoat, his gauntlets, his crest, his

shield and his sword, the veritable arms worn by the first great English soldier.

For a great soldier he was, and a great commander. He could be stern and he could be merciless, but those were stern and merciless times, and the man whose last thoughts were for his comrades-in-arms was a chief who could hold men to him and a leader whom they would follow to the death. Men no longer pray for his soul in the chapel which he founded in the crypt of the cathedral; but morning and evening the voice of the trumpet, calling English soldiers to their work and dismissing them to their rest, peals forth from the barracks without and pierces faintly into the silence of the Sanctuary, no unfitting requiem for the great warrior who, waiting for the sound of a louder trumpet, sleeps peacefully beneath the shadow of his shield.

THE HON. SIR JOHN FORTESCUE (1859–1933).
From the "History of the British Army".

*

THE MUD AT AGINCOURT

The English Army was in no handsome array. The archers were without armour, many without shoes: their heads poorly protected by caps of boiled leather or of wicker hatched with iron, and their bills and axes, stuck into their girdles, gave them the look of carpenters. Many had let down their hosen in order to be at their ease and go thoroughly to work, first at bending the bow, then at handling the axe when they should be able to leave their enclosure of stakes and hew at those immovable masses.

A strange, incredible and yet certain fact is that in reality the French Army could not stir either to fight or to fly. The rear-guard alone effected its escape.

At the decisive moment when old Sir Thomas Erpingham, having drawn up the English army, threw his truncheon into the air, exclaiming, "Now strike!" a signal which the English had answered by a formidable shout of ten thousand voices, the French Army, to their great astonishment, remained motionless. Horses and knights appeared to be enchanted or struck dead in their armour. The truth was that their big battle-steeds, weighed down with their heavy riders and lumbering caparisons of iron, had all their feet completely sunk in the deep wet clay: they were fixed there and could only struggle out to crawl on a few steps at a walk. The ground was soft and cut up by the trampling of the horses, so that they found great difficulty in extricating themselves from it. . . .

To arouse these inert masses the English archers rained, with increasing shower, ten thousand arrows right in their faces. The iron horsemen stooped their heads, otherwise the arrows would have pierced through the vizors of their casques. Then two squadrons of the French, wheeling from both wings, by dint of furious spurring moved on slowly to the charge. Neither squadron reached the English line. Not more than a hundred and twenty got clear to run upon the stakes of the English archers. The greater number had fallen by the way: men and horses rolled in the mud.

Would to Heaven all had so fallen, but those whose horses were only wounded could no longer manage the ungovernable animals which bore them back on their own ranks. One can imagine the fearful scene that took place in this serried mass, the horses startled, backing, maddened by the press, throwing their riders or bruising them in their armour between iron and iron.

Then the English came up. Quitting their fortress of stakes and throwing aside their bows and arrows they marched on at their ease with hatchets, bills, heavy swords and leaded maces to demolish this mountain of men and horses mixed together.

M. MICHELET.
(From "History of France".)

*

THE SOLDIER'S "ESSENTIAL PARTS"

To dare boldly
In a fair cause, and for their country's safety.
To run upon the cannon's mouth undaunted;
To obey their leaders, and shun mutinies;

58

To bear with patience the winter's cold
And summer's scorching heat, and not to faint
When plenty of provision fails, with hunger;
Are the essential parts make up a soldier.

MASSINGER (1583–1640).

*

ACT LIVELY: NEGLECT NO MEANS

It is no longer disputing, but Out instantly all you can. Raise all your Bands: get what volunteers you can: hasten your horses. I beseech you spare not, but be expeditious and industrious. . . . You must act lively: do it without distraction. Neglect no means.

O. CROMWELL (1643).

*

TO AVENGE THEIR DEAD ADMIRAL

Being invited to Sir Christopher Mings' funeral, I into the church and there heard the service and stayed till they buried him and then out. And there met with Sir William Coventry (Commissioner of the Navy) who was there out of great generosity and no person of quality there but he, and went with him into his coach, and being in it with him there happened this extraordinary case.

About a dozen able, proper, lusty men came to the coach-side with tears in their eyes and one of them that spoke for the rest begun and says to

Sir W. Coventry, "We are here a dozen of us that have long known and served our dead Commander Sir Christopher Mings, and have now done that last office of laying him in the ground. We would be glad we had any other to offer after him and in revenge of him. All we have is our lives: if you will please to get His Royal Highness to give us a fireship among us all, here is a dozen of us. Out of all which choose you one to be Commander and the rest of us, whoever he is, will serve him and if possible do that that shall show our memory of our dead Commander and our revenge."

Sir W. Coventry was herewith much moved (as well as I who could hardly abstain from weeping) and took their names and so parted; telling me that he would move His Royal Highness, as in a thing very extraordinary, which was done.

S. PEPYS (1666).

*

MARLBOROUGH'S LAST DAYS

It is indeed astonishing that during all these years, when he had so much leisure, Marlborough should never have left any record, even in conversation, of the critical and disputed passages in his life nor told his tales of camp and court. . . . He was by no means indifferent to his fame. His desire "to leave a good name to history" had always been strong within him; but as he looked back over his life he seems to have felt sure that

60

the facts would tell their tale and that he need not stir himself to do so. It is the truth that only a single remark of his about himself has survived. One day he paced with failing steps the state room of his palace and stood long and intently contemplating his portrait by Kneller. Then he turned away with the words, "That was once a man."

The span of mortals is short: the end universal: and the tinge of melancholy which accompanies retirement is in itself an anodyne. It is foolish to waste lamentations upon the closing phase of human life. Noble spirits yield themselves willingly to the successively falling shades which carry them to a better world or to oblivion.

The Archdeacon (Coxe) has recounted Marlborough's death in 1722 in the magniloquent terms appropriate to a ducal demise in an age when hereditary aristocracy still ruled the land. Of course, it is more becoming for a warrior to die in battle on the field, in command, with great causes in dispute and strong action surging round: like Charles XII at Frederickshald, like Berwick at Philippsburg, or Wolfe on the Heights of Abraham, or Nelson at Trafalgar. But these swift exits are not in human choice. Great captains must take their chance with the rest. Cæsar was assassinated by his dearest friend. Hannibal was cut off by poison. Frederick the Great lingered out years of loneliness in body and soul. Napoleon rotted at St. Helena. Compared with these Marlborough had a good and fair end to his life.

WINSTON S. CHURCHILL.
From "Marlborough: His Life and Times".

*

THE MEN THAT FOUGHT AT MINDEN

The old soldiers scattered about our neighbourhood were mostly the descendants of the Borderers whose propensity for war might perhaps be innate. I think, however, that the breed is thinned from the numbers of those that have been killed off in our wars. One of these, a near relative, would describe how he had his knapsack, as well as his coat-laps and the cocks of his hat, shot through and through and yet had escaped unhurt. Others of them would give similar descriptive accounts: and when a party of them met over their ale, it is not easy to depicture the warmth with which they greeted each other and prided themselves on the battles they had won.

One of these, during a walk in which I fell in with him from Newcastle to Ovingham, described the minute particulars of the Battle of Minden, and how, in the absence of Lord Sackville, they shook hands the whole length of the line, vowing to stand by each other without flinching. This tall stout man, John Cowie, though old, appeared to be in all the vigour of youth. He lived at Ovington. His associate, Ben Garlick, of Prudhow, appeared as if his constitution had been broken down. They had served in a corps called Napier's Grenadiers. Cowie appeared occasionally in his old military coat, etc. After he died this coat, which had been shot at at Minden and elsewhere, was at last hung up on a stake on the corn rigs as a scare-crow.

THOS. BEWICK (1753–1828).

From "Memoirs".

*

MANŒUVRING WITH CHERRY STONES

It happened to me to be present, and sitting next to Admiral Rodney at table, when the thought seemed first to occur to him of breaking the French line by passing through it in the heat of the action. It was at Lord George Germaine's house at Stoneland after dinner, when having asked a number of questions about the manœuvring of columns and the effect of charging with them on a line of infantry, he proceeded to arrange a parcel of cherry stones, which he had collected from the table. Forming them into two fleets drawn up in line and opposed to each other, he at once arrested our attention, which had not been very generally engaged by his preparatory enquiries, by declaring he was determined so to pierce the enemy's line of battle (arranging his manœuvre at the same time on the table) if ever it was his fortune to bring them into action.

I dare say this passed with some as mere

rhapsody, and all seemed to regard it as a very perilous and doubtful experiment, but landsmen's doubts and difficulties made no impression on the Admiral, who having seized the idea held it fast, and in his eager animated way went on manœuvring his cherry stones and throwing his enemy's representatives into such utter confusion that, already possessed of that victory in imagination, which in reality he lived to gain, he concluded his process by swearing he would lay the French Admiral's flag at his sovereign's feet, a promise which he actually pledged to his majesty in his closet and faithfully and gloriously performed.

RICHARD CUMBERLAND (1732–1811).

*

SIR RALPH ABERCROMBY

All great and true Generals, from King David, Hannibal, Cæsar, Cromwell, the great Frederic, etc., down to our own Sir Colin Campbell, have had their men's comforts, interests and lives at heart. The late Lord Dunfermline—*magni parentis filius haud degener*—when speaking with deep feeling and anger to the writer about the sufferings of the men and the frightful blunders in the Crimea, told the following story of his father, the great and good Sir Ralph Abercromby.

After his glorious victory, the dying General was being carried in a litter to the boat of the *Foudroyant* in which he died. He was in great pain from his wound and could get no place to rest. Sir John Macdonald (afterwards Adjutant-General) put something under his head. Sir Ralph smiled and said, "That is a comfort. That is the very thing. What is it, John?" "It's only a soldier's blanket, Sir Ralph." "Only a soldier's blanket, sir," said the old man, fixing his eye severely on him. "Whose blanket is it?" "One of the men's." "I wish to know the name of the man whose blanket this is"—and everything paused till he was satisfied. "It is Duncan Roy's of the 42nd, Sir Ralph." "Then see that Duncan Roy gets his blanket this very night!" And wearied and content, the soldier's friend was moved to his death-bed.

"Yes, Doctor!" said Lord Dunfermline, in his strong, earnest way, "the whole question is in that blanket—in Duncan getting his blanket that very night."

DR. JOHN BROWN (1810–1882).
From "Horæ Subsecivæ".

*

ON THE TRANSPORTS FROM THE PENINSULA

The wind increased as the night came on, and soon we had to experience all the horrors of a storm at sea. The pumps were set to work; the sails were torn to shreds; the coppers were overset; and we appeared in a fair way, I thought, of going to the bottom. Meanwhile, the pumps were kept at work night and day incessantly till they were choked; and the gale growing worse and worse, all the soldiery were ordered below, and the hatches closed; soon after which the vessel turned over on one side and lay a helpless log upon the water.

In this situation an officer was placed over us, with his sword drawn in one hand, and a lantern in the other, in order to keep us on the side which was uppermost, so as to give the vessel a chance of righting herself in the roaring tide. The officer's task was not an easy one, as the heaving waves frequently sent us sprawling from the part we clung to, over to the lowermost part of the hold where he stood, and he was obliged every minute to drive us back.

We remained in this painful situation for, I should think, five or six hours, expecting every instant to be our last, when, to our great joy, the sea suddenly grew calm, the wind abated, the vessel righted herself, and we were once more released from our prison, having tasted nothing in the shape of food for at least forty-eight hours. Soon after this we arrived in sight of Spithead, where we saw nine of our convoy, laden with troops, which had been driven on shore in the gale.

After remaining off Spithead for about five or six days, one fine morning we received orders to disembark, and our poor feet once more touched English ground. The inhabitants flocked down to the beach to see us as we did so, and they must have been a good deal surprised at the spectacle we presented. Our beards were long and ragged; almost all were without shoes and stockings; many had their clothes and accoutrements in fragments, with their heads swathed in old rags, and our weapons were covered with rust; whilst not a few had now, from toil and fatigue, become quite blind.

Let not the reader, however, think that even now we were to be despised as soldiers. Long marches, inclement weather and want of food, had done their work upon us; but we were perhaps better than we appeared, as the sequel showed. Under the gallant Crauford we had made some tremendous marches, and even galled our enemies severely, making good our retreat by the way of Vigo. But our comrades in adversity, who had retired by the other road to Corunña, under General Moore, turned to bay there, and showed the enemy that the English soldier is not to be beaten even under the most adverse circumstances.

RIFLEMAN HARRIS.

From "The Retreat to Corunna".

*

THE VETERANS OF THE PENINSULA

Dost thou remember, soldier, old and hoary,
    The days we fought and conquered side by side,
On fields of battle famous now in story,
    Where Britons triumphed, and where Britons
        died?

Dost thou remember all our old campaigning
   O'er many a field in Portugal and Spain?
Of our old comrades few are now remaining—
   How many sleep upon the bloody plain!

Dost thou remember all those marches weary,
   From gathering foes to reach Corunna's shore?
Who can forget that midnight, sad and dreary,
   When in his grave we laid the gallant Moore!
But 'ere he died our General heard us cheering,
   And saw us charge with victory's flag unfurled;
And then he slept, without his ever fearing
   For British soldiers conquering o'er the world.

Rememberest thou the bloody Albuera!
   The deadly breach in Badajoz's walls!
Vittoria, Salamanca, Talavera!
   Till Roncesvalles echoed to our balls!
Ha! how we drove the Frenchmen all before us,
   As foam is driven before the stormy breeze!
We fought right on, with conquering banners
     o'er us,
   From Torres Vedras to the Pyrenees.

Dost thou remember to the war returning,
   —Long will our enemies remember too!—
We fought again, our hearts for glory burning
   At Quatre Bras and awful Waterloo!
We thought of home upon that Sabbath morning
   When Cameron's pibroch roused our Highland
     Corps,

Then proudly marched, the mighty Emperor
    scorning,
  And vowed to die or conquer as of yore!

Rememberest thou the old familiar faces
  Of warriors nursed in many a stormy fight,
Whose lonely graves, which now the stranger
    traces,
  Mark every spot they held from morn till night?
In vain did Cuirassiers in clouds surround them,
  With cannon thundering as the tempest raves;
They left our squares, oh! just as they had found
    them,
  Firm as the rocks amidst the ocean's waves.

NORMAN MACLEOD.
From "The Starling," 1870.

*

NELSON'S THREE RIGHT ARMS

In consequence of some punctilio a coldness was
occasioned between Capt. Nelson and Capt. Bell,
or in truth a mutual prejudice. Some years after,
both their ships being together close off Minorca
and near Port Mahon, a violent storm nearly
disabled Nelson's vessel, and in addition to the
fury of the wind it was night-time and the thickest
darkness. Capt. Bell, however, brought his vessel
at length to Nelson's assistance, took his ship in
tow and used his best endeavours to bring her
and his own vessel into Port Mahon.

The difficulties and the dangers increased.

Nelson considered the case of his own ship as desperate and that unless she was immediately left to her own fate, both vessels would inevitably be lost. He, therefore, with the generosity natural to him, repeatedly requested Capt. Bell to cut him loose, and on Bell's refusal he became impetuous and enforced his demands with passionate threats. Bell then himself took the speaking trumpet and with great solemnity and without the least disturbance of temper, called out in reply, "I feel confident that I can bring you in safe: I therefore must not and, by the help of Almighty God I will not, leave you." What he promised he performed, and after they were safely anchored Nelson came on board Bell's ship and, embracing him with all the ardour of acknowledgment, exclaimed, "A friend in need is a friend indeed!" At this time and on this occasion commenced that firm and perfect friendship between these two men which was interrupted only by the death of the former.

The two men whom Lord Nelson specially honoured were Sir Thomas Trowbridge and Sir Alexander Bell; and once when they were both present, on some allusion being made to the loss of his arm, he replied, "Who shall dare tell me that I want an arm when I have three right arms— this (putting forward his own left one) and Bell and Trowbridge?"

S. T. COLERIDGE (1772–1834).
From "The Friend".

NELSON USES HIS BLIND EYE

Nelson was now in all the excitement of action, pacing the quarter-deck. A shot through the mainmast knocked the splinters about and he observed to one of his officers, with a smile, "It is warm work, and this day may be the last to many of us at a moment," and then stopping short at the gangway added with emotion: "But mark you, I would not be elsewhere for thousands." About this time the Signal Lieutenant called out that No. 39 (the signal for discontinuing the action) was thrown out by the Commander-in-Chief. The Signal Officer met him at the next turn and asked if he should repeat it. "No," he replied, "acknowledge it." Presently he called after him to know if the signal to close action was still hoisted, and being answered in the affirmative said, "Mind you keep it so." He now paced the deck, moving the stump of his lost arm in a manner which always indicated great emotion. "Do you know," he said to Mr. Ferguson, "what is shewn on board the Commander-in-Chief? Number 39!" Mr. Ferguson asked what that meant. "Why, to leave off action." Then, shrugging up his shoulders, he repeated the words—"Leave off action? No, damme if I do! You know, Foley," turning to the Captain, "I have only one eye. I have a right to be blind sometimes"—and then, putting the glass to his blind eye, in that mood of mind which sports with bitterness, he exclaimed, "I really do not see the signal."

Presently, he exclaimed, "Damn the signal! Keep mine for closer battle flying! That's the way I answer such signals. Nail mine to the mast!"

JOHN CAMPBELL.

From "Lives of the Admirals".

*

THE COB-MAN AT WATERLOO

Carew told us a capital story of the Duke. The Duke was at the Marchioness of Downshire's, and the ladies plagued him for some of his stories. For some time he declared all his stories were in print. At last he said, "Well, I'll tell you one that has not been printed."

In the middle of the battle of Waterloo he saw a man in plain clothes riding about on a cob in the thickest fire. During a temporary lull the Duke beckoned him, and he rode over. He asked him who he was, and what business he had there. He replied he was an Englishman, accidentally at Brussels; that he had never seen a fight and wanted to see one. The Duke told him he was in instant danger of his life; he said "Not more than your Grace," and they parted. But every now and then he saw the Cob-man riding about in the smoke, and at last having nobody to send to a regiment, he again beckoned to this little fellow, and told him to go up to that regiment and order them to charge—giving him some mark of authority the colonel would recognise. Away he galloped, and in a few minutes the Duke saw his order obeyed.

The Duke asked him for his card, and found in the evening, when the card fell out of his sash, that he lived at Birmingham, and was a button manufacturer! When at Birmingham the Duke inquired of the firm, and found he was their traveller, and then in Ireland. When he returned, at the Duke's request he called on him in London. The Duke was happy to see him, and said he had a vacancy in the Mint of £800 a year, where accounts were wanted. The little Cob-man said it would be exactly the thing, and the Duke installed him.

R. B. HAYDON (1786–1846).

From the "Journals".

*

THE IRISH SOLDIER

[*Speaking in the House of Commons on the Irish Municipal Bill in* 1837, *Lalor Sheil caught up a phrase of Lord Lyndhurst's, who had borrowed it from a fiery speech by O'Connell. It described the Irish as* "aliens in blood, in language and in religion".]

Aliens! good God! was Arthur, Duke of Wellington, in the House of Lords and did he not start up and exclaim, "Hold! I have seen the aliens do their duty"? The battles, sieges, fortunes he has passed through should have come back upon him. Whose were the arms that drove your bayonets at

Vimeira through the phalanxes that never reeled in the shock of war before? What desperate valour climbed the steeps and filled the moats at Badajoz? All his victories should have rushed and crowded back upon his memory—Vimeira, Badajoz, Salamanca, Albuera, Toulouse, and, last of all, the greatest——

Tell me, for you were there—I appeal to the gallant soldier before me (Sir Henry Hardinge) from whose opinions I differ, but who bears, I know, a generous heart in an intrepid breast—tell me, for you must needs remember, on that day when the destinies of mankind were trembling in the balance, when death fell in showers, when the artillery of France was levelled by the most deadly science, when her legions, incited by the voice and inspired by the example of their mighty leader, rushed again and again to the onset—tell me if for an instant, when to hesitate for an instant was to be lost, the "aliens" blenched?

And when at length the moment for the last and decisive movement had arrived and the valour which had so long been wisely checked was let loose—when with words familiar, but immortal, the great captain commanded the great assault—tell me if Catholic Ireland, with less heroic valour than the natives of this your own glorious country, precipitated herself upon the foe? The blood of England, Scotland and Ireland flowed in the same stream and drenched the same field. When the chill morning dawned, their dead lay cold and

stark together: in the same deep pit their bodies
were deposited: the green corn of spring is now
breaking from their commingled dust: the dew
falls from heaven upon their union in the grave.
Partakers in every peril—in the glory shall we
not be permitted to participate, and shall we be
told, as a requital, that we are estranged from the
noble country for whose salvation our life-
blood was poured out?

LALOR SHEIL (1791–1851).

*

SOLE SURVIVOR OF AN ARMY

At last, on the 13th of January, when the garrison
(of Jellalabad) were busy on the works, toiling
with axe and shovel, with their arms piled and
their accoutrements laid close at hand, a sentry
on the ramparts, looking out towards the Cabul
road, saw a solitary white-faced horseman struggling on towards the fort. The word was passed:
the tidings spread. Presently the ramparts were
lined with officers, looking out, with throbbing
hearts, through unsteady telescopes, or with
straining eyes tracing the road. Slowly and
painfully, as though horse and rider both were
in an extremity of mortal weakness, the solitary,
mounted man came reeling, tottering on. They
saw that he was an Englishman. On a wretched,
weary pony, clinging as one sick or wounded to
its neck, he sat or rather leaned forward: and
there were those who, as they watched his progress,

thought that he could never reach, unaided, the walls of Jellalabad.

A shudder ran through the garrison. That solitary horseman looked like the messenger of death. Few doubted that he was the bearer of intelligence that would fill their souls with horror and dismay. Their worst forebodings seemed confirmed. There was the one man who was to tell the story of the massacre of a great army. A party of cavalry were sent out to succour him. They brought him in wounded, exhausted, half-dead. The messenger was Dr. Brydon, and he now reported his belief that he was the sole survivor of Elphinstone's army of some sixteen thousand men.

JOHN WILLIAM KAYE (1814–1876).
From "History of the War in Afghanistan".

*

STONEWALL JACKSON

Washington seemed so perfectly secure that the recruiting offices had been closed and the President and the Secretary, anticipating the immediate fall of Richmond, left for Fredericksburg the next day. McDowell was to march on the 26th and the departure of his fine army was to be preceded by a grand review. . . . .

So on this night of May 22 the President and his people were without fear of what the morrow might bring forth. The end of the rebellion seemed near at hand. Washington was full of the anticipated triumph. The crowds passed to and fro in the broad avenues, exchanging congratulations on the success of the Northern arms and the approaching downfall of the slaveholders. The theatres were filled with delighted audiences, who hailed every allusion to the "Southern Chivalry" with enthusiasm and gaiety and confidence reigned supreme.

Little dreamt the light-hearted multitude that in the silent woods of the Luray Valley a Confederate army lay asleep beneath the stars. Little dreamt Lincoln, or Banks, or Stanton that not more than seventy miles from Washington and less than thirty from Strasburg, the most daring of their enemies, waiting for the dawn to rise above the mountains, was pouring out his soul in prayer:

Appealing from his native sod
In forma pauperis to God:
"Lay bare Thine arm, stretch forth Thy rod.
. Amen!" That's Stonewall's way.

It is not always joy that cometh in the morning, least of all to generals as ignorant as Banks when they have to deal with a skilful foe.

COL. G. F. R. HENDERSON.

From "Stonewall Jackson".

*

THE DERVISHES AT OMDURMAN

And the Dervishes? The honour of the fight must still go with the men who died. Our men were perfect, but the Dervishes were superb,

77

beyond perfection. It was their largest, best and bravest army, and it died worthily of the huge Empire that Mahdism won and kept so long. Their riflemen, mangled by every kind of death and torment that man can devise, clung round the black flag and the green, emptying their poor, rotten, home-made cartridges dauntlessly. Their spearmen charged death at every minute hopelessly. Their horsemen led each attack, riding into the bullets till nothing was left but three horses trotting up to our line, heads down, saying, "For goodness sake, let us in out of this." Not one rush, or two or ten—but rush on rush, company on company, never stopping though all their view—that was not unshaken enemy—was the bodies of the men who had rushed before them. A dusky line got up and stormed forward: it bent, broke up, fell apart and disappeared. Before the smoke had cleared, another line was bending and storming forward in the same track.

It was over. The avenging squadrons of the Egyptian cavalry swept over the field. The Khalifa and the Sheik-ed-Din had galloped back to Omdurman. Ali Wad Hel was borne away on an angareb with a bullet through his thigh-bone. Yakub lay dead under his brother's banner. From the green army there now came only death-enamoured desperadoes, strolling one by one towards the rifles, pausing to shake a spear, turning aside to recognise a corpse, then, caught by a sudden jet of fury, bounding forward, checking, sinking limply to the ground. Now under the black flag in a ring of bodies stood only three men, facing the three thousand of the Third Brigade. They folded their arms about the staff and gazed steadily forward. Two fell. The last dervish stood up and filled his chest; he shouted the name of his God and hurled his spear. Then he stood quite still, waiting. It took him full: he quivered, gave at the knees and toppled with his head on his arms and his face towards the legions of his conquerors.

G. W. STEEVENS (1869–1900).

From "With Kitchener to Khartoum".

*

FIGHTING-MAN AND SAINT

One of the first of my Captains was the seventh son of the last Vice-Chancellor of England, Sir Launcelot Shadwell. He was about the greatest saint on earth. The sailors called him, somewhat profanely, Our Heavenly Father. He was once heard to say "Damn" and the whole ship was upset. When, as Midshipmen, we punished one of our mess-mates for abstracting his cheese, he was extremely angry with us and asked us what right we had to interfere with his cheese. He always had the Midshipmen to breakfast with him and when we were sea-sick he gave us champagne and gingerbread nuts. As he went in mortal fear of his own steward, who bossed him utterly, he would say: "I think the aroma has rather gone out of this champagne. Give it to the young gentlemen." The steward would reply, "Now, you know very well, sir, that the aroma ain't gone out of this 'ere champagne"—but all the same we got it.

Shadwell's appearance on going into a fight I must describe. We went up a Chinese river to capture a pirate stronghold. Presently the pirates opened fire from a banana plantation on the river bank. We nipped ashore from the boats to the plantation. I remember I was armed to the teeth, like a Greek brigand, all swords and pistols, and was weighed down with my weapons. We took shelter in the plantation, but our Captain stood on the river bank. He was dressed in a pair of white trousers, yellow waistcoat and a blue tail coat with brass buttons and a tall white hat with a gold stripe up the side of it and he was waving a white umbrella to encourage us to come out of the bananas and go for the enemy. He had no weapon of any sort.

His sole desire for fame was to do good; and he requested for himself when he died that he should be buried under an apple tree, so that people might say, "God bless old Shadwell!"

When my Captain was severely wounded he asked me, when being sent home, what he could do for me. I asked him to give me a set of studs with his motto on them—*Loyal au mort*—and I have worn them daily for over sixty years.

ADMIRAL LORD FISHER (1841–1920).

From "Records".

MAXIMS OF LORD FISHER

"Time, Twiss, time is everything," said Nelson to Gen. Twiss, when chasing the French fleet under Villeneuve to the West Indies; "a quarter of an hour may mean the difference between Victory and Defeat." This was in sailing days. Now it will be quarters of a minute, not quarters of an hour.

As in war, so in the preparation for war, Rashness must have its place.

An instant offensive is obligatory. . . . All will depend on the instant start, the sudden blow.

Whoever hits soonest and oftenest will win.

Peace brings with it the reign of old men. The sacred fire never burnt in Collingwood, who was simply a naval machine, never having been his own master all his life.

Fighting conditions are all altered. The wind formerly determined the course of action: now it is only the mind of man. The man, and the best man, is wanted—not a fossil; not a careful man.

Formerly sea battles were sailors' battles, now they are officers'—the Admiral everything.

The last place to defend England will be the shores of England. The frontiers of England are the coasts of the enemy. We ought to be there five minutes before war breaks out.

Naval supremacy once destroyed is destroyed for ever. Carthage, Spain, Holland, the great commercial nations of the past had the sea wrested from them and then they fell.

A successful Mercantile Marine leads to a successful War Navy.

ADMIRAL LORD FISHER.

From "Records".

*

THE COST OF THE FIRST BATTLE OF YPRES

The British Army have fought many a defensive battle with success—Crecy, Agincourt, Albuera, Waterloo, Inkerman—and Ypres proved that the men of 1914, recruited haphazard by voluntary enlistment, were fully the equals of their forefathers in valour and determination. They were more than the equals, not only of the flower of the youth of Germany in the volunteer units of the new Reserve Corps, but also of the picked representatives of the German nation selected by a process of universal service. That British troops have fought comparatively few successful offensive battles is due mainly to their commanders never having at their disposal forces adequate for such a purpose and seldom being in a strategic situation that justified it. Yet Minden, Blenheim, Salamanca and Vittoria had shown what they were capable of in the attack: and the counter-attack at Ypres was not only crowned with success but had truly marvellous results. They indicate what might have been accomplished had General Haig been in command of numbers commensurate with his task. . . . The Germans had a numerical superiority of nearly two to one in their favour on the Ypres front as a whole, and far more favourable odds in particular sectors, but it did not avail to compensate for inferior leading and other factors. . . .

Whether the Germans were outfought or took counsel of their fears, the second great rush of their hosts was in any case stayed; but the cost was overwhelming. In the British battalions which fought at the Marne and Ypres there scarcely remained with the colours an average of one officer and 30 men of those who landed in August, 1914. The old British Army was gone beyond recall, leaving but a remnant to carry on the training of the New Armies; but the framework that remained had gained an experience and confidence that were to make those Armies invincible. Nor had the Old Army fallen in vain. It had created such an impression on the Germans that their leaders turned aside to seek for less stubborn foes and left the British sector alone, attempting no serious attack on it for three long years.

From "The Official History of the Great War".

*

THE R.A.F.

How oft do they their silver bowers leave
    To come to succour us that succour want!
How oft do they with golden pinions cleave
    The flitting skies, like flying pursuivant,
Against foul fiend to aid us militant!
    They for us fight, they watch and duly ward

And their bright squadrons round about us plant,
And all for love and nothing for reward.

EDMUND SPENSER (1552–1599).
From the "Faerie Queene".

*

YOUTH IN THE SKIES

Those who were children yesterday
Now move in lovely flight,
Swift-glancing as the shooting stars
That cleave the Summer night:

A moment flashed, they came and went,
Horizons rise and fall,
The speed of valour lifts them up
And strength obeys their call.

The downs below are breathing peace
With thyme and butterflies,
And sheep at pasture in the shade—
And now from English skies

Those who were children yesterday
Look down with other eyes:
Man's desperate folly was not theirs,
But theirs the sacrifice.

Old men may wage a war of words;
Another race are these,
Who flash to glory, dawn and night,
Above the starry seas.

THE HON. HERBERT ASQUITH (1881–   ).
From "Youth in the Skies".

84

IV

Ladies Assembly

*

God bless my dearest Albert! God bless my dearest country which has shown itself so great to-day! One felt grateful to the great God who seemed to pervade all and bless all.

> Queen Victoria's entry in her Diary
> after opening the Great Exhibition of 1851.

Mrs. Jordan made even Methodists love her.—

LEIGH HUNT.

Mrs. Garrick told me that after her husband's funeral she prayed with great composure, then went and kissed the dear bed and got into it with a sad pleasure.—

HANNAH MORE.

Were there even a few hearts and intellects like hers the earth would already become the hoped-for heaven.—From J. S. Mill's inscription on his wife's tomb at Avignon.

Ponder no more, Renny; whatever you do, do it, but ponder no more!—Dr. JOHNSON.

"It is very pleasant dining with a bachelor," said Miss Matty, softly, as we settled ourselves in the counting house. "I only hope it is not improper: so many pleasant things are."—MRS. GASKELL, from "Cranford".

> No Spring, nor Summer Beauty hath such grace
> As I have seen in one Autumnall face.

DONNE.

> Oh! I adore thee, William Lamb,
> But hate to hear thee say, "God damn"!

LADY CAROLINE LAMB.

85

Mrs. Mary Ann Clarke, on being asked by Counsel in the Court of King's Bench under whose protection she then was, bowed to the President, Lord Ellenborough, and replied, "His Lordship's".

The finest of all times for flirting is a wedding. They are all agog, poor things.

The King of Greece told his sister, who repeated it to me, that there was no lady in Europe who could enter a room like Lady Dufferin.—1ST MARQUIS OF DUFFERIN.

Think of 3,000 sitting down to Temperance tea-trays! I'd as lief be a duck and sit in a pond with my chin upon duckweed.—HON. CAROLINE NORTON (1859).

You know how ignorant I am and that I only ask for information. . . . I always like to be put right when I am wrong.—ROSA DARTLE, from "David Copperfield".

I'm not denying that women are foolish: God Almighty made 'em to match the men.—MRS. POYSER, from "Adam Bede".

ANNE HYDE, DUCHESS OF YORK

The Duchess of York died on Friday: she was opened on Saturday, embalmed on Sunday and buried last night. . . . The Duke sent for the Bishop of Oxford out of the chapel, who came but her senses were first gone. In the meantime the Duke called, "Dame, do you know me?" twice or thrice: then with much stirring she said "I?" After a little respite, she took a little courage and with what vehemency and tenderness she could she said, "Duke, Duke, death is terrible: death is very terrible," which were her last words.

From Historical MSS. Commission
7th Report.

Miss Margaret Blagge (afterwards Mrs. Sidney Godolphin), one of the Queen's Ladies in Waiting, who attended the Duchess during her illness "with an extraordinary sedulity", gave the following account of the event:

"The Duchesse died, a Princesse honoured in power: had much Wit, much Money, much Esteeme. She was full of unspeakable torture and died (poore Creature!) in Doubt of her Religion, without any Sacrament or Divine by her, like a poor Wretch; None remembered her after one Weeke: None sorry for her: She smelt extreamly: was tost and flung about, and everyone did what they would with that stately Carcasse.

"What is this World! What is Greatenesse! What to be esteemed and thought a Wit! We shall all be stript, without Sence or Remembrance. But God, if we serve Him in our Health, will give us patience in our Sicknesse."

JOHN EVELYN. (1620–1706)
From "The Life of Mrs. Godolphin".

*

A SAINT AT WHITEHALL
So then what I further find in her *Diary*, among the Resolutions she was wont to set downe. It seems she had lost at *Cards*, a Diversion which she affected not but to comply with others and unavoydabley—Behold! With what Remorse, with what Discretion!

June 2nd.

"I will never play this halfe-Yeare but at 3 peny Ombre, and then with one at halfs: I Will not: I do not Vowe: but I will not do it. What! Loose Mony at Cards? Yet not give to the Poore? 'Tis robbing of God, misspending my Time and misemploying my Talent: Three greate Sins: Three pound would have kept three people from starving a Moneth: Well, I will not play. Here's a Lesson for Ladys, who idle away and spend their precious Moments, Yeares and days as well as Mony unaccountably, unexcusably."

'Tis in this Manuscript I find a Catalogue of the particular Mercys she had received from God: Amongst which that He had given her so Religious a Mother, such good Breeding, Early Receiving the Sacrament: The Prayers of many for her and the Assistance of a Spiritual Guide, which (she says) I am confident was the Reward of my Receiving at the Charter-House.

JOHN EVELYN.
From "The Life of Mrs. Godolphin".

*

DOROTHY WANTS A PLAIN GOLD RING
Lord! there were a thousand things I remembered after you were gone that I should have said and now I am to write not one of them will come into my head. Sure as I live, it is not settled yet!

Good God! the fears and surprises, the crosses and disorders of that day, it was confused enough to be a dream and I am apt to think sometimes it was no more. But no, I saw you: when shall I do it again, God only knows! Can there be a romancer story than ours would make if the conclusion proved happy? Ah! I dare not hope it: something that I cannot describe draws a cloud over all the light my fancy discovers sometimes, and leaves me so in the dark with all my fears about me that I trouble to think on 't. . . .

Before you go I must have a ring from you, too, a plain gold one: if I ever marry it shall be my wedding ring: when I die, I'll give it you again. What a dismal story this is you sent me: but who could expect better from a love begun upon such grounds? I cannot pity neither of them, they were both so guilty. Yet they are the more to be pitied for that.

Here is a note comes to me just now; will you do this service for a fine lady that is my friend: have I not taught her well? She writes better than her mistress. How merry and pleased she is with her marrying because there is a plentiful fortune: otherwise she would not value the man at all. This is the world: would you and I were out of it, for sure we were not made to live in it.

Do you remember Arme* and the little house there? Shall we go there? that's next to being

* Now called Herm, the little island near Guernsey.

out of the world. There we might live like Baucis and Philemon, grow old together in our little cottage and for our charity to some shipwrecked strangers obtain the blessing of dying both at the same time. How idly I talk! 'Tis because the story pleases me—in Ovid—so much. I remember I cried when I read it. Methought they were the perfectest characters of a contented marriage, where piety and love were all their wealth, and in their poverty feasted the gods when evil men shut them out. I am called away,— farewell.

DOROTHY OSBORNE (1627–95).

*

BOLINGBROKE'S TRIBUTE TO HIS WIFE

I want to tell you, my dear Dean, how much my wife is obliged to you. She says she would find strength enough to nurse you, if you were here; and yet, God knows, she is extremely weak: the slow fever works under, and mines the constitution; we keep it off sometimes, but still it returns, and makes new breaches before nature can repair the old ones.

I am not ashamed to say to you that I admire her more every hour of my life: death is not to her the King of Terrors; she beholds him without the least. When she suffers much, she wishes for him as a deliverer from pain; when life is tolerable, she looks on him with dislike, because he is to separate her from those friends to whom she is more attached than to life itself.

LORD BOLINGBROKE (1733).
From a letter to Dean Swift.

*

POPE'S AFFECTION FOR HIS MOTHER

My Lord Bolingbroke has spoken justly of his lady; why not I of my mother? Yesterday was her birth-day, now entering on the ninety-first year of her age; her memory much diminished, but her senses very little hurt, her sight and hearing good; she sleeps not ill, eats moderately, drinks water, says her prayers; this is all she does. I have reason to thank God for her continuing so long a very good and tender parent, and for allowing me to exercise for some years those cares which are now as necessary to her as hers have been to me. An object of this sort daily before one's eyes, very much softens the mind, but perhaps may hinder it from the willingness of contracting other ties of the like domestic nature, when one finds how painful it is even to enjoy the tender pleasures. I have formerly made some strong efforts to get and to deserve a friend: perhaps it were wiser never to attempt it, but live extempore, and look upon the world only as a place to pass through: just pay your hosts their dues, disperse a little charity, and hurry on.

ALEXANDER POPE (1733).

91

WOMEN STORM THE HOUSE OF LORDS

A tribe of dames resolved to show that neither men nor laws could resist them. These heroines were Lady Huntingdon, the Duchess of Queensbury, the Duchess of Ancaster, Lady Westmoreland, Lady Cobham, Lady Charlotte Edwin, Lady Archibald Hamilton and her daughter, Mrs. Scott, Mrs. Pendarves and Lady Frances Sanderson. I am thus particular in their names since I look upon them to be the boldest assertors of and most resigned sufferers for liberty I ever read of.

They presented themselves at the door at 9 o'clock in the morning, where Sir William Sanderson respectfully informed them that the Chancellor had made an order against their admittance. The Duchess of Queensbury, as head of the squadron, pished at the ill-breeding of a mere lawyer and desired him to let them upstairs privately. After some modest refusals he swore by G-d he would not let them in. Her Grace, with a noble warmth, answered, by G-d, they would come in, in spight of the Chancellor and the whole House.

This being reported, the Peers resolved to starve them out: an order was made that the doors should not be opened till they raised their siege. These Amazons now showed themselves qualified for the duty even of foot-soldiers. They stood there until four in the afternoon, without either sustenance or evacuation, every now and then plying vollies of thumps, kicks and raps against the door, with so much violence that the speeches in the House were scarce heard.

When the Lords were not to be conquered by this, the two Duchesses (very well apprised of the use of stratagems in war) commanded a dead silence of half an hour, and the Chancellor, who thought this a certain sign of their absence, the Commons also being very impatient to enter, gave order for the opening of the door—upon which they all rushed in, pushed aside their competitors and placed themselves in the front rows of the gallery. They stayed there till after eleven, when the House rose: and during the debate gave applause and showed marks of dislike, not only by smiles and winks—which have always been allowed in these cases—but by noisy laughs and apparent contempts: which is supposed to be the true reason why poor Lord Hervey spoke miserably. You must own this action very well worthy of record, and I think not to be paralleled in history, ancient or modern.

LADY MARY WORTLEY MONTAGU.
(March, 1739.)

*

AN EMPRESS OF FASHION

You tell me my letters entertain you: *tant mieux*. It is my wish, but my wonder; for I live so little in the world, that I do not know the present generation by sight: for, though I pass by them in the streets, the hats with valences, the folds above the chin of the ladies, and the dirty shirts and shaggy hair of the young men, who have levelled nobility almost as much as the nobility in France have, have confounded all individuality. Besides, if I did go to public places and assemblies, which my going to roost earlier prevents, the bats and owls do not begin to fly abroad till far in the night, when they begin to see and be seen.

However, one of the empresses of fashion, the Duchess of Gordon, uses fifteen to sixteen hours of her four-and-twenty. I heard her journal of last Monday. She went first to Handel's music in the Abbey; she then clambered over the benches, and went to Hastings' trial in the (Westminster) Hall; after dinner, to the play; then to Lady Lucan's assembly; after that to Ranelagh and returned to Mrs. Hobart's faro-table; gave a ball herself in the evening of that morning, into which she must have got a good way; and set out for Scotland the next day. Hercules could not have achieved a quarter of her labours in the same space of time . . . Sir William Hamilton is arrived—his Nymph of the Attitudes* was too prudish to visit the rambling peeress.

HORACE WALPOLE (1791).
From a letter to Miss Berry.

* Emily Hart—Nelson's "Emma"—whom Sir W. Hamilton married in the following September.

MRS. JAMES ANALYSES AMELIA

"In the first place," cries Mrs. James, "her eyes are too large, and she hath a look with them that I don't know how to describe; but I know I don't like it. Then her eyebrows are too large; therefore, indeed, she doth all in her power to remedy this with her pincers: for if it were not for those, her eyebrows would be preposterous. Then her nose, as well proportioned as it is, has a visible scar on one side. Her neck likewise is too protuberant for genteel size, especially as she laces herself: for no woman, in my opinion, can be genteel who is not entirely flat before. And lastly she is both too short and too tall.

"Well, you may laugh, Mr. James, I know what I mean, though I cannot well express it. I mean she is too tall for a pretty woman and too short for a fine woman. There is such a thing as a kind of insipid medium, or a kind of something that is neither one thing nor another. I know not how to express it more clearly; but when I say such a one is a pretty woman, a pretty thing, a pretty creature, you know very well I mean a little woman: and when I say such a one is a very fine woman, a very fine person of a woman, to be sure I must mean a tall woman. Now a woman that is between both is certainly neither the one nor the other."

HENRY FIELDING (1707-1754).
From "Amelia".

*

95

THE FADED BEAUTY

"I think," said Northcote, "a great beauty is most to be pitied. She completely outlives herself. She has been used to the most bewitching homage, to have the highest court paid and the most flattering things said to her by all who approach her and to be received with looks of delight and surprise wherever she comes: and she afterwards finds herself not only deprived of all this and reduced to a cypher, but she sees it all transferred to another who has become the reigning toast and beauty of the day in her stead. It must be a most violent shock. It is like a king who is dethroned and reduced to serve as a page in his own palace.

"I remember once being struck with seeing the Duchess of ——, the same that Sir Joshua painted, and who was a miracle of beauty when she was young, and followed by crowds wherever she went:—I was coming out of Mrs. W——'s and there on the landing place she was standing by herself and calling over the bannister for her servant to come to her. If she had been as she once was, a thousand admirers would have flown to her assistance; but her face was painted over like a mask and there was hardly any appearance of life left but the restless motion of her eyes. I was really hurt."

I answered that the late Queen (Charlotte) had much the same painful look that he described— her face highly rouged and her eyes rolling in her head like an automaton, but she had not the mortification of having ever been a beauty.

"There was a Miss —— too," Northcote added, "who was a celebrated beauty when she was a girl and who also sat to Sir Joshua. I saw her not long ago and she was grown as coarse and vulgar as possible; she was like an apple-woman or one who would do to keep the Three Tuns. The change must be very mortifying. To be sure, there is one thing, it comes on by degrees."

From Hazlitt's "Conversations with
Northcote" (1746–1831).

*

LITTLE MARJORIE FLEMING

The year before Marjorie Fleming died, when in Edinburgh, she was at a Twelfth Night supper at Sir Walter Scott's, in Castle Street. The company had all come—all but Marjorie. Scott's familiars, whom we all know, were there—all were come but Marjorie; and all were dull because Scott was dull. "Where's that bairn? what can have come over her? I'll go myself and see." And he was getting up and would have gone; when the bell rang, and in came Duncan Roy and his henchman Tougald, with the sedan chair, which was brought right into the lobby, and its top raised.

And there, in its darkness and dingy old cloth, sat Maidie in white, her eyes gleaming, and Scott bending over her in ecstasy—"hung over her enamoured". "Sit ye there, my dautie, till they all see you"; and forthwith he brought them all. You can fancy the scene. And he lifted her up and marched to his seat with her on his stout shoulder, and set her down beside him; and then began the night, and such a night!

Those who knew Scott best said that night was never equalled; Maidie and he were the stars; and she gave them *Constance's* speeches and *Helvellyn*, the ballad then much in vogue—and all her *repertoire*, Scott showing her off and being oft-times rebuked by her for his intentional blunders.

JOHN BROWN (1810–1882).
From "Horæ Subsecivæ".

[Marjorie Fleming (1803–1811) died a month before her ninth birthday. Scott adored her whimsical genius and her delightful ways.]

*

LADY HOLLAND IN PETULANT MOOD

I met Lady Holland again on Thursday at Lord Sefton's. She began complaining of the slipperiness of the courtyard, and of the danger of her horse falling; to which Sefton replied that it should be gravelled the next time she did him the honour of dining there. She then began to sniff, and, turning her eyes to various pots filled with beautiful roses and all kinds of flowers, she said: "Lord Sefton, I must beg of you to have those flowers taken out of the room; they are so much too powerful for me." Sefton and his valet Paoli actually carried the table and all its contents out of the room.

Then poor dear little Lady Sefton, who has always a posy as large as life at her breast when she is dressed, took it out in the humblest manner, and said: "Perhaps, Lady Holland, this nosegay may be too much for you." But the other was pleased to allow her to keep it, tho' by no means in a very gracious manner. Then when candles were lighted at the close of dinner, she would have three of them put out, as being too much and too near her. Was there ever?

THOMAS CREEVEY (1768–1838).

*

"THEN FARE THEE WELL, FANNY!"

Then fare thee well, Fanny, thus doubly undone,
Thou frail to the many, and false to the one.
Thou art past all recalling, e'en would I recall,
For the woman so fallen for ever must fall.

These lines, about which frequent enquiry has been made, were given me by Scrope Davies. They originally formed the conclusion of a copy of verses addressed by Lord Byron to Lady Frances W. W. (Webster), to whom he was (in his manner) devotedly attached, until (early in 1815) she threw him over for the Duke of Wellington, then in the full blaze of his Peninsular glory.

"Byron," said Davies, "came one morning into

my lodgings in St. James's Street, in a towering passion, and standing before the fire, broke out, "D—— all women, and d—— that woman in particular." He tore from his watch-ribbon a seal she had given him, and dashed it into the grate. As soon as he left the room, I picked it up, and here it is."

He showed it me, and allowed me to take an impression of it, which I have still. It was a large seal, representing a ship in full sail, a star in the distance, with the motto, *Si je la perds, je suis perdu.* Two or three days afterwards his Lordship presented himself again with a copy of verses addressed to his fickle fair one, from which Davies with some difficulty induced him to omit the four concluding lines.

Lady Frances has a double claim to immortality, for at least one letter from the hero of Waterloo was addressed to her from the battle-field. Scrope Davies, who took the credit of having been high in her favour, told me her peculiar mode of manifesting preference, which I suppress.

FRANCES WILLIAMS WYNNE.

From the "Diaries of a Lady of Quality".

*

MISS JULIA DYAWAY WALTZING

It is less indelicate in such a man as Tom Belcher to give Cropley a cross buttock than an officer of hussars to put one hand on the bare back of a virgin of eighteen years, another round her waist and thus to whirl her about for a quarter of an hour in his arms, till both partners are blind, and that too in the presence of 300 spectators. A waltzing match is, we humbly suggest, a more indecent exhibition than a boxing match. What can be more so than to step ready stripped into the ring and hug in succession a long series of military men, occasionally relieved by civilians? The Amazon dismisses from her embrace captain, colonel and knight-at-arms, all panting and perspiring and reeling, while she stands victorious and unexhausted in the ring. And who compose the ring? Judges, senators, soldiers, grandmothers, matrons, maids; and among them our own shrivelled correspondent. Go, Tabitha, to Moulsey Hurst when Turner fights Young Cabbage and then, on your conscience, tell the Editor of *Blackwood's Magazine* that their conduct is as indecent as that of Captain Sabretache and Miss Julia Dyaway.

From Blackwood's Magazine, 1820.

*

LEIGH HUNT'S MOTHER

Having been born nine years later than the youngest of my brothers, I have no recollection of my mother's earlier aspect. Her eyes were always fine, and her person lady-like; her hair also retained its colour for a long period; but her brown complexion had been exchanged for a jaundiced one, which she retained through life; and her cheeks were sunken, and her mouth drawn down with sorrow at the corners. She retained the energy of her character on great occasions; but her spirit in ordinary was weakened, and she looked at the bustle and discord of the present state of society with a frightened aversion.

My father's danger, and the war-whoops of the Indians which she heard in Philadelphia, had shaken her soul as well as frame. The sight of two men fighting in the streets would drive her in tears down another road; and I remember, when we lived near the park, she would take me a long circuit out of the way rather than hazard the spectacle of the soldiers. Little did she think of the timidity with which she was thus inoculating me, and what difficulty I should have, when I went to school, to sustain all those fine theories, and that unbending resistance to oppression, which she inculcated. However, perhaps it ultimately turned out for the best. One must feel more than usual for the sore places of humanity even to fight properly in their behalf. Never shall I forget her face, as it used to appear to me coming up the cloisters, with that weary hang of the head on one side, and that melancholy smile!

One holiday, in a severe winter, as she was taking me home, she was petitioned for charity by a woman sick and ill-clothed. It was in Black-friars Road, I think, about midway. My mother, with the tears in her eyes, turned up a gateway, or some such place, and beckoning the woman to follow, took off her flannel petticoat, and gave it her. It is supposed that a cold which ensued fixed the rheumatism upon her for life. Saints have been made for charities no greater.

LEIGH HUNT (1784–1859).
From "Autobiography".

*

A GAMBLER'S DAUGHTER

Yes, my dearest, my mother's fortune was large, my father's good, legacies from both sides, a £20,000 prize in the lottery—all have vanished. My uncle's estates, his wife's, his father's and mother's (a fine old place called Old Wall in Westmorland: she, my grandmother, was a Graham of the Netherby clan) all have disappeared: so that I, the only child amongst six or seven good fortunes (for my mother, herself an only child, inherited an even splendid inheritance) have been during the better part of my life struggling with actual difficulty: and if I should live long enough, shall probably die in a workhouse—content so to die if preserved from the far bitterer misery of seeing my dear, dear father want his accustomed comforts: content, nay happy, if that far deeper wretchedness be spared.

MARY RUSSELL MITFORD (1787–1855).

*

THE TWO SISTERS

Emily is nowhere here now: her wasted mortal remains are taken out of the house. We have laid her cherished head under the church aisle beside my mother's, my two sisters' (dead long ago) and my poor hapless brother's. But a small remnant of the race is left—so my poor father thinks.

Well, the loss is ours, not hers, and some sad comfort I take, as I hear the wind blow and feel the cutting keenness of the frost, in knowing that the elements bring her no more suffering. Their severity cannot reach her grave: her fever is quieted: her restlessness soothed: her deep hollow cough is hushed for ever: we do not hear it in the night nor listen for it in the morning. We have not the conflict of the strangely strong spirit and the fragile frame before us—relentless conflict, once seen, never to be forgotten. A dreary calm reigns round us, in the midst of which we seek resignation.

My father and my sister Anne are far from well. As for me: God has hitherto most graciously sustained me. So far I have felt adequate to bear my own burden and even to offer a little help to others. I am not idle: I can get through daily duties and do something towards keeping hope and energy alive in our mourning household. My father says to me almost hourly, "Charlotte, you must bear up: I shall sink if you fail me": these words, you can conceive, are a stimulus to nature. The sight, too, of my sister Anne's very still but deep sorrow wakens in me such fear for her that

I dare not falter. Somebody must cheer the rest.

So I will not now ask why Emily was torn from us in the fulness of our attachment, rooted up in the prime of her own days, in the promise of her powers; why her existence now lies like a field of green corn trodden down, like a tree in full bearing struck at the root: I will only say, sweet is rest after labour and calm after tempest, and repeat again and again that Emily knows that now.

CHARLOTTE BRONTË (1816–55).

*

MISS JENKYNS

I had often occasion to notice the use that was made of fragments and small opportunities in Cranford; the rose-leaves that were gathered ere they fell to make into a pot-pourri for some one who had no garden; the little bundles of lavender flowers sent to strew the drawers of some town-dweller, or to burn in the chamber of some invalid. Things that many would despise, and actions which it seemed scarcely worth while to perform, were all attended to in Cranford. Miss Jenkyns stuck an apple full of cloves, to be heated and smell pleasantly in Miss Brown's room; and as she put in each clove she uttered a Johnsonian sentence. Indeed, she never could think of the Browns without talking Johnson; and, as they were seldom absent from her thoughts just then, I heard many a rolling three-piled sentence.

MRS. GASKELL (1810–65).
From "Cranford".

*

A BIRTHDAY PARTY AT THE MACREADYS'

Then the dancing—old Major Burns with his one eye—old Jerdan of the *Literary Gazette* (escaped out of the Rules of the Queen's Bench for the great occasion!) the gigantic Thackeray, etc. etc. all capering like Mænades. Dickens did all but go down on his knees to make me—waltz with him! But I thought I did my part well enough in talking the maddest nonsense with him, Forster, Thackeray and Maclise—without attempting the *impossible*.

However, after supper when we were all madder than ever with the pulling of crackers, the drinking of champagne and the making of speeches, a universal country dance was proposed—and Forster, *seizing me round the waist*, whirled me into the thick of it and *made* me dance! like a person in the treadmill who must move forward or be crushed to death. Once I cried out, "Oh for the love of Heaven let me go! You are going to dash my brains out against the folding doors!" To which he answered—you can fancy his tone— "Your *brains*! who cares about their brains *here*? *Let them go!*"

In fact the thing was rising into something not unlike the Rape of the Sabines! (Mrs. Reid was happily gone some time) when somebody looked at her watch and exclaimed "Twelve o'clock." Whereupon we all rushed to the cloak-room, and there and in the lobby and up to the last moment the mirth raged on. Dickens took home Thackeray and Forster with him and his wife to *finish the night there* and a royal night they would have of it, I fancy! Ending perhaps with a visit to the watch-house.

JANE CARLYLE.

From a letter to Jeannie Welsh. (1843).

*

MRS. DELANY

Her stature was in a middle proportion and every part and proportion perfect in their kind, fitted alike for activity and strength. Her walk was graceful beyond anything that ever I saw in woman and her dance would have been equally so, would her diffidence have permitted it. It was so always in her private practice, but the whole world could not have prevailed upon her to attempt it in public, where she would be the distinguished object of observation, as in minuets or single dances. She was bashful to an extreme and, if I may use the expression, even blameably so. The case was the same with her playing, for though she had confessedly the finest hand and execution that ever was heard, she never let anybody but her intimate acquaintance hear it. She could not bear the attention of others and whenever she found that she was attended to in a very extraordinary manner, she blushed and fluttered herself into a confusion which quickly forced her to give over.

With a person fairly proportioned she had a most lovely face of great sweetness, set off with a head of fair hair, shining and naturally curled: with a complexion which nothing could outdo or equal, in which, so to speak, in the language of poets, "the lilies and roses contended for the mastery". Her eyes were bright: indeed, I never could tell what colour they were of, but to the best of my judgment they were what Solomon called *doves' eyes*, and she is almost the only woman I ever saw whose lips were scarlet and her bloom beyond expression.

DR. DELANY (1685–1768).

*

"TELL ME YOU LOVE ME"

Tell me you love me and always will. Tell me so that when I dream I may dream of Love, and when I sleep dreamless Love may be holding me in his wings, and when I wake Love may be the spirit in my feet, and when I die Love may be the Angel that takes me home.

Laura Lyttleton to her husband,
Alfred Lyttleton (1917).
From Edith Lyttleton's account of
his life.

A CHARACTER SKETCH

I think I have imagination, born not of fancy but of feeling; a conception of the beautiful, not merely in poetry, music, art and nature, but in human beings; and I have a clear though distant vision, down dark, long and often divergent avenues, of the ordered meaning of God. I take this opportunity of saying my religion is a reality and never away from me.

I have a great longing to help those I love, which leads me to intrepid personal criticism; and I do not always know what hurts my friends' feelings. I do not think I should mind anything I have said to others being said to me, but one can never tell; I have taken adverse criticism pretty well all my life and had a lot of it, but by some gap I have not succeeded in making my friends take it well. I am not vain or touchy and it takes a lot to offend me; but when I am hurt the scar remains. I feel differently about people who have hurt me; my confidence has been shaken; I hope I am not ungenerous, but I fear I am not really forgiving. Worldly people say that explanations are a mistake; but having it out is the only chance anyone can ever have of retaining my love; and those who have neither the candour, generosity or humbleness to say they are wrong are not worth loving. I am not afraid of suffering too much in life, but much more afraid of feeling too little; and all quarrels make me profoundly unhappy. One of my complaints against the shortness of life is that there is not time enough to feel pity and love for enough people. I am infinitely compassionate and moved to my foundations by the misfortunes of others. . . .

What then are my faults?

I am fundamentally nervous, irritable and restless. These may sound slight shortcomings but they go to the foundation of my nature, crippling activity, lessening my influence and preventing my achieving anything remarkable. I wear myself out in a hundred unnecessary ways, regretting trifles I have not done, arranging and rearranging what I have got to do and what everyone else is going to do, till I can hardly eat or sleep. To be in one position for long at a time, to sit through bad plays, to listen to moderate music or moderate conversation is a positive punishment to me. I am energetic and industrious, but I am a little too quick; I am *driven* along by my temperament till I feel exhausted.

I was determined to have a life of my own and not to marry before I knew what I was about. This gave me time in which to read and reflect. I was not without application, but I learnt more from human beings than from books. I read the Prefaces of books but skipped them with people and I have always liked strangers. I hardly know the meaning of the word fear nor the derivation of shyness. I do not think that I am particularly witty or original. But if I had to confess and express an opinion upon myself which was not external I should say that it was my power of love. I have lived dangerously and loved much.

MARGOT ASQUITH.

*

INIMITABLE MRS. JORDAN

Mrs. Jordan was inimitable in exemplifying the consequences of too much restraint in ill-educated Country Girls, in Romps, in Hoydens, and in Wards on whom the mercenary have designs. She wore a bib and tucker, and pinafore, with a bouncing propriety, fit to make the boldest spectator alarmed at the idea of bringing such a household responsibility on his shoulders. To see her when thus attired shed blubbering tears for some disappointment, and eat all the while a great thick slice of bread and butter, weeping, and moaning, and munching, and eyeing at every bite the part she meant to bite next, was a lesson against will and appetite worth a hundred sermons.

The way in which she would take a friend by the cheek and kiss her, or make up a quarrel with a lover, or coax a guardian into good-humour, or sing (without accompaniment) the song "Since then I'm doom'd", or "In the dead of the night", trusting, as she had a right to do, and as the house wished her to do, to the sole effect of her sweet, mellow, and loving voice—the reader will pardon me, but tears of pleasure and regret come into my eyes at the recollection, as if she personified whatsoever was happy at that period of life, and which has gone like herself. The very sound of the little familiar word "bud" from her lips (the abbreviation of husband), as she packed it closer, as it were, in the utterance, and pouted it up with fondness in the man's face, taking him at the same time by the chin, was a whole concentrated world of the power of loving.

LEIGH HUNT (1784-1859).

From "Autobiography".

*

MDDLE. GEORGES

When I see Mddle. Georges I seem to be beholding the ruins of Palmyra in motion. Age has played terrible havoc with her, still she is not less majestic, nor less coquettish. Coquetry in old age is like a rose in a grinning death's head. Mddle. Georges came to ask me yesterday to give a performance for her benefit.

"You'll save me from starving," she said.

I looked at her in surprise, for she wore a magnificent hat and feathers and primrose kid gloves.

"You are thinking how well all this still becomes me, are you not, my dear Director?" she asked, smiling.

Thereupon she took a small glass from her pocket and looked at herself mincingly. I became thoroughly alarmed, for she looks seventy-five when she speaks and eighty when she smiles.

She proposed to me to edit her "Memoirs". I took her at her word there and then, and tried to gather material for the chapters on Napoleon.

"Is it true that he sent for you long after midnight and that he forgot that you were there until morning, absorbed as he was in the map of Europe?"

"Pure slander," she replied with dignity. "He knew what was due to me and what was due to himself. His map of Europe! I was his map of Europe."

ARSÈNE HOUSSAYE.
(Director of the Théâtre Français.)

*

A WOMAN IN WHITE

Not many years ago an English gentleman, who in an encounter by night in the streets of Madrid had the misfortune to kill his man, fled into a church porch for sanctuary. Leaning against the door he was surprised to find it open and a glimmering light in the Church. He had the courage to advance against the light, but was terribly startled at the sight of a woman in white who ascended from a grave with a bloody knife in her hand.

The phantom marched up to him and asked him what he did there. He told her the truth without reserve, believing that he had met a ghost. Upon which she spoke to him in the following manner: "Stranger, thou art in my power! I am a murderer as thou art. Know then that I am a nun of a noble family! A base perjured man undid me and boasted of it. I soon had him dispatched: but not content with the murder, I have bribed the sexton to let me enter his grave and have now plucked out his false heart from his body, and thus I use a traitor's heart."

At these words she tore it in pieces and trampled it under her feet.

From "The Spectator" (1714).

*

114

V

The Tide of the Spirit

Religion is always decaying in the hands of the multitude: it has to be revived by individuals.—BISHOP CREIGHTON.

Heaven is first a *temper* and then a *place*.—WHICHCOTE.

To come from a gaze at the stars—Orion and shaking Sirius below him—is to catch a glance at the unscrutable face of Him that hurries us on, as on a wheel, from dust to dust.—G. MEREDITH.

"Some of the rabbins tell us that the cherubims are a set of angels who know most, and the seraphims a set of angels who love most.—"The Spectator."

Miracles are the swaddling clothes of infant churches.—FULLER.

Let no man be hasty to eat the fruits of Paradise before his time.—JEREMY TAYLOR.

Man must and will have religion: if he has not the religion of Jesus, he will have the religion of Satan and will erect a synagogue of Satan.—BLAKE.

After all, man knows mighty little and may some day learn enough of his own ignorance to fall down and pray.—HENRY ADAMS.

You say you believe the Gospel; you live as if you were sure not one word of it is true.—BISHOP WILSON.

All that I have read about what happens in a future existence makes the life beyond the grave seem an uncomfortable adventure. I have no desire for eternal bliss.—LOGAN PEARSALL SMITH.

I always wear my thickest greatcoat in the parish church as the fungi grow in great number about the Communion table.—ED. FITZGERALD.

I am one of the very few examples in this country of one who has not thrown off religious belief but has never had it.—J. S. MILL.

Destroy the Church of England! You must be mad! It is the only thing which stands between us and real religion.—CH. BULLER.

The English Sunday—a day of sanctity in which indolent ineptitude passes for religious repose.—BERNAL OSBORNE.

"No, my Lord," said Lord Melbourne to the Archbishop of York, who had invited him to attend evening service, "once is orthodox, twice is puritanical."

Things are coming to a pretty pass when religion is allowed to invade private life.—LORD MELBOURNE.

The Supreme Being must be an entirely different individual from what I have every reason to believe Him to be, if He would care in the least for the society of your relations.—C. DICKENS.

MY SOUL, THERE IS A COUNTRY

My soul, there is a country
Far, far beyond the stars,
Where stands a wingèd sentry
All skilful in the wars.

There above noise and danger
Sweet Peace sits crowned with smiles,
And One born in a manger
Commands the beauteous files

116

If thou canst get but thither,
There grows the flower of peace,
The Rose that cannot wither,
Thy fortress and thy ease.

Leave then thy foolish ranges,
For none can thee secure,
But One, who never changes,
Thy God, thy life, thy cure.

HENRY VAUGHAN (1622–95).

*

I PRAISED THE EARTH

I praised the earth, in beauty seen,
With garlands gay of various green:
I praised the sea, whose ample field
Shone glorious as a silver shield.
And earth and ocean seemed to say,
"Our beauties are but for a day".

I praised the sun whose chariot rolled
On wheels of amber and of gold:
I praised the moon whose softer eye
Gleamed sweetly through the summer sky,
And moon and sun in answer said,
"Our days of light are numberèd".

O God, O good beyond compare,
If thus thy meaner works are fair,
If thus thy bounties gild the span
Of ruined earth and sinful man,
How glorious must the mansion be
Where thy redeemed shall dwell with thee.

BISHOP HEBER (1783–1826).

*

ILLUMINATUS

Whoso hath felt the vision of the Highest
    Cannot confound nor doubt Him nor deny:
Yea, with one voice though thou, O world, deniest,
    Stand thou on that side, for on this am I.

Who that one moment has the least descried Him
    Dimly and faintly, hidden and afar,
Doth not despise all excellence beside Him,
    Pleasures and powers that are not and that are?

Yea, amid all men bear himself hereafter,
    Smit with a solemn and a sweet surprise,
Dumb to their scorn, and turning on their laughter
    Only the dominance of earnest eyes.

F. H. MYERS (1843–1901).

Stanzas from "St. Paul".

*

118

THE GODHEAD

As the bee through the garden ranges
From world to world the Godhead changes:
As the sheep go feeding in the waste,
From form to form he maketh haste:
This vault which glows immense with light
Is the inn where he lodges for a night.
What recks such Traveller of the bowers
Which bloom and fade like meadow flowers
A bunch of fragrant lilies be,
Or the stars of eternity?
Alike to him the better, the worse—
The glowing angel, the outcast corse.
Thou meetest him by centuries,
And lo! he passes like a breeze:
Thou seek'st in globe and galaxy,
He hides in pure transparency:
Thou askest in fountains and in fires—
He is the essence that inquires.
He is the axis of the star,
He is the sparkle of the spar,
He is the heart of every creature,
He is the meaning of every feature:
And his mind is the sky,
Than all it holds more deep, more high.

R. W. EMERSON (1803–1882),
From "Woodnotes".

*

ALL SAINTS

One feast, of holy days the crest,
  I, though no churchman, love to keep;
All Saints, the unknown good that rest
  In God's still memory folded deep;
The bravely dumb that did their deed,
  And scorned to blot it with a name,
Men of the plain heroic breed,
  That loved Heaven's silence more than fame.

Such lived not in the past alone,
  But thread to-day the unheeding street,
And stairs to Sin and Famine known
  Sing with the welcome of their feet;
The den they enter grows a shrine,
  The grimy sash an oriel burns,
Their cup of water warms like wine,
  Their speech is filled from heavenly urns.

About their brows to me appears
  An aureole traced in tenderest light,
The rainbow-gleam of smiles through tears
  In dying eyes by them made bright,
Of souls that shivered on the edge
  Of that chill ford repassed no more,
And in their mercy felt the pledge
  And sweetness of the farther shore.

J. R. LOWELL (1819–1891).

*

DOUBT

I have a life with Christ to live,
    But, ere I live it, must I wait
Till learning can clear answer give
    Of this and that book's date?

I have a life in Christ to live;
    I have a death in Christ to die,
And must I wait till science give
    All doubts a full reply?

Nay rather, while the sea of doubt
Is raging wildly round about,
Questioning of life and death and sin,
    Let me but creep within
Thy fold, O Christ, and at Thy feet
    Take but the lowest seat,
And hear Thine awful voice repeat
In gentlest accents, heavenly sweet,
    Come unto Me and rest;
    Believe me and be blest.

        J. C. SHAIRP (1819-1885)

*

INATTENTION AT PRAYER

When we consider with a religious seriousness
the manifold weaknesses of the strongest devotions
in time of prayer, it is a sad consideration. I
throw myself down in my chamber and I call in

and invite God and his Angels, but lose attention for the noise of a flie, for the rattling of a coach, for the whining of a doore. I talk on, in the same posture of praying: eyes lifted up: knees bowed down, as though I prayed to God and if God or his Angels should ask me when I thought last of God in that prayer, I cannot tell. Sometimes I find that I had forgot what I was about, but when I began to forget it, I cannot tell. A memory of yesterday's pleasures, a fear of to-morrow's dangers, a straw under my knee, a noise in my ear, a light in mine eye, an anything, a nothing, a fancy, a Chimera in my brain, troubles me in my prayer. So certainly is there nothing, nothing in spirituall things, perfect in this world.

DR. DONNE (1573–1631).

*

SEEK GOD WITHIN THY OWN SOUL

To seek our divinity merely in books and writings is to seek the living among the dead; we do but in vain seek God many times in these, where His truth too often is not so much enshrined as entombed. No, seek for God within thine own soul; He is better discerned, as Plotinus phraseth it, by an intellectual touch of Him; we must see with our eyes and hear with our ears, and our hands must handle the word of life. The soul itself hath its sense as well as the body; and therefore David, when he would teach us to know what the divine goodness is, calls not for speculation but sensation—Taste and see how good the Lord is.   That is not the best and truest knowledge of God which is wrought out by the labour and sweat of the brain, but that which is kindled within us by a heavenly warmth in our hearts.

JOHN SMITH (1618–1652).

*

ANY EXCUSE FOR NOT ATTENDING CHURCH

There is no excuse so trivial that will not pass upon some men's consciences to excuse their attendance at the public worship of God.   Some are so unfortunate as to be always indisposed on the Lord's day, and think nothing so unwholesome as the air of a church.   Others have their affairs so oddly contrived, as to be always unluckily prevented by business.   With some it is a great mark of wit and deep understanding to stay at home on Sundays.   Others again discover strange fits of laziness, that seize them particularly on that day, and confine them to their beds. Others are absent out of mere contempt of religion.   And, lastly, there are not a few who look upon it as a day of rest, and therefore claim the privilege of their cattle, to keep the Sabbath by eating, drinking, and sleeping, after the toil and labour of the week.   Now in all this the worst circumstance is, that these persons are such whose companies are most required, and who stand most in need of a physician.

JONATHAN SWIFT (1667–1745).

From "A Sermon on Sleeping in Church".

*

THE NATURE OF RELIGION

Such is the nature of religion, that it keeps the mind in a good frame and temper; it establishes a healthful complexion of soul, and makes it fit to discharge itself duly in all its offices towards God, with itself, and with men. Whereas the mind of a wicked and profane man is a very wilderness, where lust and exorbitant passions bear down all before them, and are more fierce and cruel than wolves and tigers. . . . The heavenly state consists in the mind's freedom from these kinds of things. It doth clear the mind from all impotent and insatiable desires, which do abuse a man's soul, and make it restless and unquiet; it sets a man free from eager impetuous loves, from vain and disappointing hopes, from lawless and exorbitant appetites, from frothy and empty joys, from dismal presaging fears and anxious cares, from inward heart-burnings, from self-eating envy, from swelling pride and ambition, from dull and black melancholy, from boiling anger and raging fury, from a gnawing, aching conscience, from arbitrary presumption, from rigid sourness and severity of spirit; for these make the man that is not biassed and principled with religion inwardly to boil, to be hot with the fervours of hell, and like the troubled sea when it cannot rest, whose waters cast up mire and dirt.

BENJAMIN WHICHCOTE (1609–1683).

*

WHEN RELIGION IS OUR RULING TEMPER

Religion is not ours till we live by it, till it is the religion of our thoughts, words and actions, till it goes with us into every place, sits uppermost on every occasion, and forms and governs our hopes and fears, our cares and pleasures. He is the religious man who watches and guards his spirit, and endeavours to be always in the temper of religion; who is as fearful of foolish thoughts, irregular tempers, and vain imaginations at one time as at another; who is as wise and heavenly at home or in the field as in the house of God. For when once religion has got possession of a man's heart, and is become, as it ought to be, his ruling temper, it is as agreeable to such a one in all places and at all times to speak and act according to its directions, as it is to the ambitious man to act according to the motions of ambition. We must therefore take it for granted, that if we are not religious in our conversation and common temper, we are not of a religious spirit.

WILLIAM LAW (1688–1761).

*

A SCEPTIC ON "ARTIFICIAL THEOLOGY"

The authority of the schools lasted till the resurrection of letters, but as soon as real knowledge was enlarged and the conduct of the understanding better understood, it fell into contempt. The advocates of artificial theology have had since that time a very hard task. They have been obliged to defend in the light what was composed in the dark, and to acquire knowledge in order to justify ignorance. They were drawn to it with reluctancy: but learning that grew up among the laity and controversies with one another, made that unavoidable which was not eligible on the principles of ecclesiastical policy. They have done with these new arms all that great parts, great pains, and great zeal could do under such disadvantages. But this Troy cannot be defended: irreparable breaches have been made in it. They have improved in learning and knowledge, but this improvement is as remarkable at least among the laity as among the clergy, besides which it must be owned that the former have had in this respect a sort of direct obligation to the latter; for whilst these men (the clergy) have searched into antiquity, have improved criticism, and almost exhausted subtlety, they have furnished so many arms the more to such of the others as do not submit implicitly to them, but examine and judge for themselves. By refuting one another when they differ, they have made it no hard matter to refute them all when they agree; and, I believe, there are few books written to propagate or defend the received notions of artificial theology which may not be refuted by the books themselves.

LORD BOLINGBROKE (1678–1751).

*

DR. JOHNSON REFLECTS

Good Friday, 1773.

I hope in time to take pleasure in public worship.

Good Friday, 1775.

We then took tea by Boswell's desire and I eat one bun, I think, that I might not seem to fast ostentatiously.

Easter Day, 1776.

My reigning sin, to which perhaps many others are attendant, is waste of time and general sluggishness, to which I was always inclined, and in part of my life have been almost compelled by morbid melancholy and disturbance of mind. Melancholy has had in me its paroxysms and remissions, but I have not improved the intervals, nor sufficiently resisted my natural inclination or sickly habits. I will resolve henceforth to rise at eight in the morning, so far as resolution is proper, and will pray that God will strengthen me. I have begun this morning.

DR. JOHNSON (1709–1784).

*

BOSWELL AND VOLTAIRE TALK RELIGION

At last we came upon Religion. Then did he rage. The company went to Supper. M. de Voltaire and I remained in the drawing-room with a great Bible before us; and if ever two mortal men disputed with vehemence we did. Yes, upon that occasion He was one Individual and I another. For a certain portion of time there was a fair opposition between Voltaire and Boswell. The daring bursts of his Ridicule confounded my understanding. He stood like an Orator of ancient Rome. Tully was never more agitated than he was. He went too far. His aged frame trembled beneath him. He cried, "O, I am very sick; My head turns round," and he let himself gently fall upon an easy chair. He recovered.

I resumed our Conversation, but changed the tone. I talked to him serious and earnest. I demanded of him an honest confession of his real sentiments. He gave it me with candour and with a mild eloquence which touched my heart. I did not believe him capable of thinking in the manner that he declared to me was "from the bottom of his heart." He exprest his veneration —his love—of the Supreme Being, and his entire resignation to the will of Him who is Allwise. He exprest his desire to resemble the Author of Goodness, by being good himself. His sentiments go no farther. He does not inflame his mind with grand hopes of the immortality of the Soul. He says it may be; but he knows nothing of it. And his mind is in perfect tranquillity.

I was moved; I was sorry. I doubted his Sincerity. I called to him with emotion, "Are you sincere? are you really sincere?" He answered, "Before God I am."

JAMES BOSWELL (1740–1795).

From a letter to W. J. Temple.

*

AGNOSTIC TO BROAD CHURCHMAN

I write this the more readily to you, because it is clear to me that if that great and powerful instrument for good or evil, the Church of England, is to be saved from being shivered into fragments by the advancing tide of science—an event I should be very sorry to witness, but which will infallibly occur if men like Samuel Wilberforce of Oxford are to have guidance of her destinies—it must be by the efforts of men who, like yourself, see your way to the combination of the practice of the Church with the spirit of science.

Understand that all the younger men of science whom I know intimately are *essentially* of my way of thinking. (I know not a scoffer or an irreligious or an immoral man among them, but they all regard orthodoxy as you do Brahmanism.) Understand that this new school of the prophets is the only one that can work miracles, the only one that can constantly appeal to nature for evidence that it is right, and you will comprehend that it is of no use to try to barricade us with shovel hats and aprons, or to talk about our doctrines being "shocking."

I don't profess to understand the logic of yourself, Maurice, and the rest of your school, but I have always said that I would swear by your truthfulness and sincerity, and that good must come of your efforts. The more plain this was to me, however, the more obvious the necessity to let you see where the men of science are driving, and it has often been in my mind to write to you before.

THOMAS HENRY HUXLEY (1825–1895).

*

THE SPIRIT OF A FAITH

It is intensely difficult to enter into the spirit of a system not our own. Particular principles and doctrines are easily mastered: but a system answering all the spiritual cravings, all the intellectual capabilities of man, demands more than a mere mental effort—a submission of the intellect, an act of faith, a temporary suspension of the critical faculty.

This applies not merely to the Christian religion with its unfathomable mysteries and its inexhaustible fund of truth, but to the fruits of human speculation. Nobody has ever succeeded in writing a history of philosophy without incurring either the reproach that he is a mere historian, incapable of entering into the genius of any system, or a mere metaphysician, who can discern in all other philosophies only the relation they bear to his own.

In religion the difficulty is greater still and greatest of all with Catholicism. For the Church is to be seen not in books but in life. No divine can put together the whole body of her doctrine: no canonist the whole fabric of her law: no historian the infinite vicissitudes of her career. The Protestant who wishes to be informed on all these things can be advised to rely on no one manual, on no encyclopædia of her deeds and of her ideas; if he seeks to know what these have been he must be told to look around. And to one who surveys her teaching and her fortunes through all ages and all lands, ignorant or careless of that which is essential, changeless and immortal in her, it will not be easy to discern through so much outward change a regular development, amid such variety of forms the unchanging substance, in so many modifications fidelity to constant laws: or to recognise in a career so chequered with failure, disaster and suffering, with the apostasy of heroes, the weakness of rulers and the errors of doctors, the unfailing hand of a heavenly Guide.

LORD ACTON.

*

THACKERAY'S RELIGIOUS FEELING

I cannot resist recalling one Sunday evening in December, when Thackeray was walking with two friends along the Dean Road, to the west of Edinburgh—one of the noblest outlets to any city. It was a lovely evening—such a sunset as one never forgets; a rich dark bar of cloud hovered over the sun, going down behind the Highland hills, lying bathed in amethystine bloom; between this cloud and the hills there was a narrow slip of the pure ether, of a tender cowslip colour, lucid, and as if it were the very body of heaven in its clearness; every object standing out as if etched upon the sky.

The north-west end of Corstophine Hill, with

its trees and rocks, lay in the heart of this pure radiance, and there a wooden crane, used in the quarry below, was so placed as to assume the figure of a cross; there it was, unmistakable, lifted up against the crystalline sky. All three gazed at it silently. As they gazed, Thackeray gave utterance in a tremulous, gentle, and rapid voice, to what all were feeling, in the word "CALVARY!" The friends walked on in silence, and then turned to other things. All that evening he was very gentle and serious, speaking, as he seldom did, of divine things—of death, of sin, of eternity, of salvation; expressing his simple faith in God and in his Saviour.

JOHN BROWN (1810–1882).

From "Horæ Subsecivæ".

*

THE EVOLUTION OF A POSITIVIST

I was brought up as a High Churchman, my godfather being an intimate ally of Henry Phillpotts, Bishop of Exeter, and he took care to give me a thorough training in orthodox divinity. At school I had been something of a neo-Catholic and took the sacrament with a leaning towards transubstantiation. As a student at college, I slowly came to regard the entire scheme of theology as an open question: and I ultimately left the

University without assured belief in any form of supernatural doctrine. But as the supernatural died out of my view, the natural took its place, and amply covered the same ground.

The change was so gradual, and the growth of one phase of thought out of another was with me so perfectly regular, that I have never been able to fix any definite period of change, nor indeed have I ever been conscious of any real change of mind at all. I have never known any abrupt break in mental attitude: nor have I ever felt change of belief to involve moral deterioration, loss of peace, or storms of the soul. I never parted with any belief till I had found its complement: nor did I ever look back with antipathy or contempt on the beliefs I had outgrown. That which was objective law to me as a youth had become subjective duty to me as a man.

I have found theology to be a fine moral training, when it ceased to be an external dogma. I have at no time in my life lost faith in a supreme Providence, in an immortal soul, and in spiritual life; but I came to find these much nearer to me on earth than I had imagined, much more real, more vivid and more practical. . . . Theology, with its religious machinery and its spiritual consolations, has gained a fresh meaning to me, now that I look on it as a mode of moral evolution and not as historical reality. I read the Bible, my Christian mystics and poets still, and with greater pleasure and deeper insight than I did

when I was told to believe in thirty-nine "articles"
and to repeat the three creeds and the catechism.

FREDERIC HARRISON (1890).
From "Memories and Thoughts".

*

CHRISTIANITY WILL FIND A WAY

Who can with just and firm hand sever the
transitory from the durable and the accidental
from the durable in old opinions? Who can
combine in the measures which reason would
prescribe reverence and gratitude to the past with
a sense of the new claims, new means, new duties
of the present? Who can be stout and earnest
to do battle for the Truth and yet hold sacred,
as he ought, the freedom of enquiry, and cherish,
as he ought, a chivalry of controversy like the
ancient chivalry of arms? One persuasion at
least let us embrace: one error let us avoid. Let
us be persuaded of this, that Christianity will by
her inherent resources find for herself a philosophy
equal to all the shifting and the growing wants of
the time. Let us avoid the error of seeking to
cherish a Christianity of isolation. The Christianity which is now and hereafter to flourish and
through its power in the inner circles of human
thought to influence ultimately, in some manner
more adequately than now, the masses of mankind, must be such as of old the Wisdom of God
was described.

For in her is an understanding spirit, holy, one only, manifold, subtile, lively, clear, undefiled, plain, not subject to hurt, loving the thing that is good, quick, which cannot be letted, ready to do good, kind to man, steadfast, sure, free from care, having all power, overseeing all things. . . . For she is the brightness of the everlasting light, the unspotted mirror of the power of God and the image of His goodness.

W. E. GLADSTONE.

From a speech at Edinburgh, 1865.

*

SLIPPING INTO ACCIDIE

There is something very terrible and humiliating in the swiftness with which a great deal of energy and aspiration is unstrung the moment even a light wreath of mist passes over the aspect of the truths that held it up. So much less time and reasoning may suffice for the relaxation of a high demand than were required to enforce its recognition. And thus the thinnest rumour of negative teaching seems enough in some cases to take the heart out of a man's struggle against sloth or worldliness.

If a considerable number of articles in magazines imply that it is impossible to know God it does not seem worth while to get up half an hour earlier in the morning to seek Him before the long day's work begins: if in various quarters and on various grounds the claims of Christ are being set aside or disregarded, then, though the arguments against those claims may never have been carefully examined, the standard of the Sermon on the Mount begins to seem more than can be expected of a man, and if it is often hinted that sins which Christianity absolutely and unhesitatingly condemns may be condoned in an ethical system which takes man as it finds him and recognises all the facts of human nature, the resolute intention of the will is shaken and the clear cherished purpose of a pure and noble life recedes further and further, till it seems almost beyond the possibility of attainment, beyond the range of reasonable ambition.

And so there settles down upon the soul a dire form of accidie: the dull refusal of the highest aspiration in the moral life: the acceptance of a view of one's self and of one's powers which once would have appeared intolerably poor, unworthy and fainthearted: an acquiescence in discouragement which reaches the utmost depth of sadness when it ceases to be regretful: a despondency concerning that goodness to which the love of God has called men, and for which His grace can make them strong.

FRANCIS PAGET, Bishop of Oxford.

From "The Spirit of Discipline".

*

RENAN AND SABATIER

Many years afterwards I had a long talk about Renan with Sabatier, the famous authority on St. Francis. Sabatier was born at Nimes, a great Protestant stronghold. So fanatical was his mother in her Protestantism that she would draw down the blinds rather than that any inmate of her household should set eyes upon a Catholic procession passing along the street. As a very small boy Sabatier was distressed by the thought of these wicked Catholics, creatures so wicked that it was pollution to gaze upon them. Very secretly he determined to make those wicked Catholics better, to convert them, but first to know all about them. So he would steal into Catholic churches, listen to Catholic music, study Catholic ritual. Very soon he became so learned in matters of ritual that priests came to consult him.

Then he sought a deeper kind of learning. He became a University student in Paris, and one day, since his subject was theology, found himself standing right at the back of Renan's lecture-room, as I had done. Something in his appearance, perhaps his rare personal beauty and flaming dark eyes, attracted the old man's attention. "Avez-vous compris?" he asked. "Pas un mot, Monsieur," was the reply. Thereupon, to his intense astonishment and delight this raw young provincial student was taken up into the great man's study and treated to such a lecture on theology as he would never have thought possible.

At the end he started to take his leave. It was raining hard. He had no great coat, no umbrella, and his poor garret was on the other side of Paris. Renan escorted him home, holding his umbrella over him all the way and all the time talking like a God. At the end of their journey Sabatier was too shy to interrupt the talk, and so back they walked to the Collège de France and back again across Paris to the student's lodgings, the famous old man steadily holding up the umbrella and steadily talking, the enraptured young student trotting by his side.

As may be imagined, from that time onwards Sabatier was Renan's slave. It was to Renan that he owed the chief inspiration of his life. "You wish," said the great savant, "to reconcile the Catholic and Protestant Churches. Study St. Francis. He is what Catholics and Protestants have in common."

H. A. L. FISHER.

From "An Unfinished Autobiography".

*

THE BAD HABIT OF PERSECUTION

It needs no weighty scholar, pressed down and running over with the produce of immense research, to demonstrate how common people in a barbarous age were tempted and demoralised by the tremendous power over pain and death and hell. We have to learn by what reasoning process, by what ethical motive, men trained to charity and mercy came to forsake the ancient ways and made themselves cheerfully familiar with the mysteries of the torture chamber, the perpetual prison and the stake. And this cleared away, when it has been explained why the gentlest of women chose that the keeper of her conscience should be Conrad of Marburg, and inversely how that relentless slaughterer directed so pure a penitent as Saint Elizabeth, a larger problem follows.

After the first generation we find that the strongest, the most original, the most independent minds in Europe, men born for opposition, who were neither awed nor dazzled by common law and scholastic theology, by the master of sentences, the philosopher and the gloss, fully agreed with Gucha and Raymond. And we ask how it came about that as the rigour of official zeal relaxed and there was no compulsion, the fallen cause was taken up by the Council of Constance, the University of Paris, the States General, the House of Commons and the first reformers; that Ximenes outdid the early Dominicans, while Vives was preaching toleration, that Fisher, with his friend's handy book of revolutionary liberalism in his pocket, declared that violence is the best argument with Protestants, that Luther, excommunicated for

condemning persecution, became a persecutor?
Force of habit will not help us, nor love, nor fear
of authority, nor the unperceived absorption of
circumambient fumes.

LORD ACTON.

From the "Essay on the Inquisition".

*

THE PRIEST OF ARICIA

Who does not know Turner's picture of the
Golden Bough? The scene, suffused with the
golden glow of imagination in which the divine
mind of Turner steeped and transfigured even
the fairest natural landscape, is a dream-like
vision of the little woodland lake of Nemi, Diana's
Mirror, as it was called by the ancients. No one
who has seen that calm water, lapped in a green
hollow of the Alban Hills, can ever forget it.
The two characteristic Italian villages which
slumber on its banks and the equally Italian
palace, whose terraced gardens descend simply
to the lake, hardly break the stillness and even the
solitariness of the scene. Diana herself might
still linger by this lonely shore, still haunt these
woodlands wild.

In antiquity this sylvan landscape was the
scene of a strange and recurring tragedy. On
the northern shore of the lake, right under the
precipitous cliffs on which the modern village

of Nemi is perched, stood the sacred grove and sanctuary of Diana Nemorensis, or Diana of the Wood. The lake and the grove were sometimes known as the lake and grove of Aricia. In this sacred grove there grew a certain tree round which at any time of the day and probably far into the night a grim figure might be seen to prowl. In his hand he carried a drawn sword, and he kept peering warily about him as if every instant he expected to be set upon by an enemy. He was a priest and a murderer; and the man for whom he looked was sooner or later to murder him and hold the priesthood in his stead. Such was the rule of the sanctuary. A candidate for the priesthood could only succeed to office by slaying the priest and, having slain him, he retained office till he was himself slain by a stronger or a craftier.

Year in year out, in summer and winter, in fair weather and foul, he had to keep his lonely watch; and whenever he snatched a troubled slumber it was at peril of his life. The least relaxation of his vigilance, the smallest abatement of his strength of limb or skill of fence, put him in jeopardy: grey hairs might seal his death warrant. To gentle and pious pilgrims at the shrine the sight of him may well have appeared to darken the fair landscape, as when a cloud suddenly blots the sun on a bright day. The dreamy blue of Italian skies, the dappled shade of sun in woods, and the sparkle of waves in the

sun can have accorded but ill with that stern
and sinister figure.

J. G. FRAZER.

From "The Golden Bough".

*

PERSEVERANCE MATTERS MOST

As to much frequentation of the Cathedral,
(Salisbury), you know well how greatly I love this
for you. Yet there is one warning I would give
you and would beg you to bear in mind. *Do not
overdo it:* I mean do not take your utter fill, while
the attraction is thus strong. If we want our
fervour to last, we must practise moderation even
in our prayer, even in our Quiet.

And certainly it is perseverance in the spiritual
life, on and on, across the years and the changes
of our moods and trials, health and environment,
it is this that supremely matters. And you will
add greatly to the probabilities of such perseverance, if you will get into the way (after having
settled upon the amount of time that it is wise
for you to give to the Cathedral, or your prayer
of quiet in general) of keeping a little even beyond
this time, when you are dry, and a little short of
this time, when you are in consolation.

You see why, don't you? Already the Stoics
had the double rule *Abstine et sustine:* abstain and
sustain: i.e. moderate thyself in things attractive
and consoling; persevere, hold out, in things

repulsive and desolating. There is nothing God loves better, or rewards more richly, than such double self-conquest as this. Whereas all those who heedlessly take their glut of pleasant things, however sacred these things may be, are in grave danger of soon outliving their fervour, even if they do not become permanently disgusted.

BARON VON HÜGEL (1919)
TO HIS NIECE "G.G."
From "Selected Letters".

*

"LAYING THE MATTER BEFORE THE LORD"

I remember, on one occasion, when the Browns, a family of Baptists who kept a large haberdashery shop in a neighbouring town, asked for the pleasure of my company "to tea and games," and carried complacency so far as to offer to send that local vehicle "the midge," to fetch me and bring me back—my Father's conscience was so painfully perplexed, that he desired me to come up with him to the now-deserted "boudoir" of the departed Marks (lately the housekeeper) that we might "lay the matter before the Lord."

We did so, kneeling side by side, with our backs to the window and our foreheads pressed upon the horse-hair cover of the small, coffin-like sofa. My Father prayed aloud, with great fervour, that it might be revealed to me, by the voice of God, whether it was or was not the Lord's will that I should attend the Browns' party. My Father's attitude seemed to me to be hardly fair, since he did not scruple to remind the Deity of various objections to a life of pleasure and of the snakes that lie hidden in the grass of evening parties. It would have been more scrupulous, I thought, to give no sort of hint of the kind of answer he desired and expected.

It will be justly said that my life was made up of very trifling things, since I have to confess that this incident of the Browns' invitation was one of its landmarks. As I knelt, feeling very small, by the immense bulk of my Father, there gushed through my veins like a wine the determination to rebel. Never before, in all these years of my vocation, had I felt my resistance take precisely this definite form. We rose presently from the sofa, my forehead and the backs of my hands still chafed by the texture of the horsehair, and we faced one another in the dreary light. My Father, perfectly confident in the success of what had really been a sort of incantation, asked me in a loud, wheedling voice, "Well, and what is the answer which our Lord vouchsafes?" I said nothing, and so my Father, more sharply, continued, "We have asked Him to direct you to a true knowledge of His will. We have desired Him to let you know whether it is, or is not, in accordance with His wishes that you should accept this invitation from the Browns."

He positively beamed down at me; he had no

doubt of the reply. He was already, I believe, planning some little treat to make up to me for the material deprivation. But my answer came, in the high-piping accents of despair: "The Lord says I may go to the Browns." My Father gazed at me in speechless horror. He was caught in his own trap, and though he was certain that the Lord had said nothing of the kind, there was no road open for him but just sheer retreat. Yet surely it was an error in tactics to slam the door.

EDMUND GOSSE (1849–1928).

From "Father and Son".

*

A THEOLOGICAL "PREAMBLE"!

"The Catholic Church," I said, "holds it better for the sun and moon to drop from heaven, for the earth to fail, and for all the many millions on it to die of starvation in extreme agony, as far as temporal affliction, than that one soul, I will not say should be lost, but commit one single venial sin, should tell one wilful untruth, or should steal one poor farthing without excuse." I think the principles here enumerated to be the mere preamble in the formal credentials of the Catholic Church, as an Act of Parliament might begin with "*Whereas*."

CARDINAL NEWMAN (1801–1890).

From "Apologia pro Vita Sua".

Chap. VII.

146

REAL AND NOMINAL CREEDS

The truth is becoming more and more manifest that real creeds continually diverge from nominal creeds and adapt themselves to new social and individual requirements. The contrast between mediæval Christianity and the present Christianity of Protestant countries, or again the contrast between the belief in a devil appointed to torment the wicked, strenuously held early this century and spreading denial both of a devil and of eternal punishment, or again the recent expression of opinion by a Roman Catholic that there may be happiness in hell, suffice to show the re-moulding of what is nominally the same creed into what is practically quite a new creed, and when we observe, too, how in modern preaching theological dogmas are dropping into the background and ethical doctrines coming into the foreground, it seems that in course of time we shall reach a stage in which, recognising the mystery of change as insoluble, religious organisations will be devoted to ethical culture.

Thus I have come more and more to look calmly on forms of religious habit to which I had in early days a pronounced aversion. Holding that they are in the main naturally adapted to their respective peoples and times, it now seems to me well that they should severally live and work as long as the conditions permit and further that sudden changes of religious institutions as of political institutions are certain to be followed by frictions.

If it be asked why, thinking thus, I have persevered in setting forth views at variance with current creeds, my reply is: It is for each to utter that which he sincerely believes to be true, and adding his unit of influence to all other units, leave the results to work themselves out.

HERBERT SPENCER (1820–1903).

From "Autobiography".

*

EVANGELICAL ASCETICISM

Cold dinners on Sunday! Yes, they are hateful! I loathe them not so much for their culinary shortcomings as for their kill-joy associations. Even my saintly aunt, afterwards known as Lady Mount Temple, used to say as a girl that when married she would certainly give them up. For myself they made me as little look forward to a heaven where "Sabbaths never end," as to one where "congregations ne'er break up."

Of course my father ascribed our cold Sabbatical fare to his desire to give rest to the servants. But this was not his only motive. Without suspecting it he was in favour of a periodical recurrence of a Protestant fast-day. He wished there to be at least one day in a week when the elect gave up what other men enjoyed. Religion is nothing if not ascetic, and a quaint proof of our Sabbath-worship was that although my father often had large parties staying with him on Sunday, yet his guests were on that day not only deprived of hot meat but also given chablis instead of champagne.

This Sabbatical substitution of chablis for champagne recalls the story—I think a true one—told of the late Canon Bull, of Christ Church, who half a century ago was famous throughout Oxford for his excellent dinners. One of these dinners was given to a party of Oxonians in Lent. Neither salmon nor roast beef was lacking, but at the outset he most apologetically declared: "At this holy season we have no side-dishes." It ought to be added that though we always had cold meals on Easter Day, we had excellent hot joints on Good Friday, for, as my father once said to me, "I don't look upon Good Friday as quite like Sunday."

LIONEL A. TOLLEMACHE (1838–1919).

From "Old and Odd Memories".

VI

A Company of Worthies

*

SIR GERVASE CLIFTON

He received from me the certain notice of his approaching death, as he was wont to do an invitation of his good friends to his own Bowling Green, one of the most pleasant imaginable, and thereupon called for his old chaplain, Mr. Robert Thirlby, to do the office of his confessor, and when he had done with him, he called for his children, whom, Patriarch-like, he particularly blessed and admonished, with the smartness and ingenuity of a practised and well-studied orator. The day following he received visits from divers friends, in the old dining-room near his bed-chamber (in which room his portrait hangs to this day) who were not so sensible of his danger, because he entertained them after his usual manner, yet that night (as I easily foretold him) his sleepiness began which could never be taken away.

DR. THOROTON (1665).

[Sir Gervase Clifton, Bart., of Clifton Hall, Notts, was known to his contemporaries as "Gervase the Gentle". He was married seven times. The Clifton Baronetcy was one of the original creation of 1611.]

151

OLIVER DIES IN A GREAT STORM

On Monday, August 30, 1658, there roared and howled all day a mighty storm of wind. Ludlow, coming up to town from Essex, could not start in the morning for wind: tried it in the afternoon, still could not get along in his coach, for head-wind: had to stop at Epping. . . .

It was on this stormy Monday, while rocking winds, heard in the sickroom and everywhere, were piping aloud, that Thurloe and an official person entered to enquire, who, in the case of the worst, was to be his Highness's Successor. The Successor is named in a sealed paper already drawn up, above a year ago, at Hampton Court: now lying in such and such a place. The Paper was sent for, searched for: it could never be found. Richard's (Cromwell) is the name understood to have been written in that Paper: not a good name, but in fact one does not know. . . . Or perhaps it was Fleetwood's name and the Paper by certain parties was stolen. None knows.

On the Thursday night following, "and not till then," his Highness is understood to have formally named "Richard"—or perhaps it might only be some heavy laden, Yes, Yes, spoken out of the thick death-slumbers, in answer to Thurloe's *question* "Richard?" The thing is a little uncertain. . . .

To-morrow is September 3, always kept as a Thanksgiving Day, since the victories of Dunbar and Worcester. . . . He said: "I would be willing to live to be further serviceable to God and His People, but my work is done. Yet God will be with His People."

He was very restless most part of the night, speaking often to himself. And there being something to drink offered him, he was desired to take the same, and endeavour to sleep. Unto which he answered: "It is not my desire to drink or sleep, but my design is to make what haste I can to be gone."

T. CARLYLE (1795–1881).
From "Oliver Cromwell's Letters
and Speeches".

*

A SECOND SIR ROGER

To his religious duties this good man (Lord Sackville) was not only regularly but respectfully attentive. On the Sunday morning he appeared in gala, as if he was dressed for a drawing-room. He marched out his whole family in grand cavalcade to his parish church, leaving only a centinel to watch the fires at home and mount guard upon the spits. His deportment in the house of prayer was exemplary and more in character of times past than of times present; he had a way of standing up in sermon time for the purpose of reviewing the congregation, and awing the idlers into decorum that never failed to remind me of Sir Roger de Coverley at church. Sometimes, when he had been struck by passages in the discourse which he wished to point out to the audience as rules for moral practice worthy to be noticed, he would mark his approbation of them with such cheering nods and signals of assent to the preacher, as were often more than my muscles could withstand. But when to the total overthrow of all gravity, in his zeal to encourage the efforts of a very young declaimer in the pulpit, I heard him cry out to the Rev. Mr. Henry Eatoff in the middle of his sermon "Well done, Harry!" it was irresistible: suppression was out of my power. What made it more intolerably comic was the unmoved sincerity of his manner, and his surprise to find that anything had passed that could provoke a laugh so out of time and place. He had nursed up with no small care and cost in each of his parish churches a corps of rustic psalm-singers to whose performances he paid the greatest attention, rising up and with his eyes directed to the singing gallery, marking time, which was not always rigidly adhered to, and once when his ear, which was very correct, had been tortured by a tone most glaringly discordant, he set his mark upon the culprit by calling out to him by name and loudly saying, "Out of tune, Tom Baker!"

RICHARD CUMBERLAND (1732–1811).

*

A FAMOUS LEICESTERSHIRE WHIG

Sir John Danvers was a man of sound common sense, though in some things highly eccentric.

He was remarkably fond, like the Chinese, of painting everything red, so much so that every door, window shutter, and gatepost in the little towns of Swithland and Mountsorrel was so decorated. He did not stop here: he adopted it in his own dress: but the glaring effect of red was tempered with a mixture of black. If I remember right, his coat was of a dull scarlet, with black buttons, black waistcoat and small clothes, red buttons and red stockings. Being a thick, broad-set man, his appearance was like that of the Knave of Spades.

Sir John, like his ancestors, was a great friend to the liberal principles of our Constitution. It was his ancestor who joined with the Greys of Groby and Hazelrig of Noseley to maintain our liberties in the time of Charles I and signed with them the order for his execution. His Whiggism was so strong that he wrote his own epitaph, desirous that this part of his character, as a lover of the Constitution, should be perpetuated in his family.

When a boy I remember visiting the old hall, which stands in a most romantic part of the county of Leicester. One of his singularities was that no coal should be used in his house: and in every corner of the mansion were piled up short billets cut from the neighbouring woods. Whenever he appeared abroad it was in a sort of stage coach richly emblazoned with his arms and when at home a flag was kept flying upon the topmost turret.

Sir John possessed a good library but used to say that a gentleman's library was complete if it consisted of four books only—the Bible, the Book of Common Prayer, Don Quixote and the Court Calendar.

WILLIAM GARDINER (1770–1853).
From "Music and Friends".

*

THURLOW RETORTS ON THE DUKE OF GRAFTON

Lord Chancellor Thurlow, being reproached by the Duke of Grafton in the House of Lords with his mean origin, rose from the Woolsack and advanced slowly to the place from which the Chancellor generally addresses the House. Then, fixing the Duke with the look of Jove when he grasped the thunder, "I am amazed," he said in a loud tone of voice, "at the attack the noble Duke has made upon me. Yes, my lords," considerably raising his voice, "I am amazed at His Grace's speech. The noble Duke cannot look before him, behind him, or on either side of him, without seeing some noble peer who owes his seat in this House to successful exertions in the profession to which I belong. Does he not feel that it is as honourable to owe it to these as to being the accident of an accident? To all these noble lords the language of the noble Duke is as applicable and insulting as it is to myself. But I don't fear to meet it singly and alone.

"No one venerates the peerage more than I do, but, my lords, I must say that the peerage solicited me, and not I the peerage. Nay more, I can say and will say that as a Peer of Parliament, as Speaker of this right honourable House, as Keeper of the Great Seal, as guardian of His Majesty's conscience, as Lord High Chancellor of England, nay, even in that character alone in which the noble Duke would think it an affront to be considered—as a man—I am at this moment as respectable, I beg leave to add, I am at this moment as much respected as the proudest peer I now look down upon."

The effect of this speech, both within the walls of Parliament and out of them, was prodigious. It gave Lord Thurlow an ascendancy in the House which no Chancellor had ever possessed; it invested him in public opinion with a character of independence and honour, and this, though he was ever on the unpopular side of politics, made him always popular with the people. From this time every Peer shrank from the risk of an encounter with Thurlow and he ruled the House with a rod of iron.

LORD CAMPBELL (1779–1861).
From "Lives of the Chancellors".

*

IMPORTANT VISITORS AT DROPMORE

I was about sixteen or seventeen when, at Dropmore—where I was with Lord and Lady

Grenville only—Mr. Pitt arrived for a visit of two days. First, I was disappointed in that turned-up nose, and in that countenance, in which it was so impossible to find any indication of the mind, and in that person which was so deficient in dignity that he had hardly the air of a gentleman.

After this first disappointment my every faculty seemed to me to be absorbed in listening. If not tropes, I fully expected the dictums of wisdom each time that he opened his mouth. From what I then heard and saw, I should say that mouth was made for eating; as to speaking, there was very little, and that little was totally uninteresting to me, and I believe would have been so to everybody. I was certainly not capable of a very accurate judgment, but I was as certainly in a mood very much to overrate instead of underrating what fell from the great man, and to be quite sure that what I did not understand must be mighty fine.

On the second day arrived Lord Wellesley, whom I thought very agreeable; partly, I fancy, from his highbred manners, and still more from his occasionally saying a few words to *me*, and thus making me feel treated as a reasonable creature. After I had retired for the night, I heard from the library, which was under my room, the most extraordinary noises—barking, mewing, hissing, howling, interspersed with violent shouts of laughter. I settled that the servants had come into the room, and had got drunk and riotous; and I turned to sleep when the noise had ceased.

Never can I forget my dismay (it was more than astonishment) when next day at breakfast I heard that my wise uncle and his two wise guests, whom we had left talking, as I supposed, of the fate of Europe, had spyed in the room a little bird; they did not wish it to be shut up there all night: therefore, after having opened every window, these great wise men tried every variety of noise they could make to frighten out the poor bird.

FRANCES WILLIAMS WYNN.

From the "Diaries of a Lady of Quality".

*

"HIS MEDIOCRITY WAS HIS MERIT"

Lord Liverpool governed England in the greatest crisis of the (Napoleonic) war and for twelve troubled years of peace, chosen not by the nation but by the owners of the land. The English gentry were well content with an order of things by which for a century and a quarter they had enjoyed so much prosperity and power. Desiring no change they wished for no ideas. They sympathised with the complacent respectability of Lord Liverpool's character and knew how to value the safe sterility of his mind. He distanced statesmen like Grenville, Wellesley and Canning not in spite of his inferiority but by reason of it. His mediocrity was his merit.

The secret of his policy was that he had none. For six years his Administration outdid the Holy Alliance. For five years it led the liberal movement throughout the world. The Prime Minister hardly knew the difference. He it was who forced Canning on the King. In the same spirit he wished his Government to include men who were in favour of the Catholic claims and men who were opposed to them. His career exemplified not the accidental combination but the natural affinity between the love of conservatism and the fear of ideas.

LORD ACTON (1834–1902).

*

THE "DEVIL" IN LORD BROUGHAM

There is a last quality in which Lord Brougham excels which has perhaps been of more value to him than all his other qualities put together. In the speech of ordinary men it is called "devil". What it is one can hardly express in a single sentence. It is most easily explained by physiognomy. There is a glare in some men's eyes which seems to say, "Beware! I am dangerous. *Noli me tangere.*" Lord Brougham's face has this. A mischievous excitability is the most obvious expression of it. If he were a horse nobody would buy him: with that eye, no one could answer for his temper. Such men are often not really resolute, but they are not pleasant to be near in a difficulty. They have an aggressive eagerness which is formidable. They would kick against the pricks rather than not kick at all. A little of the demon is excellent for an agitator.

Lord Grey was most unwilling to make Brougham Lord Chancellor. . . . He was too mobile: you could not fancy him droning. He had attacked Lord Eldon for many years, of course: but did he know law? He was a most active person; would he sit *still* on the Woolsack? Of his inattention to his profession men circulated idle tales. "Pity he hadn't known a little law, and then he would have known a little of everything," was the remark of one who certainly knows only one thing.

A more circumstantial person recounted that when Brougham had been a pupil of Sir Nicholas Tindal, in the Temple, an uncle of his, having high hopes of his abilities, asked the latter: "I hope my nephew is giving himself up, soul and body, to his profession?" "I don't know anything," replied the distinguished special pleader, "as to his *soul*, but his body is very seldom in my Chambers." . . . His practice at the Bar, large and lucrative as it was, had not shown him to possess the finer discretion, the more delicate tact of the advocate. Mr. Scarlett stole verdicts away from him. "He strikes hard, sir," said an attorney, "but he strikes wrong." His appointment as Chancellor scarcely strengthened the Ministry of the time. . . . It was like Mr. Disraeli being Chancellor of the Exchequer.

WALTER BAGEHOT (1826–1877).

*

LORD CLARENDON ON LORD DERBY

Clarendon spoke to me with the utmost bitterness of Lord Derby. "Had studied him ever since he (Clarendon) was in the House of Lords. No generosity, never, to friend or foe: never acknowledged help, a great aristocrat, proud of family wealth. He had only agreed to the Reform Bill as he would of old have backed a horse at Newmarket: hated Disraeli but believed in him as he would have done in an unprincipled trainer: he wins—that is all. He knows the garlic given, etc. He says to those without, 'All fair, gentlemen.'"

BISHOP WILBERFORCE (1867).

*

LORD PALMERSTON AT HOME

When at Broadlands Lord Palmerston was a regular attendant at Romsey Church, but was occasionally late. Once when he did not appear till towards the end of the second lesson, the sermon was more than ordinarily long, which a guest attributed to the complacent consideration of the clergyman who was determined that his lordship should gain in one way what he lost in another. "I never saw it in that light before," he said. "I will take care not to tax his kindness again."

He passed some hours of every day on horseback, except on Sundays when he walked. On a cold Sunday in the November of 1864, after luncheon, he proposed a walk and led the way to the paddocks, which he opened one after the other with an enormous key produced from his coat pocket, pointing out and speculating on the qualities of the colts. "That filly," he said, "will run for the Derby the year after next." He then took the party over the river by the ferry-boat, which he tugged backwards and forwards by a hard rope over a stiff pulley, taking an obvious pleasure in the exertion and declining help.

Returning home, after nearly two hours' brisk exercise, in the dusk across the park, his foot struck against a hidden stump, and he fell flat, but was up again in a moment saying, "There is no damage except to the knees of my trousers." The party looked anxiously at one another, remembering the regretted death of Lord Lansdowne, and were not quite at ease till the next morning, when he joined the breakfast table with unshaken spirits and his wonted buoyancy of step.

He was fond of billiards and when at Brocket or Broadlands, played three games, neither more nor less, before retiring for the night. He was about on the level of those who play a good deal without taking rank as players. His best strokes were the winning hazards, and fortune favoured him as much in this as in the political game. After three or four *flukes* he would say, "I think I had better not name my stroke." He was never the least put out by losing, though he enjoyed winning, especially if Lady Palmerston was looking on.

From "Fraser's Magazine" (Nov. 1865)

O CAPTAIN! MY CAPTAIN!

O Captain! my Captain! our fearful trip is done,
The ship has weather'd every rack, the prize we
    sought is won,
The port is near, the bells I hear, the people all
    exulting,
While follow eyes the steady keel, the vessel grim
    and daring;
        But O heart! heart! heart!
        O the bleeding drops of red,
           Where on the deck my Captain lies,
           Fallen cold and dead.

O Captain! my Captain! rise up and hear the bells;
Rise up—for you the flag is flung—for you the
    bugle trills,
For you bouquets and ribbon'd wreaths—for you
    the shores a-crowding,
For you they call, the swaying mass, their eager
    faces turning,
        Here Captain! dear father!
        This arm beneath your head!
           It is some dream that on the deck,
           You've fallen cold and dead.

My Captain does not answer, his lips are pale and
    still,
My father does not feel my arm, he has no pulse
    nor will,
The ship is anchor'd safe and sound, the voyage
    closed and done,

From fearful trip the victor ship comes in with
    object won;
        Exult O shores, and ring O bells!
        But I with mournful tread,
           Walk the deck my Captain lies,
           Fallen cold and dead.
               WALT WHITMAN.
         From "Leaves of Grass".
      (On the death of Abraham Lincoln.)

*

A VICTORIAN SPORTSMAN

The announcement of the Earl of Glasgow's
death falls cruelly upon those who have been
accustomed to see him getting upon his horse,
without overcoat, on the rawest November days,
watching the races during the Houghton meeting
with his old and staunch friend, General Peel.
But perhaps the scene in which he shone most
brightly was at a dinner in the Newmarket Rooms
some twenty years ago when he was surrounded
by Lord Derby, General Peel, Lord Exeter,
Mr. Greville, Lord Strafford and Mr. Payne.
With what glee and quiet drollery would he dis-
parage the staying powers of some flying two-
year-old like Tadmor or Dervish! With what
sanguine over-confidence would he match against
them something got by Gameboy out of Miss
Whip!

Nor, if he was staunch in adhering to particular

strains of blood, however unsuccessful they might be, can it be said that he showed less tenacity in clinging to old haunts. Of all racecourses in England the one which was dearest to his heart was the "Knavesmire" at York: and of all hostelries none was so grateful to him as the Black Swan in that ancient city. It was at this time-honoured inn that, in 1824, he made his first match for 1,000 guineas between his Jock the Laird's Brother and Lord Kennedy's Negotiator, which match it is hardly necessary to add he lost: and it was at the same place that in 1824 he bet Lord Kennedy 1,000 to 10 that Jem Robinson would not win the Derby and the Oaks and be married within the same week. Few now living remember how triumphantly the great jockey won the Derby upon Cedric, the Oaks upon Cobweb, and made his fiancée his wife, all by the appointed date.

It may be doubted whether in all the long and splendid annals of the Turf, anyone ever initiated or contributed to more waggish drolleries than Lord Glasgow. Without a tinge of bitterness or vindictiveness he loved to banter such old friends as "the Clerk of the Council"—for thus he always styled Mr. C. G. Greville—or to depreciate the horses bred by Lord Derby and General Peel. Sometimes, no doubt, in his intercourse with his trainers he employed language that was more forcible than elegant: nor was there even an imaginary dialogue conceived by Lucian or Walter Savage Landor which could compare with some which have actually taken place between Lord Glasgow and Thomas Dawson.

HON. FRANCIS LAWLEY.

From *The Daily Telegraph* of March 13, 1869.

*

SIR TATTON SYKES OF SLEDMERE

The reverence felt for him in Yorkshire was akin to idolatry. To see him riding out of the Eddlesthorpe paddock after a September ram-letting on his Colwick black, which then numbered with its rider a hundred and eight years, accompanied by the clergyman of Sledmere, and returning the greeting of friends and tenants and to hear the half-whispered: "God bless him! How hearty he is—he'll put in for a hundred!" read to me like a chapter out of the *Spectator*.

"How's Sir Tatton looking?" was one of the first questions asked as each York and Doncaster meeting came round. Strangers might well descend from the Grand Stand as soon as he had been pointed out to them at his wonted place by the rails, and make a series of mysterious gyrations around him in order to do full justice to the assertion: "You'll never see such a man again!"

There they would hear the regular string of anecdotes which have been told of him by the workmen's firesides—how he had seen every St. Leger but Charles XII's since he was fourteen

—how he nearly missed Blacklock's by riding seven hundred and twenty miles to "cannie Aberdeen" for a mount on Kutusoff, with only a clean shirt and a razor for his baggage—how he rose with the lark and slashed his own hedges, and how bluff Jack Shirley, the huntsman, complimented him on the excellence of his work, near the Eddlesthorpe Kennels before he guessed who "my old gentleman" was—how he helped to dig the big pond in his park—how deftly he could rebuke forwardness in the field or on the carpet, or give the retort courteous to a bizarre politician—how he often walked by the side of his young horses to and fro the marshes and drove his first lot of Leicester ewes a three days' journey from Lincoln to Barton Ferry—how "Gentleman Jackson" and Jem Belcher had taught him their best hits and to "clear a lane of such men" as once chose to measure the gentleness of his fist by his voice and insult him at a wayside inn—and how he had consistently nurtured himself for these deeds of daring on ale and apple pie.

Time had nearly taken off all his old acquaintances . . . but it never made him faithless to the old garb of Yorkshire—the long, straight-cut, black coat, the ample frill, the beaver gloves, the expansive umbrella, the drab breeches and the mahogany tops which were quite as much part and parcel of the Constitution as "Old Glory's". He had been fashioned in stirring times, and there was not the faintest analogy to him in life or book.

He could almost recollect the Declaration of Independence and he had got one glimpse of Doctor Johnson after much judicious perseverance. . . .

His forty seasons as Master of Foxhounds began some years before he succeeded to the baronetcy, and from 1823, the year of his marriage, his Sledmere life had flown on in one almost unvaried round. "Statesmen might howl and patriots bray," but he did not care to be one of the "faithful Commons" for the privilege of hearing them. His friend, Sir George, could tell him all about them when he came down in August; and as for eloquence, his quotation from Mr. Jorrocks of "Muck's your man" could bring far heartier cheers at a Malton or Driffield agricultural dinner than any which were echoed back from the panels of St. Stephen's.

HENRY HALL DIXON (1822–1870).

From "The Druid".

*

CHARLES SUMNER

Garlands upon his grave,
    And flowers upon his hearse,
And to the tender heart and brave
    The tribute of this verse.

His was the troubled life,
    The conflict and the pain,
The grief, the bitterness of strife,
    The honour without stain.

Like Winkelreid, he took
Into his manly breast
The sheaf of hostile spears, and broke
A path for the oppressed.

Then from the fatal field
Upon a nation's heart,
Borne like a warrior on his shield!—
So should the brave depart.

Death takes us by surprise,
And stays our hurrying feet;
The great design unfinished lies,
Our lives are incomplete.

But in the dark unknown
Perfect their circles seem,
Even as a bridge's arch of stone
Is rounded in the stream.

Alike are life and death,
When life in death survives,
And the interrupted breath
Inspires a thousand lives.

Were a star quenched on high,
For ages would its light,
Still travelling downward from the sky,
Shine on our mortal sight.

So when a great man dies,
  For years beyond our ken
The light he leaves behind him lies
  Upon the paths of men.

          H. W. LONGFELLOW (1875).

*

CHARLES DARWIN'S SELF-ANALYSIS

I have no great quickness of apprehension or wit which is so remarkable in some clever men, for instance, Huxley. I am, therefore, a poor critic: a paper or book, when first read, generally excites my admiration, and it is only after considerable reflection that I perceive the weak points. My power to follow a long and purely abstract train of thought is very limited, and therefore I could never have succeeded with metaphysics or mathematics. My memory is extensive, yet hazy: it suffices to make me cautious by vaguely telling me that I have observed or read something opposed to the conclusion which I am drawing, or on the other hand in favour of it: and after a time I can generally recollect where to search for my authority. So poor in one sense is my memory that I have never been able to remember for more than a few days a single date or a line of poetry.

Some of my critics have said, "Oh! he's a good observer, but he has no power of reasoning": I do not think that this can be true, for the *Origin of Species* is one long argument from beginning to end, and it has convinced not a few able men. No one could have written it without some power of

171

reasoning. I have a fair share of invention, and of common sense and judgment, such as every fairly successful lawyer or doctor must have, but not, I believe, to any high degree.

On the favourable side of the balance, I think that I am superior to the common run of men in noticing things which easily escape attention, and in observing them carefully. My industry has been nearly as great as it could have been in the observation and collection of facts. What is far more important, my love of natural science has been steady and ardent. . . .

I have steadily endeavoured to keep my mind free so as to give up any hypothesis, however much beloved (and I cannot resist forming one on every subject) as soon as facts are shown to be opposed to it. Indeed, I have had no choice but to act in this matter, for with the exception of the Coral Reefs, I cannot remember a single first-formed hypothesis which had not after a time to be given up or greatly modified. This has naturally led me to distrust greatly deductive reasoning in the mixed sciences. . . .

My habits are methodical and this has been of not a little use for my particular line of work. Lastly, I have had ample leisure from not having to earn my own bread. Even ill-health, though it has annihilated several years of my life, has saved me from the distractions of society and amusement.

CHARLES DARWIN (1809–1882).
From "Autobiography".

ROBERT LOWE, LORD SHERBROOKE

Here lie the bones of Robert Lowe,
A faithless friend, a bitter foe—
Whither his restless spirit's fled,
Is guess-work: one thing's sure—he's dead.
Should he have gone to realms above,
Farewell to peace and heavenly love,
But if he's sought a lower level,
The Lord have mercy on the Devil!

ANON.

*

THE DEATH OF LORD BEACONSFIELD

He often said he knew he had no chance and seemed to wish almost that the doctors would tell him so. But they did not know—or would not tell him—and so he glided on till the ship of his life got among the clouds and the breakers and he began to sink without knowing where he was. And so it came that he had not the opportunity of sending a word to some for whom, as I thought I could see, he would have sent a loving message had he known what was so near. I never doubted what the end must be. I knew too well how little of reserve force for long past was left in him.

I am very unhappy! But I won't dwell on that. My life is dreadfully changed. But I have often thought of you and Lady Chesterfield and known how your dear kind hearts were aching.

Will you give her my love? and ask her to forgive my not writing to her?

Indeed, till to-day, I have scarcely been physically able to do so. Day and night was I with him trying to help him over all his pains and troubles as each arose, or to dispel some of the confusions which came over his poor tired brain. It was weary work that sitting with my hand in his in the night watches, trying to guide that mighty mind as a child has to be led!—that trying to be cheerful when I could scarcely help weeping! And I was thankful more than I could ever have deemed possible when the great peace came over him.

MONTY CORRY (LORD ROWTON) (1838–1903).

*

LORD SALISBURY
(THE 8TH MARQUESS)

If this be pride in one of ancient birth
  Not much to heed the clamour of the crowd,
But, being worthy, to believe in worth,
  Then he was proud.

Sincere in aim he spoke the thing he felt,
  With single heart the ancient ways he trod,
Self-confident the more, because he knelt
  And trusted God.

Others have held it blessed to receive:
  He lavished all his life to make the name
Of England greater, well content to leave
  His own the same.

174

It was enough for him to save the State,
  To shield the Church from wrong, to guard the
    throne,
Amid the shocks of change he dared to wait
  Unchanged, alone.

Therefore to him who sought no selfish fame,
  But lived for duty, as the noble must,
Came the free guerdon of the world's acclaim,
  The nation's trust.

He is a part of all that shall endure
  Of England's heritage; while time shall last,
While faith and honour stand, he lives secure,
  And has not passed.

Still shall the spirit of his fiery youth
  His loftier age ennoble all our strife,
Because he sought the way and loved the truth
  And has the life.

                    HUGH MACNAGHTEN.
          From "Fifty Years at Eton".

*

LORD D'ABERNON AT BERLIN

Lord D'Abernon, who, contrary to prevailing rumour, relied very little on his diplomatic staff and dictated all his despatches himself, relied a good deal on "Tich" Whelan, his private secretary, whom he always addressed as "Corporal" and in his hours of boredom unbent before him. It was "Tich" who daily wrote up, to Lord D'Abernon's dictation, the diary record of the great man's ambassadorship. When the task was completed, Lord D'Abernon would rise, shake his shoulders like a great bear, and say, "Corporal, we will now play billiards."

Then the six-foot-three of the Ambassador would engage in solemn contest with the five-foot-two of the private secretary, who with flushed face and puffed out chest would spreadeagle himself across the table with a cue more than twice as long as himself. It was an unequal contest, but it brought joy and relaxation to the Ambassador and increased the hero-worship of the private secretary.

Lord D'Abernon was an impressive figure in a double-breasted blue suit and a stiff white shirt, on the cuffs of which he jotted down his memoranda of important conversations. It was the duty of his private secretary to prevent the shirt and the cuffs being sent to the wash until the notes had been faithfully entered in his lordship's famous diary.

Lord D'Abernon, then just beginning his reign of glory in Berlin, impressed me as the greatest Ambassador I have ever met. His carelessness in dress and his loose collar, nearly always detached from its stud and floating tie detracted nothing from the nobility of his commanding presence. There was always a far-away expression in his eyes, doubtless cultivated in order to increase the impression of disinterested detachment which he sought to give to all his utterances. But he spoke as one having authority, and his conversation was first class—witty and to the point. He had, too, strong views of his own, and but for the intransigence of the French, might have given to the German Republic the permanence and stability which it never acquired.

Certainly, no Ambassador of modern times has ever wielded such influence over the statesmen of the country to which he was accredited. During his seven years in Berlin, the German Government rarely, if ever, issued a Note without first discussing its terms with this most unorthodox of British Ambassadors and accepting his advice.

R. H. BRUCE LOCKHART.

From "Retreat from Glory".

*

A. J. BALFOUR

Just as Rosebery was a seventeenth century type so there was much of the eighteenth century in Balfour, for he had its aversion to too roseate dreams about humanity, but also its profound consciousness of homely worth and homely wisdom. His enthusiasm, slow to kindle, was for what was practicable, for the business of carrying out the work of the world, and his hero was the man who was willing to take a hand.

He had few of the attributes of a popular leader since he was unrhetorical and fastidious and hated all that was showy and glossy, and his mental processes were often too subtle for popular

177

comprehension. Yet he was a great party leader because of his overwhelming power in debate and because of a moral elevation of which the nation became increasingly aware.

His character will be a puzzle for future historians, and it sometimes puzzled even his friends, since it united so many assumed contradictions. He combined a real earnestness and a thoroughgoing scepticism. . . .

Another rare combination was his pessimism and optimism. He had none of the Victorian belief in progress. He saw no golden age in the future, and doubted the existence of any in the past. Hope and dream, he seemed to say, but if you are wise, do not look for too much: this world is a bridge to pass over, not to build upon. But at the same time he revealed the fortitude of human nature, the courage with which men stumbled up the steep ascent of life. . . . Above all, he trusted his countrymen. . . . He revised the doctrine of the Empire so as to shift the emphasis from constitutional bonds to human loyalties.

But the most remarkable union of opposites was his devotion to what was old and his aliveness to what was new. He had the eighteenth-century sense of living in a world which was not made yesterday and emphatically would not be remade to-morrow, and he saw the long descent of the most novel problems. Like Burke, he would not destroy what many generations had built merely because some of the plasterwork was shaky. At the same time he was wholly in tune with his age and aware of every *nuance* of the modern world. He would never admit that there was any merit in a thing merely because it was new, but he gave it a judicial examination.

He had his shortcomings too. Sometimes he used his powers on behalf of an obscurantism which was not his true creed. But he was a very great servant of the State and a great human being. To many there was something chilly in his aloofness from the passions of the market place, something not quite human. Could he suffer and rejoice like an ordinary creature? Assuredly he could. I have seen him in old age show the light-heartedness of a boy, and he could mourn long and deeply, though silently, for the loss of friends. As the phrase goes, he "maximised" life, getting and giving of the best and on his death-bed he looked forward to the end calmly and hopefully as the gateway to an ampler world.

JOHN BUCHAN (Lord Tweedsmuir) (1875–1940).
From "Memory Hold-the-Door".

*

F. E. SMITH
(EARL OF BIRKENHEAD)

Everything "F. E." undertook he did easily, as if with his left hand, and with a superb gesture of unconcern. He was Aristotle's Magnificent

Man, the last exponent of the eighteenth-century Grand Manner. . . . He liked the good things of life and made no bones about it: ginger remained for him hot in the mouth and he refused to relinquish cakes and ale because of the frowns of the anæmic. He had his own strict code of honour, hard as a stone and plain as a pikestaff, and he never departed from it. One of its articles was loyalty to friendship. . . .

"F. E." had plenty of foibles and plenty of critics, but, as has been well said, it is only at the tree loaded with fruit that people throw stones. He had talents of the first order and in a dazzling variety. He was a great lawyer, a great advocate and a great judge. . . . He was a great orator. Not in the highest rank, perhaps, for here, too, he had a limited range and I was never much moved by his solemnities: but in supple argument and devastating controversial skill he had no equal in our time. He had a beautiful voice and his sentences seemed to flow with a contemptuous ease. The fluency of the ordinary man suggests the shallow and the ineffective, but his proclaimed an insolent mastery. . . .

The Magnificent Man is apt to lack the small prudential virtues "F. E." took no thought for the morrow: he was resolved to get what he sought by the sheer weight of brains and will and not by any tactical adroitness. I question whether, if he had lived, he would have gone much further: certainly he would never have been Prime Minister, for he was too much the brilliant individualist for our queer synthetic policy. There has been no one quite like him in our history, for audacious figures like Thurlow had usually something rotten and cankered about them, whereas "F. E." had most of the wholesome virtues. Sometimes he seemed to cultivate a kind of Regency grossness, but the coarseness of grain was superficial: he was capable of the most delicate consideration and chivalry. Above all, he had magnanimity: next to a stout ally he loved a stout opponent.

JOHN BUCHAN (Lord Tweedsmuir) (1875–1940). From "Memory Hold-the-Door".

*

"HARRY" CUST

"Harry" Cust combined in his personality a variety of accomplishments and interests rare even in the days of Crabbet,* now hardly ever found together. Like most commodities of life they are now distributed amongst a larger number of persons: the gold is beaten thinner. The physical and the intellectual sides of life—sport and letters—have been divorced. Bloomsbury and Chelsea are steeped in thought—the only horses they have ever seen are the bronze horses of St. Mark, while Newmarket and Melton could (in Macaulay's phrase) as soon decipher a Baby-

* Wilfrid Blunt's place in Sussex, where the Society wits of the 'nineties often assembled.

Ionian brick as a *Cantica* of Dante. Harry read the *Georgics* driving in his dog-cart to the Meet. Like Charles James Fox he would cap quotations from Horace while walking down St. James's Street after a dance at three in the morning. His kindness and the trouble he would take for a neighbour (in the Samaritan sense) were un-bounded, and he would give a no less concentrated and eager attention to a humble stranger or obscure kinsman than to a wit or a statesman. Never could he be at less than concert pitch. Twice only have I felt myself close to the springs of life: when under the "deep questionings that probe to endless dole" of T. E. Lawrence, and when I drank at that fountain of joy—Henry Cust. . . . To be with him was delight. . . . I think that even now, a score of years after his death, there are still some who, remembering him, sigh in Shakespeare's tremendous homage, "Would I were with him, wheresomever he is!"

SIR RONALD STORRS (1881–   ).

*

A THANKSGIVING

I who the watcher of your ways have been,
I who the radiance of your days have seen,
Thank God.

I who the fire of your mind have known,
I who in flame of your soul have grown,
Thank God.

I who to you owe each least thought,
I who by you are less than nought,
   Thank God.

I who in you found all life's stay,
I who for you lived all life's day,
   Thank God.

I who from you draw all life's light,
I who for you live through life's night,
   Thank God, thank God.
      Mrs. Henry Cust.

[Henry John Cockayne Cust, 1861–1917, great-grandson of the first Lord Brownlow, sat in Parliament 1890–1895 and 1900–1906, and most brilliantly edited the *Pall Mall Gazette* 1892–1896.]

     *

SAUNDERS, L.C.J.

Lord Chief Justice Saunders succeeded in the room of Pemberton. His character and his beginning were equally strange. He was at first no better than a poor beggar boy, if not a parish foundling, without known parents or relations. He had found a way to live by obsequiousness in Clement's Inn, as I remember, and by courting the attorneys' clerks for scraps. The extraordinary observance and diligence of the boy made the Society willing to do him good.

He appeared very ambitious to learn to write,

and one of the attorneys got a board knocked up at a window at the top of a staircase, and that was his desk where he sat and wrote after copies of court and other hands the clerks gave him. He made himself so expert a writer that he took in business and earned some pence by hackney-writing. And thus by degrees he pushed his faculties and fell to forms, and by books that were lent him, became an exquisite entering clerk, and by the same course of improvement of himself an able counsel, first in special pleading, then at large: and after he was called to the bar had practice in the King's Bench Court equal to any of them.

As to his person he was very corpulent and beastly: a mere lump of morbid flesh. He used to say, "By his troggs" (such a humorous way of talking he affected) "none could say he wanted issue of his body, for he had nine in his back." He was a fetid mass, that offended his neighbours at the bar in the sharpest degree. Those, whose ill fortune it was to stand near him, were confessors and in summer time, almost martyrs.

This hateful decay of his carcass came upon him by continual sottishness, for to say nothing of brandy, he was seldom without a pot of ale at his nose, or near him. That exercise was all he used: the rest of his life was sitting at his desk or piping at home: and home was a tailor's house in Butcher Row, called his lodging, and the man's wife was his nurse or worse: but by virtue of his money, of which he made little account, though he got a good deal, he soon became master of the family: and being no changeling, he never removed, but was true to his friends and they to him to the last hour of his life.

ROGER NORTH (1653–1734).
From "Life of Lord Keeper Guilford".

*

A CORRUPT LORD CHANCELLOR

Giving evidence as to his appointment to a Mastership, Master Elde said: His lordship (Lord Macclesfield) said he had no manner of objection to me: he had known me a considerable time, and he believed I should make a good officer. He desired me to *consider of it* and come to him again and I did so.

I came again in a day or two and told him I had considered of it and desired to know if his lordship would admit me, and I would make him a present of £4,000 or £5,000; I cannot say which of the two I said, but I believe it was £5,000. My lord said, "Thee or Thou, or You and I" (my lord was pleased to treat me as a friend) "must not make bargains." He said if I was desirous of having the office he would treat with me in a different manner than he would with any man living.

I made no further application at all, but spoke to Mr. Cottingham, meeting him in Westminster Hall, and told him I had been at my lord's and my lord was pleased to speak very kindly to me, and I had proposed to give him £5,000. Mr. Cottingham answered "*Guineas are handsomer. . . .*" I immediately went to my lord's: I was willing to get into the office as soon as I could. I did carry with me £5,000 guineas in gold and banknotes. I had the money in my chambers, but could not tell how to convey it: it was a great burthen and weight; but recollecting I had a basket in my chambers I put the guineas into the basket and the notes with them. I went in a chair and took the basket with me in my chair.

When I came to my lord's house, I saw Mr. Cottingham there and I gave him the basket and desired him to carry it up to my lord. I saw him go upstairs with the basket and when he came down he intimated to me that he had delivered it. (Cottingham subsequently stated that he carried it up to Lord Macclesfield and left it covered up in his study without saying a word.)

When I was admitted my lord invited me to dinner and some of my friends with me: and he was pleased to treat me and some members of the House of Commons in a very handsome manner. I was after dinner sworn in before them. Some months after I spoke to my lord's gentleman and desired him if he saw such a basket that he would give it me back, and some time after he did so.

Q. "*Was any money returned in it?*"
A. "*No, there was not.*"

From evidence given at the Trial of
Lord Macclesfield (1725).

ALMOST "AN ODD INCIDENT"

We had a week with Haldane at Cloan. I preached at Auchterarder on the Sunday. Every day I had abundant talking and walking with Haldane. I had one adventure with him. He took me for a walk along a ravine where he had not been for a long time. The path disappeared, the sides were precipitous, loose earth and many of the little trees, which were abundant, were decayed and gave no hold and the earth slithered away. Haldane, who is most agile, would not go further and I think he was right, but when he tried to get up the bank on our return, he stuck and for some minutes I was seriously alarmed that he would slip into the ravine below—a really serious matter. However, I got above him and hauled him up with my stick. He is not a good climbing companion. He recognised it to the full and even exaggerated the perils in which he had been. We felt it would have been an odd incident if the Archbishop and a Lord Chancellor had together tumbled down a valley and been killed. But the thing was really not impossible.

DR. RANDALL DAVIDSON (1918).
From a letter in the Bishop of Chichester's (Dr. Bell)
"Life of Archbishop Davidson".

*

BUDDING LORD CHANCELLORS AT PLAY

J. A. Simon and F. E. Smith were close friends at Oxford, though intimacy, I suppose, would hardly be the word for the relationship of such very opposite characters. They were at the same college as undergraduates, and Simon was a member of that historic Wadham Rugby team which was captained by "F. E." and whose record of triumphs has never, I believe, been equalled in college football. Simon worked, as "F. E." did not, hard and regularly, but he had plenty of other interests, including politics: there was never the faintest trace in him of the slavish student whom Max Beerbohm, in a lyric of his undergraduate days, unkindly addressed in the opening lines:

> Smug! in your attic crooning
> Your Aristotle through,
> The sun himself is swooning
> At sight of you. .   .

Once, after a dinner given by the Warden of Merton, "F. E." took Simon and myself over to his rooms, where they plunged immediately into a vehement argument about the Government's Chinese policy. It ended at midnight with Simon tipping "F. E." out of his chair, and "F. E." squirting soda-water at Simon. "F. E." at that time was a Fellow of Merton, Simon of All Souls.

E. C. BENTLEY.
From "Those Days".

*

THE COMPLETE GAMESTER

It was a tradition of Limmers* that Mr. George Payne and Lord Albert Denison, afterwards the first Lord Londesborough, sat up all night in that famous but now extinguished hostelry, and that when they separated in the morning, Lord Albert, having lost about £30,000, proceeded to the adjoining Temple of Hymen at St. George's, Hanover Square, to be married to his first wife, Miss Henrietta Maria Forester, the sister of Lady Chesterfield, Mrs. Anson and Lady Bradford.

With the same antagonist, and playing at the same game (écarté) Payne once set out from London in a post-chaise to pay a visit to a country house in the New Forest. They played all day, and when night fell a lamp in the roof of the chaise was lighted and they proceeded to deal and propose without intermission.

Mr. Payne was in the midst of a capital turn of luck, with £100 staked on each game, when they both became aware that the chaise had stopped and that the bewildered post-boy, who had lost his way, was tapping lustily with the butt end of his whip at the window of the post-chaise to solicit the attention of its occupants. "What do you want?" said Mr. Payne testily. "Please, Sir, I have lost my way." "Come and tell me when you

---

* Limmers was a fashionable private hotel at the corner of Conduit Street and George Street.

have found it," was all the rejoinder he could elicit.

JAMES RICE (1843–1882).
From the "History of the British Turf".

*

THE THIRD AND LAST MARQUIS OF HASTINGS

"The Spider and the Fly" drama is ended. That poor coronetted youth, who has crowded into six years more Corinthian excitement and weightier Turf cares than many fast men know in a lifetime, has laid down his weary load at last. He was only twenty-six in July and had already frittered away two fine family estates. Betting is said to be the touchstone of an Englishman's sincerity: but with the Marquis a craving for the odds had become a passion, or even a disease.

He worshipped chance with all the ardour of a fanatic. His wits were, he considered, worth to him in the betting ring at least £20,000 a year, and he sometimes threaded his way through the mazes of tricks and public cunning with all the sagacity of a wizard. His public coups were so often brilliant that it was hardly to be wondered at that he believed in his own destiny and his power to break the Ring. It mattered nothing to him whether the draining or other improvements on his Donington Estate were stopped, if he only got fresh supplies for another Newmarket campaign. The Rings, on the other hand, had marked him for their own and never left him.

They would cluster beneath the Jockey Club balcony at Epsom, holding up their hands to claim his attention, and catching at his replies like a flock of hungry hawks. There he would stand, smiling at the wild tumult below, wearing his hat jauntily on one side, a red flower in his button-hole, and his colours round his neck, perfectly cool and unruffled while "the talent" made his horse a hot favourite at once, and a few slipped back to the Ring to follow his lead. For a time he was a perfect Cocker: but he fell at last in the unequal strife, and the men who had drawn him most copiously were among the first to set their faces sternly against him, when, bereft of resources, he wished to see the Heath once more.

H. H. DIXON ("The Druid").

Nov. 1868.

[Hermit's victory in the Derby of 1868 and Achievement's defeat in the Oaks had resulted in the Marquis having to find £103,000 on the following Monday morning. Dixon's reference to his many brilliant coups—soon forgotten after his catastrophic fall—is corroborated by the anecdote told of Steel, the bookmaker, who was once heard to mutter as the Marquis left him, "Ah, my Lord, Heaven's been very gracious to you, for you look a fool and you ain't one." Nevertheless, he committed almost every folly generally encountered on the road to ruin, even to that of wilfully accelerating the pace.]

*

MR. WALKER "DETERMINES TO BE WELL"

During my early youth and for a long time after I felt no security of my health. At last, one day when I had shut myself up in the country and was reading with some attention Cicero's treatise "De Oratore", some passage—I quite forget which—suggested to me the expediency of making the improvement of my health my study. *I rose from my book, stood bolt upright and determined to be well.* In pursuance of my resolution I tried many extremes, amidst the remonstrances and ridicule of those around me. I persevered, nevertheless, and it is now, I believe, full sixteen years since I have had any medical advice or taken any medicine.

During that period I have lived constantly in the world—for the last six years in London without ever being absent during any one whole week—and I have never foregone a single engagement of business or pleasure, or been confined an hour, with the exception of two days in the country from over-exertion. For nine years I have worn neither great-coat nor cloak, though I ride and walk at all hours and in all weathers. My dress has been the same in summer and winter, *my under garments being single and only of cotton, and I am always light shod.* The only inconvenience I suffer is occasionally from colds, *but with a little more care I could entirely prevent them: or if I took the trouble I could remove the most severe in twenty-four hours.*

T. WALKER.

From "The Original" (1835).

*

A STORY OF A BLIND OLD PAUPER

David Jones began his life as one of the scarlet penny-posts, and rode with his horn and saddle-bags between the General Post Office and Hampstead Heath three times a day. Then followed a stable apprenticeship under old Chifney*, and from being a head lad at Newmarket he rose to be head groom to the Marquis of Westminster and General Grosvenor and was one of the first two persons who ever slept in Eaton Hall. He sailed next to India and Spain and was all through the Peninsular War, as head groom to a General of Brigade, and came home—speaking three languages—to train and ride once more. Priam winning the Derby (1830) was about the last image that impressed itself on his failing retina.

Total blindness and the ruin of the London season by the death of George IV, which left his Mayfair lodging-house unlet, broke him down in

* George IV's favourite jockey.

the same year and at last the workhouse at Chelsea was his lot. In the summer time we would often go to meet him in the Brompton lanes, led by a little girl, with a flower in his button-hole, "to show 'em I've been in the country," and the year before he died he assured us that he would like to get a match on to walk any man of his age five miles yet.

Such stories he would tell, over and over again, of old times. How, for example, in his hunting-groom days he out-manœuvred the crafty Mat Milton; how he "wasted" from Hampton to Hyde Park Corner; how his three terriers killed and ate one of Mr. Grantley Berkeley's best fox-hound whelps at walk; how General Grosvenor once despatched him to the Newmarket turnpike for a bladder of hog's lard, when his horse's feet got snowballed just before a match: how Robson the trainer looked "for all the world like a clergyman" and seldom did more to a boy than hit him with a black glove; how Cork and Tiny knew each other 300 yards off on the heath and instantly desired battle; how he fed a golden roan Egyptian on tamarinds off Lisbon and cantered him to try his paces between the guns on deck; how he spent an anxious night before Waterloo; how one master shot himself through the head almost in his presence; and how his only hope of "leaving the house" went for ever when his soldier-son died at Scutari.

At last he fell fainting in the heat on his way

back, early in June, from "The Corner", where he went once a week to receive a small allowance left him by the late Mr. Edmund Tattersall, and when we next saw him he was on his death-bed. He dared not speak, and after handing over his scissors and a few old letters he would insist on retaining only eighteenpence out of the few shillings he had left.

When we pressed him for the reason, he stealthily clutched with his hand as he lay—to indicate that the other paupers in the ward, who leant forward and glared savagely in their beds, or hobbled within earshot to catch the faintest whisper that might pass between us would, as he knew from hard experience, rob him the instant he died, and that he was determined to foil them.

All was over when next we called, but we learnt that even in his death-throes he had been once more with his string at Hampton Wick and was calling for champagne into the weighing house to toast a winner. That weary, chequered story of eight-and-seventy-years was closed at last and relief, not indoor or outdoor, had come in a far grander shape, as we claimed him from the dead-house and laid him to his rest on the morning of the longest day.

HENRY HALL DIXON.

("The Druid").

*

MR. JORROCKS IS LOST

Night now drew on apace and heavy darkening clouds proclaimed a fast approaching storm. At Staunton-Snivey, Mr. Jorrocks learned that the hounds had just passed the turnpike on to the Downs with the fox "dead beat close afore them" and, still unwilling to give in, he groped open a bridle gate and entered upon the wide extending Plain. The wind had now risen and swept with uncommon keenness over the unprotected open. The drizzling rain, too, became changed into larger, heavier drops; and, thrusting his hat upon his brow, Mr. Jorrocks buttoned his coat up to his throat and wrapping its laps over his thighs tucked them in between his legs and the saddle. Dismal and disheartening were his thoughts and many his misgivings for his rashness.

"Oh! dear, oh! dear," muttered he, "wot a most momentous crisis—lost! lost! lost! completely lost! Dinner lost! 'ounds lost! self lost! all lost together! Oh! wot evil genius ever tempted me from the lovely retirement of Great Coram Street! Oh! why did I neglect the friendly warnin' o' Gabriel Junks? Change, change, storm, storm, was in his every scream, and yet I would go. Cuss the rain, it's gettin' down my werry back, I do declare!" saying which he turned the blue collar of his coat up to his ears, and both laps flew out with a desperate gust of wind. "Ord rot it," said he, "it's not never no use perserverin', may as well give in at once and 'ark back to Snivey: my Berlins are wet through, and I shall be drenched in another second. Who-ay, 'oss! who-ay: stand still, you hugly beast and let me listen!" The ducking-headed brute at length obeyed.

"It *is* the 'orn," exclaimed Mr. Jorrocks, after sitting listening for some time, with his hand to his ear: "it is the 'orn; Pigg's not far off! There it goes again, but the 'owling wind carries so many ways, there's no sayin' whereabouts he is. I'll blow and see if I can 'ail him."

Mr. Jorrocks then drew out his horn and puffed and blew most lustily, but the raging tempest scattered the notes before they were well out of his mouth, and having exhausted his breath he again paused, horn in hand, to listen. Between each blast of the raging hurricane the faint notes of the horn were heard, some coming more fully as the gale blew more favourably, and a fuller one falling on his ear during a period of partial lull, Mr. Jorrocks determined on advancing and endeavouring to rejoin his lost huntsman.

"Come hup, I say, you hugly beast!" exclaimed he, getting Artaxerxes short by the head, and digging his spurs freely into his sides. The lumbering brute acknowledged the compliment with a sort of half hitch of a kick. "Great henterpriseless brute—do believe you'd rayther 'ave a feed o' corn than the finest run wot ever was seen," observed Mr. Jorrocks, cropping him.

Night had now closed in and even the sort of

light of darkness that remains to the traveller who journeys onward with the closing day, deserted him and earth and sky assumed the same sombre hue:

The dragon wing of night o'erspread the earth.

Scarce a star was visible in the firmament and the few scattered lights that appeared here and there about the country, seemed like snatches of hope lit up for the moment to allure and perplex the wanderer.

ROBERT SURTEES (1803–1864).
From "Handley Cross".

*

VII

The Country Scene

*

Who that hath reason and his smell
Would not among roses and jasmine dwell?

A. COWLEY.

The new moon hangs like an ivory bough
In the naked frosty blue.

E. THOMAS.

The blackbird in a thorn of waving white
Sang bouquets of small tunes.

FRANCIS LEDWIDGE.

Or listen with enchanted ears
From the dark dingles to the nightingales.

M. ARNOLD.

Green pasturage and the grace of standing corn
And meadow and marsh with springs and unblown leaves,
Flocks and swift herds and all that bite sweet grass.

A. C. SWINBURNE.

It is more pleasant to me to sit in a clean room, with a
clear air outside, and hedges just coming into leaf rather
than in the Tavistock or an upper floor of Charlotte
Street.—ED. FITZGERALD (1846).

*Rura mihi et rigui placeant in vallibus amnes,
Flumina amem silvasque—inglorius!*

VIRGIL.

[Let the fields and the running brooks of the valleys
delight me: let me love the rivers and the woods—to
fame unknown!]

The very shades on hill and tree and plain
Where they have fallen doze and where they doze remain.
                                        F. THOMPSON.

  Scenes must be beautiful which daily viewed
  Please daily, and whose novelty survives
  Long knowledge and the scrutiny of years.
                                WILLIAM COWPER.

————

ENGLAND

No lovelier hills than thine have laid
    My tired thoughts to rest,
No peace of lovelier valleys made
    Like peace within my breast.

Thine are the woods whereto my soul
    Out of the noontide beam,
Flees for a refuge green and cool
    And tranquil as a dream.

Thy breaking seas like trumpets peal,
    Thy clouds—how oft have I
Watched their bright towers of silence steal
    Into infinity!

My heart within me faints to roam
    In thought even far from thee:
Thine be the grave whereto I come
    And thine my darkness be!
                    WALTER DE LA MARE (1873–   ).

*

THE QUESTION

I dreamed that, as I wandered by the way,
   Bare Winter suddenly was changed to Spring,
And gentle odours led my steps astray,
   Mixed with a sound of waters murmuring
Along a shelving bank of turf, which lay
   Under a copse, and hardly dared to fling
Its green arms round the bosom of the stream,
But kissed it and then fled, as thou mightest in
     dream.

There grew pied wind-flowers and violets,
   Daisies, those pearled Arcturi of the earth,
The constellated flower that never sets;
   Faint oxslips; tender bluebells, at whose birth
The sod scarce heaved; and that tall flower that
     wets—
   Like a child, half in tenderness and mirth—
Its mother's face with Heaven's collected tears,
When the low wind, its playmate's voice, it hears.

And in the warm hedge grew lush eglantine,
   Green cowbind and the moonlight-coloured
     may,
And cherry-blossoms, and white cups, whose wine
   Was the bright dew, yet drained not by the day;
And wild roses, and ivy serpentine,
   With its dark buds and leaves, wandering astray;
And flowers azure, black, and streaked with gold,
Fairer than any wakened eyes behold.

And nearer to the river's trembling edge
　　There grew broad flag-flowers, purple pranked
　　　with white,
And starry river buds among the sedge,
　　And floating water-lilies, broad and bright,
Which lit the oak that overhung the hedge
　　With moonlight beams of their own watery
　　　light;
And bulrushes, and reeds of such deep green
As soothed the dazzled eye with sober sheen.

Methought that of these visionary flowers
　　I made a nosegay, bound in such a way
That the same hues, which in their natural bowers
　　Were mingled or opposed, the like array
Kept these imprisoned children of the Hours
　　Within my hand—and then, elate and gay,
I hastened to the spot whence I had come,
That I might there present it!—O to whom?
　　　　　　　P. B. SHELLEY (1792–1822).

*

A GARDEN CLOSE

I know a little garden close
Set thick with lily and red rose,
Where I would wander if I might
From dewy dawn to dewy night
　　And have one with me wandering.
And though within it no birds sing,
And though no pillared house is there,

And though the apple boughs are bare
Of fruit and blossom, would to God
Her feet upon the green grass trod,
    And I beheld them as before!
        WILLIAM MORRIS (1834–1896).
            From "Jason".

*

IN A GARDEN

Here at the fountain's sliding foot,
Or at some fruit-tree's mossy root,
Casting the body's vest aside
My soul into the boughs does glide;
There, like a bird, it sits and sings,
Then whets and combs its silver wings,
And, till prepared for longer flight,
Waves in its plumes the various light.
        ANDREW MARVEL (1621–1678).

*

THE PEERLESS RED ROSE

Whenas the mildest month
Of jolly June doth spring,
And gardens green with happy hue
Their famous fruits do bring;
When eke the lustiest time
Reviveth youthful blood,
Then springs the finest featured flower
In border fair that stood.
Which moveth me to say,
In time of pleasant year,

203

Of all the pleasant flowers in June,
The red rose hath no peer.
                THOMAS HOWELL (1594–1666).

*

THE ROSE UPON HER BRIAR

The lily has a smooth stalk
    Will never hurt your hand,
But the rose upon her briar
    Is the lady of the land.

There's sweetness in the apple tree,
    And profit in the corn,
But the lady of all beauty
    Is a rose upon a thorn.

When with moss and honey
    She tips her bending briar,
And half unfolds her glowing heart,
    She sets the world on fire.
            CHRISTINA ROSSETTI (1830–1894).

*

DAPPLED THINGS

Glory be to God for dappled things—
For skies of couple-colour as a brindled cow;
For rose-moles all in stipple upon trout that swim,
Fresh-firecoal chestnut falls: finches' wings;
Landscape plotted and pieced—fold, fallow and
    plough;
And all trades, their gear and tackle trim.
        GERARD MANLY HOPKINS (1844–1889).

DAFFODILS

The daffodils were fair to see:
They nodded lightly on the lea,
   Persephone, Persephone.
Lo! one she marked of rarer growth
   Than Orchis or Anemone:
For it the maiden left them both
   And parted from their company.
Drawn nigh, she deemed it fairer still
And stooped to gather by the rill,
   The Daffodil, the Daffodil.
        JEAN INGELOW (1820–1897).

*

JENNY WREN

Of all the birds that rove and sing,
Near dwellings made for men,
None is so nimble, feat, and trim,
   As Jenny Wren.

With pin-point bill, and tail a-cock,
   So wildly shrill she cries,
The echoes on her roof tree knock
   And fill the skies.

Never was sweeter seraph hid
   Within so small a house—
A tiny, inch-long, eager, ardent,
   Feathered mouse.
      W. DE LA MARE (1873–   ).
      From "Poems 1919–1934".

THE LINNET

Upon this leafy bush
With thorns and roses in it,
Flutters a thing of light,
A twittering linnet;
And all the throbbing world
Of dew and sun and air
By this small parcel of life
Is made more fair;
As if each bramble-spray
And mounded gold-wreathed furze,
Harebell and little thyme,
Were only hers;
As if this beauty and grace
Did to one bird belong,
And, at a flutter of wing,
Might vanish in song.

W. DE LA MARE (1873–   ).
From "Poems 1901–1918".

*

MARTINS: SEPTEMBER

At secret daybreak they had met—
Chill mist beneath the welling light
Screening the marshes green and wet—
An ardent legion wild for flight.

Each preened and sleeked an arrowlike wing,
Then eager throats with lapsing cries
Praising whatever fate might bring—
Cold wave, or Africa's paradise.

206

Unventured, trackless leagues of air,
England's sweet summer narrowing on
Her lovely pastures; nought they care—
Only this ardour to be gone.

A tiny, elflike, ecstatic host . . .
And I neath them, on the highway's crust,
Like some small mute belated ghost,
A sparrow pecking in the dust.

W. DE LA MARE (1873–   ).
From "Memory and other Poems".

*

AUTUMN

I love the fitful gust that shakes
    The casement all the day,
And from the glossy elm-tree takes
    The faded leaves away,
Twirling them by the window pane
With thousand others down the lane.

I love to see the shaking twig
    Dance till the shut of eve,
The sparrow on the cottage rig,
    Whose chirp would make believe
That Spring was just now flirting by
In Summer's lap with flowers to lie.

I love to see the cottage smoke
    Curl upwards through the trees,

The pigeons nesting round the cote
    On November days like these;
The cock upon the dunghill crowing,
The mill sails on the heath a-going.

The feather from the raven's breast
    Falls on the stubble lea,
The acorns near the old crow's nest
    Drop pattering down the tree;
The grunting pigs, that wait for all,
Scramble and hurry where they fall.
            JOHN CLARE (1793–1864).

*

FROST AT MIDNIGHT

Therefore all seasons shall be sweet to thee,
Whether the summer clothe the general earth
With greenness, or the redbreast sit and sing
Betwixt the tufts of snow on the bare branch
Of mossy apple-tree, while the nigh thatch
Smokes in the sun-thaw; whether the eave-drops
    fall
Heard only in the trances of the blast,
Or if the secret ministry of frost
Shall hang them up in silent icicles,
Quietly shining to the quiet Moon.

           S. T. COLERIDGE (1772–1834).

*

WHAT OF THE NIGHT?

Is the night chilly and dark?
The night is chilly but not dark.
The thin grey cloud is spread on high,
It covers but not hides the sky.
The moon is behind and at the full
And yet she looks both small and dull.
The night is chill, the cloud is grey:
Tis a month before the month of May,
And the spring comes slowly up this way.

S. T. COLERIDGE (1772–1834).
From "Christabel".

*

NIGHT

The sun descending in the west,
The evening star does shine;
The birds are silent in their nest,
And I must seek for mine.
The moon, like a flower
In heaven's high bower,
With silent delight
Sits and smiles on the night.

Farewell, green fields and happy grove
Where flocks have ta'en delight;
Where lambs have nibbled, silent move
The feet of angels bright.
Unseen they pour blessing,
And joy without ceasing,
On each bud and blossom,
On each sleeping bosom.

209

They look in every thoughtless nest,
Where birds are covered warm;
They visit caves of every beast,
To keep them all from harm.
If they see any weeping
That should have been sleeping,
They pour sleep on their head,
And sit down by their bed.

WILLIAM BLAKE (1757–1827).

*

THE OLD PACKHORSE ROAD

Well, people say this hollow track
    Was never made for wheels and springs;
    But worn by packhorses in strings,
With wares, on ev'ry horse a pack.

Before, by yonder plain and ridge,
    The road was stean'd two-waggons wide,
    Where wheels now spin and horsemen ride,
On high-cast bank and high-bowed bridge.

The road climb'd up, onwinding deep
    Beside the ashes on the height,
    Where elderflow'rs are hanging white
O'er yonder crowds of cluster'd sheep.

And up at Holway men would shout
    "Hold hard," or else would blow a horn
    On their side of the way, to warn
Oncomers back, till they were out.

And then it struck along the glades
   Above the brook, to Rockley spring,
   And meads, where now you hear the ring
Of mowers' briskly-whetted blades.

And then it sunk, the slope to dive
   Through Pebbleford, where uncle took
   His way across the flooded brook,
But never reach'd his home alive.

And then it touch'd the ridgy ground
   With marks of walls, where Deanton stood;
   Though now the houses, stone and wood,
Are gone, with all their tongues and sound.

Our elders there, as we are told,
   Had once their homes, and doors to close
   Between warm hearths and winter snows;
And there play'd young, and there grew old.

       WILLIAM BARNES (1801–1886).

*

THE BROOK

Seated once by a brook, watching a child
Chiefly that paddled, I was thus beguiled.
Mellow the blackbird sang and sharp the thrush
Not far off in the oak and hazel bush,
Unseen.   There was a scent like honeycomb
From mugwort dull. And down upon the dome
Of the stone the cart-horse kicks against so oft
A butterfly alighted. From aloft

He took the heat of the sun, and from below,
On the hot stone he perched contented so,
As if never a cart would pass again
That way; as if I were the last of men
And he the first of insects to have earth
And sun together and to know their worth.
I was divided between him and the gleam,
The motion, and the voices, of the stream,
The waters running frizzled over gravel,
That never vanish and for ever travel.
A grey flycatcher silent on a fence
And I sat as if we had been there since
The horseman and the horse lying beneath
The fir-tree-covered barrow on the heath,
The horseman and the horse with silver shoes,
Galloped the downs last. All that I could lose
I lost. And then the child's voice raised the dead.
"No one's been here before" was what she said
And what I felt, yet never should have found
A word for, while I gathered sight and sound.

EDWARD THOMAS (1878–1917).

*

MARCH

Now I know that Spring will come again,
Perhaps to-morrow: however late I've patience
After this night following on such a day.

While still my temples ached from the cold burning
Of hail and wind, and still the primroses
Torn by the hail were covered up in it,

212

The sun filled earth and heaven with a great light
And a tenderness, almost warmth, where the hail
  dripped,
As if the mighty sun wept tears of joy.
But 'twas too late for warmth. The sunset piled
Mountains on mountains of snow and ice in the
  west:
Somewhere among their folds the wind was lost,
And yet 'twas cold, and though I knew that Spring
Would come again, I knew it had not come.
That it was lost too in those mountains chill.

What did the thrushes know? Rain, sun, hail,
  sleet
Had kept them quiet as the primroses.
They had but an hour to sing. On boughs they
  sang,
On gates, on ground: they sang while they changed
  perches
And while they fought, if they remembered to fight,
So earnest were they to pack into that hour
Their unwilling hoard of song before the moon
Grew brighter with the clouds. Then 'twas no time
For singing merely. So they could keep off silence
And night, they cared not what they sang or
  screamed,
Whether 'twas hoarse or sweet or fierce or soft:
And to me all was sweet; they could do no wrong.
Something they knew—I also while they sang
And after. Not till night had half its stars
And never a cloud, was I aware of silence.

Stained with all that hour's songs, a silence
Saying that Spring returns, perhaps to-morrow.
E. THOMAS (1878–1917).

*

FOR THESE

An acre of land between the shore and the hills,
Upon a ledge that shows my kingdoms three,
The lovely visible earth and sky and sea
Where what the curlew needs not, the farmer tills:

A house that shall love me as I love it,
Well-hedged, and honoured by a few ash trees
That linnets, greenfinches and goldfinches
Still often visit and make love in and flit:

A garden I need never go beyond,
Broken but neat, whose sunflowers every one
Are fit to be the sign of the Rising Sun:
A spring, a brook's bend, or at least a pond.

For these I ask not, but, neither too late
Nor yet too early, for what men call content,
And also that something may be sent
To be contented with, I ask of Fate.
E. THOMAS (1878–1917).

*

PRINCESS OF RIVERS

O my beloved Nymph! fair Dove,
Princess of rivers, how I love
Upon thy flow'ry banks to lie
And view thy silver stream,

214

When gilded by a summer's beam,
And in it all thy wanton fry
    Playing at liberty,
And with my angle upon them
    The all of treachery
I ever learned to practise and to try.
            C. COTTON (1630–1687).

*

POMONA

I am the ancient Apple-Queen,
As once I was so am I now;
For evermore a hope unseen
Betwixt the blossom and the bough.

Ah, where's the river's hidden Gold!
And where the windy grave of Troy?
Yet come I as I came of old
From out the heart of Summer's joy.

        WILLIAM MORRIS (1834–1896).
            From "Poems by the Way".

*

FOREFATHERS

Here they went with smock and crook,
    Toiled in the sun, lolled in the shade,
Here they mudded out the brook
    And here their hatchet cleared the glade.
Harvest-supper woke their wit,
Huntsman's moon their wooings lit.

From this church they led their brides,
    From this church themselves were led
Shoulder-high; on these waysides
    Sat to take their beer and bread.
Names are gone—what men they were
These their cottages declare.

Names are vanished, save the few
    In the old brown Bible scrawled;
These were men of pith and thew,
    Whom the city never called;
Scarce could read or hold a quill,
Built the barn, the forge, the mill.

On the green they watched their sons
    Playing till too dark to see,
As their fathers watched them once,
    As my father once watched me;
While the bat and beetle flew
On the warm air webbed with dew.

Unrecorded, unrenowned,
    Men from whom my ways begin,
Here I know you by your ground
    But I know you not within—
All is mist, and there survives
Not a moment of your lives.

Like the bee that now is blown
    Honey-heavy on my hand,

From the toppling tansy-throne
   In the green tempestuous land—
I'm in clover now, nor know
Who made honey long ago.

       EDMUND BLUNDEN (1896–   ).

*

A HOUSE AND GROUNDS

Were this impossible, I know full well
What sort of house should grace my garden-
   bell—
A good, old country lodge, half hid with blooms
Of honied green, and quaint with straggling rooms,
A few of which, white-bedded and well swept,
For friends, whose names endear'd them, should
   be kept.
Of brick I'd have it, far more broad than high,
With green up to the door, and elm trees nigh;
And the warm sun should have it in his eye.
The tiptoe traveller, peeping through the boughs
O'er my low wall, should bless the pleasant house,
And that my luck might not seem ill-bestow'd,
A bench and spring should greet him on the road.
My grounds should not be large; I like to go
To Nature for a range, and prospect too,
And cannot fancy she'll comprise for me,
Even in a park, her all-sufficiency.
Besides, my thoughts fly far; and when at rest,
Love, not a watch tower, but a lulling nest.

But all the ground I had should keep a look
Of Nature still, have birds'-nests and a brook;
One spot for flowers, the rest all turf and trees;
For I'd not grow my own bad lettuces.
I'd build a walk, however, against rain,
Long, peradventure, as my whole domain,
And so be sure of generous exercise,
The youth of age, and med'cine of the wise.
And this reminds me, that behind some screen
About my grounds, I'd have a bowling-green;
Such as in wits' and merry women's days
Suckling preferred before his walk of bays.
You may still see them, dead as haunts of fairies,
By the old seats of Killigrews and Careys,
Where all, alas, is vanished from the ring,
Wits and black eyes, the skittles and the king!

LEIGH HUNT.

*

LOB

The man was wild

And wandered.   His home was where he was free
Everybody has met one such man as he.
Does he keep clear old paths that no one uses
But once a lifetime when he loves or muses?
He is English as this gate, these flowers, this mire.
And when at eight years old Lob-lie-by-the-fire
Came in my books, this was the man I saw.
He has been in England as long as dove and daw,
Calling the wild cherry-tree the merry tree,
The rose campion Bridget-in-her-bravery;

And in a tender mood he, as I guess,
Christened one flower Love-in-idleness,
And while he walked from Exeter to Leeds
One April called all cuckoo-flowers Milkmaids.
From him old herbal Gerard learnt, as a boy,
To name wild clematis the Traveller's-joy.
Our blackbirds sang no English till his ear
Told him they called his Jan Toy "Pretty dear."
(She was Jan Toy the Lucky, who, having lost
A shilling, and found a penny loaf, rejoiced.)
For reasons of his own to him the wren
Is Jenny Pooter.   Before all other men
'Twas he first called the Hog's Back the Hog's
    Back.
That Mother Dunch's Buttocks should not lack
Their name was his care.   He could explain
Totteridge and Totterdown: and Juggler's Lane
He knows, if any one: why Tumbling Bay,
Inland in Kent, is called so, he might say.

> EDWARD THOMAS (1878–1917).
>
> Lines from "Lob".

*

THE ROSE AND THE LARK

But so have I seen a Rose newly springing from
the cleft of its hood, and at first it was fair as the
Morning and full with the dew of Heaven, as a
lamb's fleece: but when a ruder breath had forced
open its virgin modesty and dismantled its too
youthful and unripe retirements, it began to put

on darknesse and to decline to softnesse and the symptomes of a sickly age: it bowed the head and broke its stalk, and at night having lost some of its leaves and all its beauty, it fell into the portion of weeds and outworn faces.

*   *   *   *

For so have I seen a lark rising from his bed of grass and soaring upwards singing as he rises and hopes to get to heaven and climb above the clouds; but the poor bird was beaten back with the loud sighings of an eastern wind and his motion made irregular and unconstant, descending more at every breath of the tempest than it could recover by the libration and frequent weighing of its wings: till the little creature was forced to sit down and pant and stay till the storm was over, and then it made a prosperous flight and did rise and sing as if it had learned musick and motion from an Angell as he passed sometimes through the air about his ministries here below.

JEREMY TAYLOR (1613–1667).

*

THE LANE IN ITS BEAUTY

How beautiful the lane is to-day, decorated with a thousand colours! The brown road, and the rich verdure that borders it, strewed with the pale yellow leaves of the elm, just beginning to fall; hedgerows glowing with long wreaths of the bramble in every variety of purplish red; and overhead the unchanged green of the fir, contrasting with the spotted sycamore, the tawny beech, and the dry, sere leaves of the oak, which rustle as the light wind passes through them; a few common hardy yellow flowers (for yellow is the common colour of flowers, whether wild or cultivated, as blue is the rare one), flowers of many sorts, but almost of one tint, still blowing in spite of the season, and ruddy berries glowing through all. How very beautiful is the lane!

MARY RUSSELL MITFORD (1787–1855).

*

A SHEPHERD OF THE WILTSHIRE DOWNS

He agreed that it was very quiet on the downs, and that he loved their quiet. "Fifty years," he said, "I've been on the downs and the fields, day and night, seven days a week, and I've been told that it's a poor way to spend a life, working seven days for ten or twelve, or at most thirteen shillings. But I never seen it like that; I liked it, and I always did my best. You see, sir, I took a pride in it. I never left a place but I was asked to stay. When I left it was because of something I didn't like. I couldn't never abide cruelty to a dog or any beast. And I couldn't abide bad language. If my master swore at the sheep or the dog I wouldn't abide with he—no, not for a pound a week. I liked my work, and I liked knowing things about the sheep. Not things in books, for I never had no books, but what I found out with my own sense, if you can understand me."

After our long Sunday talk we were silent for a time, and then he uttered these impressive words: "I don't say that I want to have my life again, because 'twould be sinful. We must take what is sent. But if 'twas offered to me and I was told to choose my work, I'd say, 'Give me my Wiltsheer Downs again and let me be a shepherd there all my life long.'"

W. H. HUDSON (1841–1922).
From "A Shepherd's Life".

*

TOLD AT THE COTTAGE DOOR

And we didn't drink no tea then. Eight shillings a pound, or maybe seven-and-six—dear, dear, how was we to buy it! We had beer for breakfast and it did us good. It were better than all these nasty cocoa stuffs we drink now. We didn't buy it at the public-house—we brewed it ourselves. And we had a brick oven then, and could put a pie in, and a loaf, and whatever we wanted, and it were proper vittals. We baked barley bread, and black bread, and all sorts of bread, and it did us good and made us strong.

These iron ranges and stoves we have now—what's the good o' they? You can't bake bread in 'em. And the wheat bread you gits from the shop, what's it good for? 'Tisn't proper vittals—it fills 'e with wind. No, I say, I'm not going to git the fruit—let the birds have it! Just look at the greedy things—them starlings! I've shouted, and thrown sticks and all sorts of things, and shaken a cloth at 'em, and it's like calling the fowls to feed. The more noise I make the more they come.

What I say is, if I can't have the fruit I wish the blackbirds 'ud git it. People say to me, "Oh, don't talk to me about they blackbirds—they be the worst of all for fruit." But I never minded that—because—well, I'll tell 'e. I mind when I were a little thing at Old Alresford, where I were born, I used to be up at four in the morning, in the summer, listening to the blackbirds. And mother she used to say, "Lord, how she do love to hear a blackbird!" It's always been the same. It's always up at four, and in summer I goes out to hear the blackbird when it do sing so beautiful.

But them starlings that come messing about, pulling the straws out of the thatch, I've no patience with they. We didn't have so many starlings when I were young. But things is very different now; and what I say is, I wish they wasn't—I wish they was the same as when I were a girl. And I wish I was a girl again.

W. H. HUDSON (1841–1922).
From "Hampshire Days".

NOTHING LIKE FRESH AIR

It's indoors, sir, as kills half the people; being indoors three parts of the day, and next to that taking too much drink and vittals. Eating's as bad as drinking; and there ain't nothing like fresh air and the smell of the woods. You should come out here in the spring, when the oak timber is throwed (because, you see, the sap be rising, and the bark strips then), and just sit down on a stick fresh peeled—I means a trunk, you know—and sniff up the scent of that there oak bark. It goes right down your throat, and preserves your lungs as the tan do leather. And I've heard say as folks who work in the tanyards never have no illness.

There's always a smell from trees, dead or living—I could tell what wood a log was in the dark by my nose; and the air is better where the woods be. The ladies up in the great house sometimes goes out into the fir plantations—the turpentine scents strong, you see—and they say it's good for the chest; but, bless you, you must live in it. People go abroad, I'm told, to live in the pine forests to cure 'em: I say these here oaks have got every bit as much good in that way.

I never eat but two meals a day—breakfast and supper: what you would call dinner—and maybe in the middle of the day a hunch of dry bread and an apple. I take a deal for breakfast, and I'm rather lear (hungry) at supper; but you may lay your oath that's why I'm what I am in the way of health. People stuffs theirselves, and by consequence it breaks out, you see. It's the same with cattle; they're overfed, tied up in stalls and stuffed, and never no exercise, and mostly oily food too. It stands to reason they must get bad; and that's the real cause of these here rinderpests and pleuro-pneumonia and what-nots. At least that's my notion.

I'm in the woods all day, and never comes home till supper—'cept, of course, in breeding-time, to fetch the meal and stuff for the birds—so I gets the fresh air, you see; and the fresh air is the life, sir. There's the smell of the earth, too—'specially just as the plough turns it up—which is a fine thing; and the hedges and the grass are as sweet as sugar after a shower. Anything with a green leaf is the thing, depend upon it, if you want to live healthy.

RICHARD JEFFERIES (1848–1887).
From "The Gamekeeper at Home".

*

THE LOVE OF TREES

I like flowering plants, but I like trees more. There are forests in England whose leafy noises may be shaped into Agincourt and the names of the battlefields of the Roses: oaks that dropped their acorns in the year that Henry VIII held his Field of the Cloth of Gold and beeches that gave shelter to the deer when Shakespeare was a boy.

There they stand, in sun and shower, the broad-armed witnesses of perished centuries. A great English tree, the rings of centuries in its boll, touches the imagination no less than the eye, for it grows out of tradition and a past order of things and is pathetic with the suggestion of dead generations.

Trees are your best antiques. There are cedars on Lebanon which the axes of Solomon spared, they say, when he was busy with his Temple: there are others on Olivet that might have rustled in the ears of the Master and the Twelve: there are oaks in Sherwood which have tingled to the horn of Robin Hood and have listened to Maid Marian's laugh. Think of an existing Syrian cedar which is nearly as old as history, which was middle aged before the wolf suckled Romulus: think of an existing English elm in whose branches the heron was reared which the hawks of Saxon Harold killed! If you are a notable and wish to be remembered, better plant a tree than build a city or strike a medal—it will outlive both.

My trees are young enough, and if they do not take me away into the past they project me into the future. When I planted them I knew I was performing an act the issues of which would outlast me long. My oaks are but saplings, but what undreamed of English Kings will they not survive! I pluck my apples, my pears, my plums, and I know that from the same branches other hands will pluck apples, pears and plums when this body of mine will have shrunk into a pinch of dust.

ALEXANDER SMITH (1830–1867).
From "Dreamthorpe".

*

THE GRACIOUS SERVICE OF MOSS

No words that I know of will say what these mosses are. None are delicate enough, none perfect enough, none rich enough. How is one to tell of the rounded bosses of furred and beaming green—the starred divisions of rubied bloom, fine-filmed, as if the Rock Spirits could spin porphyry as we do glass—the traceries of intricate silver and fringes of amber, lustrous, arborescent, burnished through every fibre into fitful brightness and glossy traverses of silken change, yet all subdued and pensive, and framed for simplest, sweetest offices of grace? They will not be gathered, like the flowers, for chaplet or lovetoken; but of these the wild bird will make its nest, and the wearied child his pillow.

And, as they are the earth's first mercy, so they are its last gift to us. When all other service is vain from plant and tree, the soft mosses and grey lichen take up their watch by the headstone. The woods, the blossoms, the gift-bearing grasses, have done their parts for a time, but these do service for ever. Trees for the builder's yard, flowers for the bride's chamber, corn for the granary, moss for the grave.

JOHN RUSKIN (1819–1900).
From "Modern Painters".

*

TWO WILD GEESE

Arctic and Antarctic geese are alike in their devotion to their distant breeding-ground, the cradle and true home of the species or race. Witness an incident related to me many years ago by a brother who was sheep-farming in a wild and lonely district on the southern frontier of Buenos Ayres.

Immense numbers of upland geese in great flocks used to spend the cold months on the plains where he had his lonely hut; and one morning in August in the early spring of that southern country, some days after all the flocks had taken their departure to the South, he was out riding and saw at a distance before him on the plain a pair of geese. They were male and female—a white and a brown bird. Their movements attracted his attention and he rode to them.

The female was walking steadily on in a southerly direction, while the male, greatly excited, and calling loudly from time to time, walked at a distance ahead, and constantly turned back to see and call to his mate, and at intervals of a few minutes he would rise up and fly, screaming, to

228

a distance of some hundreds of yards, then finding that he had not been followed, he would return and alight at a distance of forty or fifty yards in advance of the other bird, and begin walking on as before. The female had one wing broken, and, unable to fly, had set out on her long journey to the Magellanic Islands on her feet; and her mate, though called to by that mysterious imperative voice in his heart, yet would not forsake her, but flying a little distance, to show her the way, and returning again and again, and calling to her with his wildest and most piercing cries, urged her still to spread her wings and fly with him to their distant home.

And in that sad, anxious way they would journey on to the inevitable end, when a pair or family of carrion eagles would spy them from a great distance—the two travellers left far behind by their fellows, one flying, the other walking, and the first would be left to continue the journey alone.

W. H. HUDSON (1841–1922).

From "Birds and Man".

*

THE OWL'S FATAL FASCINATION

Is it imagining quite wildly to suppose that the extraordinary, eccentric figure which the owl cuts in the daytime in itself exercises a strong fascination over the nervous and highly sensitive nature

229

of many small birds which he draws to him as irresistibly as the magnet draws steel? If the hooded serpent fascinates by its bizarre and sinister aspect may not the owl exercise in some degree a similar power through his glittering and blinking eye and—with some species—his horn-like ears, horns of Satan for his victims. May he not fascinate, too, by the wonderful facial disc and the immense mass of quaintly patterned and fluffy feathers as well as by the extreme, almost uncanny silence of his flight, and the uncouth attitudes of stillness which he adopts on his perch?

I have never seen the owl strike when thus encircled by a crowd of agitated spectators. But it is very hard for the human watcher, in cases like these, to see the play played right out. For one thing, he usually intrudes only to break the spell. It is so with the stoat and the rabbit, and no doubt with the serpent and its prey. Again, how few, if any, who have seen the stoat or weasel capering to a gallery, have seen the fell spring that ends the play? There is no fascination about a man intruding—there is only fright. But we do know for sure that the owl strikes small birds, and is it likely that he withholds when hungry and his prey is fluttering and agitated all around him?

G. A. B. DEWAR (1862–1934).
From "This Realm, this England".

*

230

BETTY

Where there was never any open water before I have cleared away the mosses and made ponds and raised all sorts of wild fowl in their vicinity. In doing this, a wonderfully small and pretty little milk-white bantam hen, whose name is Betty, and who knows her name as well as any dog ever knew his, reared one of the finest broods of fowl of the smaller kind and was taken with her callow young and placed in one of the swamps in the valleys on the moors. Betty had no place to roost in other than the heather and she so adapted herself to the necessities of her foster children that she might be seen wading in the swamps up to her breast—her clothes so to speak held very high or kilted—and catching insects for them as assiduously as if she had been on dry land. She remained with her brood of ducks till they took flight from her and then she was *brought home*.

Since then she has reared both pheasants and partridges on dry land, and her conduct when her covey of twelve partridges—one day in the September of 1866—flew away from her immensely amused me. I saw it happen. She stood up as erect as she could make herself and watched their flight as if she desired to mark them down, and then pretended to find food, and for a few minutes called them to come to it as loudly as she could. Finding they did not come, she leisurely and in an offended manner, walked home to my lawn, never looked for her birds again and very shortly knocked at the window of the kitchen to be let in, to lay under a boiler in the scullery not in use, where she had invariably deposited her eggs for the last two years: laying more frequently than any hen in my possession and continuing to lay throughout the summer and winter.

HON. G. C. GRANTLEY-BERKELEY (1800–1881).

*

VIII

Winged Words

*

MAN

I know my soul hath power to know all things,
    Yet she is blind and ignorant in all;
I know I'm one of nature's little kings,
    Yet to the least and vilest things am thrall.

I know my life's a pain, and but a span;
    I know my sense is mock'd in everything;
And, to conclude, I know my self a Man—
    Which is a proud, and yet a wretched thing.

              SIR JOHN DAVIES (1569–1626).

*

I LIVE, AND YET METHINKS

I live, and yet methinks I do not breathe;
I thirst and drink, I drink and thirst again;
I sleep and yet do dream I am awake;
I hope for that I have; I have and want;
I sing and sigh; I love and hate at once.
O, tell me, restless soul, what uncouth jar
Doth cause in store such want, in peace such war?
              ANON. (1609).

EVEN SUCH IS MAN

Like to the falling of a star,
Or as the flights of eagles are,
Or like the fresh spring's gaudy hue,
Or silver drops of morning dew,
Or like a wind that chafes the flood,
Or bubbles which on water stood:
Even such is man, whose borrow'd light,
Is straight call'd in, and paid to night.

The wind blows out; the bubble dies;
The Spring entomb'd in Autumn lies;
The dew dries up; the star is shot;
The flight is past, and man forgot.
BISHOP HENRY KING (1592–1669).

*

JOY AND GRIEF

The grateful heart for all things blesses;
Not only joy, but grief endears:
I love you for your few caresses,
I love you for your many tears.
W. S. LANDOR (1775–1864).

*

A HAPPY LIFE

My friend, the things that do attain
The happy life be these, I find:
The riches left, not got with pain;
The fruitful ground, the quiet mind;

234

The equal friend; no grudge, no strife;
  No charge of rule, no governance;
Without disease the healthy life;
  The household of continuance;

The mean diet, no dainty fare;
  Wisdom joined with simpleness;
The night dischargèd of all care,
  Where wine and wit may not oppress;

The faithful wife, without debate;
  Such sleeps as may beguile the night;
Content thyself with thine estate;
  Neither wish death nor fear his might.

HENRY HOWARD, EARL OF SURREY (1517–1547).

*

HIGH AND LOW

Were I as base as is the lowly plain,
And you, my love, as high as heaven above,
Yet should the thoughts of me your humble
    swain
Ascend to heaven in honour of my love.
Were I as high as heaven above the plain,
And you, my love, as humble and as low
As are the deepest bottoms of the main,
Wheresoe'er you were, with you my love should go
Were you the earth, dear love, and I the skies,
My love should shine on you like to the sun,
And look upon you with ten thousand eyes,

235

Till heaven waxed blind, and till the world were
 done.
  Wheresoe'er I am, below, or else above you,
  Wheresoe'er you are, my heart shall truly love
   you.

       J. SYLVESTER (1602).

*

WHEN TO HER LUTE

When to her lute Corinna sings
Her voice revives the leaden strings,
And doth in highest notes appear,
As any challenged echo clear;
But when she doth of mourning speak,
Ev'n with her sighs the strings do break.
And as her lute doth live or die,
Led by her passion, so must I;
For when of pleasure she doth sing,
My thoughts enjoy a sudden spring;
But if she doth of sorrow speak,
Ev'n from my heart the strings do break.

    THOMAS CAMPION (1567–1620).

*

THERE IS A GARDEN IN HER FACE

There is a garden in her face
 Where roses and white lilies grow:
A heavenly paradise is that place,
 Wherein all pleasant fruits do flow,
There cherries grow, which none may buy,
 Till "Cherry Ripe" themselves do cry.

    THOMAS CAMPION (1567–1620).

LOVE STANDS GUARD

Love guards the roses of thy lips
   And flies about them like a bee;
If I approach he forward skips,
   And if I kiss he stingeth me.

Love in thine eyes doth build his bower,
   And sleeps within their pretty shrine;
And if I look the boy will lower,
   And from their orbs shoot shafts divine.

Love works thy heart within his fire,
   And in my tears doth firm the same;
And if I tempt it will retire,
   And of my plaints doth make a game.

Love, let me cull her choicest flowers;
   And pity me, and calm her eye;
Make soft her heart, dissolve her lowers;
   Then will I praise thy deity.

But if thou do not, Love, I'll truly serve her
In spite of thee, and by firm faith deserve her.
          THOMAS LODGE (1558–1625).

*

THE UNFADING BEAUTY

He that loves a rosy cheek,
   Or a coral lip admires,
Or from star-like eyes doth seek
   Fuel to maintain his fires:
As old Time makes these decay,
So his flames must waste away.

But a smooth and steadfast mind,
    Gentle thoughts and calm desires,
Hearts with equal love combined,
    Kindle never-dying fires.
Where these are not, I despise
Lovely cheeks or lips or eyes.

THOMAS CAREW (1595-1639).

*

IT IS NOT BEAUTY I DEMAND

It is not Beauty I demand,
    A crystal brow, the moon's despair,
Nor the snow's daughter, a white hand,
    Nor mermaid's yellow pride of hair.

Tell me not of your starry eyes,
    Your lips that seem on roses fed,
Your breast where Cupid tumbling lies,
    Nor sleeps for kissing of his bed.

A bloomy pair of vermeil cheeks,
    Like Hebe's in her ruddiest hours,
A breath that softer music speaks
    Than summer winds a-wooing flowers.

These are but gauds; nay, what are lips?
    Coral beneath the ocean-stream,
Whose brink when your adventurer sips
    Full oft he perisheth on them.

And what are cheeks but ensigns oft
  That wave hot youth to fields of blood?
Did Helen's breast, though ne'er so soft,
  Do Greece or Ilium any good?

Eyes can with baleful ardour burn,
  Poison can breath that erst perfumed,
There's many a white hand holds an urn
  With lovers' hearts to dust consumed.

For crystal brows—there's naught within,
  They are but empty cells for pride;
He who the Syren's hair would win
  Is mostly strangled in the tide.

Give me, instead of beauty's bust,
  A tender heart, a loyal mind,
Which with temptation I could trust,
  Yet never linked with error find.

One in whose gentle bosom I
  Could pour my secret heart of woes,
Like the care-burthened honey-fly,
  That hides his murmurs in the rose.

My earthly comforter! whose love
  So indefeasible might be,
That when my spirit won above
  Hers could not stay for sympathy.
          GEORGE DARLEY (1828).

*

WHEN PHOEBE'S AWAY

My time, O ye Muses, was happily spent
When Phoebe went with me wherever I went:
Ten thousand sweet pleasures I felt in my breast:
Sure never fond shepherd like Colin was blest!
But now she is gone and has left me behind,
What a marvellous change on a sudden I find!
When things were as fine as could possibly be,
I thought 't was the Spring: but, alas! it was she.

When my lambkins around me would oftentimes
    play
And when Phoebe and I were as joyful as they,
How pleasant their sporting, how happy the time,
When Spring, love and beauty were all in their
    prime?
But now in their frolics when by me they pass,
I fling at their fleeces an handful of grass:
Be still then, I cry, for it makes me quite mad
To see you so merry, when I am so sad.

When walking with Phoebe what sights I have
    seen!
How fair was the flower, how fresh was the green!
What a lovely appearance the trees and the shade,
The cornfields and hedges and everything made!
But now she has left me, though all still are there,
They none of 'em now so delightful appear:
'Twas naught but the magic, I find, of her eyes,
Made so many beautiful prospects arise.

Sweet music went with us both all the wood
    through,
The lark, linnet, throstle, and nightingale too:
Winds over us whispered, flocks by us did bleat,
And chirp went the grasshopper under our feet.
But now she is absent, though still they sing on,
The woods are but lonely, the melody's gone:
Her voice in the concert, as now I have found,
Gave everything else its agreeable sound.

Rose, what is become of that delicate hue?
And where is the violet's beautiful blue?
Does aught of its sweetness the blossom beguile,
That meadow, those daisies, why do they not
    smile?
Ah! rivals, I see what it was that you dressed
And made yourselves fine for: a place in her breast:
You put on your colours to pleasure her eye,
To be plucked by her hand, in her bosom to die.

How slowly time creeps, till my Phoebe return!
While amidst the soft zephyrs' cold breezes I burn:
Methinks if I knew whereabouts he would tread,
I could breathe on his Wings, and 't would melt
    down the lead.
Fly swifter, ye minutes, bring hither my dear,
And rest so much longer for 't when she is here,
Ah! Colin, old time is full of delay,
Nor will budge one foot faster for all thou canst say.

REV. JOHN BYROM (1692-1763).
From "The Spectator", 1714.

241

ILLUMINATION

I have been here before,
  But when or how I cannot tell:
I know the grass beyond the door,
  The sweet, keen smell,
The sighing sound, the lights around the shore.

You have been mine before—
  How long ago I may not know:
But just, when at that swallow's soar
  Your neck turn'd so,
Some veil did fall—I knew it all of yore.

D. G. ROSSETTI (1828–1882).

*

LIFE

Stop and consider! life is but a day;
A fragile dew-drop on its perilous way
From a tree's summit; a poor Indian's sleep
While his boat hastens to the monstrous steep
Of Montmorenci.   Why so sad a moan?
Life is the rose's hope while yet unblown;
The reading of an ever-changing tale;
The light uplifting of a maiden's veil;
A pigeon tumbling in clear summer air;
A laughing school-boy, without grief or care,
Riding the springy branches of an elm.

JOHN KEATS (1795–1821).

*

JOY

Every night and every morn
Some to misery are born;
Every morn and every night
Some are born to sweet delight;
Some are born to endless night.
Joy and woe are woven fine,
A clothing for the soul divine;
Under every grief and pine
Runs a joy with silken twine.
It is right it should be so;
Man was made for joy and woe;
And when this we rightly know
Safely through the world we go.

WILLIAM BLAKE (1757–1827).

*

I LOOK INTO MY GLASS

I look into my glass
And view my wasting skin,
And say, "Would God it came to pass
My heart had shrunk as thin!"

For then I, undistrest
By hearts grown cold to me,
Could lonely wait my endless rest
With equanimity.

But Time to make me grieve
    Part steals, part lets abide,
And shakes this fragile frame at eve
    With throbbings of noontide.

              THOMAS HARDY.
              From "Wessex Poems".

*

"SHUT OUT THAT MOON"

Close up the casement, draw the blind,
    Shut out that sad-shaped moon,
She wears too much the guise she wore
    Before our lutes were strewn
With years-deep dust, and names we read
    On a white stone were hewn.

Step not out on the dew-dashed lawn
    To view the Lady's Chair,
Immense Orion's glittering form,
    The Small and Greater Bear:
Stay in; to such sights we were drawn
    When faded ones were fair.

Brush not the bough for midnight scents
    That come forth lingeringly,
And wake the same sweet sentiments
    They breathed to you and me
When living seemed a laugh, and love
    All it was said to be.

Within the common lamp-lit room
   Prison my eyes and thought;
Let dingy details crudely loom,
   Mechanic speech be wrought:
Too fragrant was Life's early bloom,
   Too tart the fruit it brought!

              THOMAS HARDY.

*

HERE LIES A DOVE

Here lies a Dove, and was the same
As innocent as is her name:
Her inward virtues to rehearse
Exceed the bounds of any verse.
For outward beauties and sweet feature
Nature strived to form a creature.
All poets' subject by death's doome
Is shut up in this narrow roome.

    A memorial in Upton Church, Northants.

*

A CHILD'S GRAVE

Long night succeeds thy little day:
   O blighted blossom!   Can it be
That this grey stone and grassy clay
   Have closed our anxious care of thee?

The half-formed speech of artless thought
   That spoke a mind beyond thy years:
The song, the dance, by nature taught,
   The sunny smiles, the transient tears:

The symmetry of face and form,
　The eye with light and life replete:
The little heart so fondly warm,
　The voice so musically sweet.

These lost to hope, in memory yet
　Around the hearts that loved thee cling,
Shadowing with long and vain regret
　The too fair promise of thy spring.

> T. L. PEACOCK (1785–1866).
> On his daughter (aged 3) in
> 　　　　Shepperton Church yard.

*

REQUIESCAT

Strew on her roses, roses,
　And never a spray of yew!
In quiet she reposes;
　Ah, would that I did too!

Her mirth the world required;
　She bathed it in smiles of glee.
But her heart was tired, tired,
　And now they let her be.

Her life was turning, turning.
　In mazes of heat and sound.
But for peace her soul was yearning,
　And now peace laps her round.

Her cabined ample spirit,
    It fluttered and failed for breath.
To-night it doth inherit
    The vasty hall of death.
            MATTHEW ARNOLD (1822–1888).

*

AS SOME LONE BIRD

As some lone bird, without a mate,
My weary heart is desolate:
I look around and cannot trace
One friendly smile or welcome face,
And even in crowds am still alone
Because I cannot love but one.
            P. B. SHELLEY (1792–1822).

*

THE VINE

The wine of Love is music,
    And the feast of Love is song;
And when Love sits down to the banquet,
    Love sits long.

Sits long and arises drunken,
    But not with the feast and the wine;
He reeleth with his own heart,
    That great, rich Vine.
            JAMES THOMSON (1834–1882).

A BIRTHDAY

My heart is like a singing bird
    Whose nest is in a watered shoot;
My heart is like an apple-tree
    Whose boughs are bent with thickset fruit:
My heart is like a rainbow shell
    That paddles in a halcyon sea;
My heart is gladder than all these
    Because my love is come to me.

Raise me a daïs of silk and down;
    Hang it with vair and purple dyes;
Carve it in doves and pomegranates,
    And peacocks with a hundred eyes;
Work it in gold and silver grapes,
    In leaves and silver fleurs-de-lys;
Because the birthday of my life
    Is come, my love is come to me.

            CHRISTINA ROSSETTI (1830–1894).

*

ALL BUT HER SWEET BASIL FORGOTTEN

And she forgot the stars, the moon, and sun,
And she forgot the blue above the trees,
And she forgot the dells where waters run,
And she forgot the chilly autumn breeze,
She had no knowledge when the day was done,
And the new morn she saw not: but in peace,
Hung over her sweet Basil evermore,
And moistened it with tears unto the core.

            JOHN KEATS (1795–1821).

MUSIC AT SEA

Around, around, flew each sweet sound,
Then darted to the Sun;
Slowly the sounds came back again,
Now mixed, now one by one.

Sometimes a-dropping from the sky
I heard the sky-lark sing;
Sometimes all little birds that are,
How they seemed to fill the sea and air
With their sweet jargoning!

And now 'twas like all instruments,
Now like a lonely flute;
And now it is an angel's song
That makes the heavens be mute.

It ceased; yet still the sails made on
A pleasant noise till noon,
A noise like of a hidden brook
In the leafy month of June,
That to the sleeping woods all night
Singeth a quiet tune.

> S. T. COLERIDGE (1772-1834).
> From "The Ancient Mariner".

*

VIBRATIONS

Music, when soft voices die,
Vibrates in the memory—
Odours, when sweet violets sicken,
Live within the sense they quicken.

Rose leaves, when the rose is dead,
Are heaped for the beloved's bed;
And so thy thoughts, when thou art gone,
Love itself shall slumber on.

PERCY BYSSHE SHELLEY (1792-1822).

*

THE IMPRISONED SOUL

At the last, tenderly,
From the walls of the powerful, fortress'd house
From the clasp of the knitted locks—from the
keep of the well-closed doors.
Let me be wafted.

Let me glide noiselessly forth;
With the key of softness unlock the locks—with
a whisper.

Set open the doors, O soul!
Tenderly! be not impatient!

(Strong is your hold.   O mortal flesh!
Strong is your hold.   O love!)

WALT WHITMAN (1819-1892).

*

BEYOND

When youthful faith hath fled
Of loving take thy leave:
Be constant to the dead,
The dead cannot deceive.

Sweet modest flowers of Spring
How fleet your balmy day!
And man's brief year can bring
No secondary May:

250

No earthly burst again
  Of gladness out of gloom,
Fond hope and vision vain
  Ungrateful to the tomb.

But 'tis an old belief
  That on some solemn shore,
Beyond the sphere of grief
  Dear friends shall meet once more.

Beyond the sphere of Time
  And Sin and Fate's control,
Serene in endless prime
  Of body and of soul.

That creed I fain would keep,
  That hope I'll not forego:
Eternal be the sleep
  Unless to waken so!
          JOHN GIBSON LOCKHART (1794-1854).

*

DUTY

Stern daughter of the Voice of God!
  O Duty! if that name you love,
Who art a light to guide, a rod
  To check the erring and reprove;
Thou who art victory and law
When empty terrors overawe;
From vain temptations dost set free,
And calms the weary strife of frail humanity.

Serene will be our days and bright,
   And happy will our nature be,
When love is an unerring light,
   And joy its own security.
And they a blissful course may hold
Even now, who, not unwisely bold,
Live in the spirit of this creed;
Yet seek thy firm support according to their need.

Stern lawgiver! Yet thou dost wear
   The Godhead's most benignant grace;
Nor know we anything so fair
   As is the smile upon thy face:
Flowers laugh before thee on their beds
And fragrance in thy footing treads;
Thou dost preserve the stars from wrong,
And the most ancient heavens through thee are
     fresh and strong.

To humbler functions, awful Power,
   I call thee: I myself commend
Unto thy guidance from this hour;
   O let my weakness have an end!
Give unto me, made lowly wise,
The spirit of self-sacrifice;
The confidence of reason give;
And in the light of truth thy bondman let me live!

        WILLIAM WORDSWORTH (1770–1850).

*

252

KING'S COLLEGE CHAPEL, CAMBRIDGE

Tax not the royal saint with vain expense,
With ill-matched aims the architect who planned—
Albeit labouring for a scanty band
Of white-robed scholars only—this immense
And glorious work of fine intelligence.
Give all thou canst; high Heaven rejects the lore
Of nicely-calculated less or more—
So deemed the man who fashioned for the sense
These lofty pillars, spread that branching roof
Self-poised, and scooped into ten thousand cells,
Where light and shade repose, where music dwells
Lingering, and wandering on as loth to die;
Like thoughts whose very sweetness yieldeth proof
That they were born for immortality.

WILLIAM WORDSWORTH (1770–1850).

*

ALL THROUGH THE NIGHT

(To an old Welsh air)
Deep the silence round us spreading,
    All through the night;
Dark the path that we are treading
    All through the night.
Still the coming day discerning,
By the hope within us burning,
To the dawn our footsteps turning,
    All through the night.

Star of faith, the dark adorning
    All through the night,

253

Leads us fearless toward the morning
    All through the night.
Though our hearts be wrapt in sorrow
From the hope of dawn we borrow
Promise of a glad to-morrow,
    All through the night.

ANON.

*

THE PASSING OF KING ARTHUR

And slowly answered Arthur from the barge:
The old order changeth, yielding place to new,
And God fulfils himself in many ways,
Lest one good custom should corrupt the world
Comfort thyself: what comfort is in me?
I have lived my life and that which I have done
May he within himself make pure! but thou,
If thou shouldst never see my face again,
Pray for my Soul! More things are wrought by
    prayer
Than this world dreams of. Wherefore, let thy
    voice
Rise like a fountain for me night and day.
For what are men better than sheep or goats
That nourish a blind life within the brain,
If knowing God, they lift not hands of prayer
Both for themselves and those who call them
    friend?
For so the whole round earth is every way
Bound by gold chains about the feet of God.

But now farewell! I am going a long way
With these thou seest—if indeed I go
(For all my mind is clouded with a doubt)
To the island valley of Avilion:
Where falls not hail, or rain, or any snow,
Nor ever wind blows loudly: but it lies
Deep-meadowed, happy, fair with orchard lawns
And bowery hollows crowned with summer sun,
Where I will heal me of my grievous wound.

So said he and the barge with oar and sail
Moved from the brink, like some full breasted
    swan
That, fluting a wild carol ere her death,
Ruffles her pure cold plume and takes the flood
With swarthy webs. Long stood Sir Bedivere,
Revolving many memories, till the hull
Looked one black dot against the verge of dawn
And on the mere the wailing died away.

TENNYSON (1809–1892.)
From "The Idylls of the King":

*

THE WORLD'S GREAT AGE BEGINS ANEW

The world's great age begins anew,
    The golden years return,
The earth doth like a snake renew
    Her winter weeds outworn:
Heaven smiles, and faiths and empires gleam,
Like wrecks of a dissolving dream.

255

A brighter Hellas rears its mountains
   From waves serener far;
A new Peneus rolls his fountains
   Against the morning star.
Where fairer Tempes bloom, there sleep
Young Cyclads on a sunnier deep.

A loftier Argo cleaves the main,
   Fraught with a later prize;
Another Orpheus sings again,
   And loves, and weeps, and dies.
A new Ulysses leaves once more
Calypso for his native shore.

Oh, write no more the tale of Troy,
   If earth Death's scroll must be!
Nor mix with Laian rage the joy
   Which dawns upon the free:
Although a subtler Sphinx renew
Riddles of death Thebes never knew.

Another Athens shall arise,
   And to remoter time
Bequeath, like sunset to the skies,
   The splendour of its prime;
And leave, if nought so bright may live,
All earth can take or Heaven can give.

Saturn and Love their long repose
   Shall burst, more bright and good
Than all who fell, than One who rose,
   Than many unsubdued:

Not gold, not blood, their altar dowers
But votive tears and symbol flowers.

Oh, cease! must hate and death return?
   Cease! must men kill and die?
Cease! drain not to its dregs the urn
   Of bitter prophecy.
The world is weary of the past,
Oh, might it die or rest at last!

P. B. SHELLEY.

From "Hellas" (1822).

*

PROUD MAISIE

Proud Maisie's in the wood
   Walking so early;
Sweet Robin sits on the bush,
   Singing so rarely.

"Tell me, thou bonnie bird,
   When shall I marry me?"
"When six braw gentlemen
   Kirkward shall carry ye."

"Who makes the bridal bed,
   Birdie, say truly?"
"The grey-headed sexton
   That delves the grave duly.

"The glow-worm o'er grave and stone
   Shall light thee steady:
The owl from the steeple sing,
   'Welcome, proud lady!'"

SIR WALTER SCOTT (1771-1832).

I   257

RAVELSTON'S MOURNING GHOST

The murmur of the mourning ghost
  That keeps the shadowy kine.
O Keith of Ravelston,
  The sorrows of thy line!

Ravelston, Ravelston,
  The merry path that leads
Down the golden morning hill,
  And through the silver meads.

Ravelston, Ravelston,
  The stile beneath the tree,
The maid that kept her mother's kine,
  The song that sang she!

She sang her song, she kept her kine,
  She sat beneath the thorn,
When Andrew Keith of Ravelston,
  Rode through, the Monday morn.

His henchmen sing, his hawk-bells ring,
  His belted jewels shine.
O Keith of Ravelston,
  The sorrows of thy line!

I lay my hand upon the stile,
  The stile is lone and cold,
The burnie that goes babbling by
  Says nought than can be told.

Yet, stranger, here from year to year,
  She keeps her shadowy kine.
O Keith of Ravelston,
  The sorrows of thy line!

Step out three steps where Andrew stood;
  Why blanch thy cheeks for fear?
The ancient stile is not alone,
  'Tis not the burn I hear!

She makes her immemorial moan,
  She keeps her shadowy kine.
O Keith of Ravelston,
  The sorrows of thy line!

SYDNEY DOBELL (1824–1874).

*

THE ROOM OF JOHN KEATS AT HAMPSTEAD

"What happened here?" said the Stranger,
"In this bare and narrow room
With one dim window looking on the grass?
A shelf of books in the gloom
And those panes of misty glass—
This is all that the eye can see—
Low foliage that leans to the lawn ·
Dark thews of a twisted tree."

Stranger, in this bare room
Was an empire of bounds unknown—
Beyond the horizon of Time;
Its pillars were not of stone,
There were heights that none could climb:
Its marches no force could enfold,
They could not be won by arms
Or bought with the stealth of gold.

On yonder boughs the nightingale made his
    nest
And sang his song before the whitening dawn,
And winged long since to his immortal rest—
Beside that shadowy lawn
Here Cortez stood, here glowed the life in Psyche's
    cheek

And proud Hyperion in a cloud of fire
'Lit on his granite peak
And raised his gleaming lyre.
Where now is a naked floor
The flowers were washed in the dew;
Beside that narrow door
The great oaks spread in the gloom.
With orbs of beauty and doom
The stars were throbbing above:
Here gods were born anew,
And the moon stooped down to her love.

"Does nothing remain, nothing of all that was?
Has Time burnt all those shapes upon his pyre?"
"Stranger, behind that blurred and misty glass
These things have happened here: they do not
    pass."

                HERBERT ASQUITH.
          From "Youth in the Skies".

*

THE OXEN

Christmas eve, and twelve of the clock,
  "Now they are all on their knees,"
An elder said as we sat in a flock
  By the embers in hearthside ease.

We pictured the meek mild creatures where
  They dwelt in their strawy pen,
Nor did it occur to one of us there
  To doubt they were kneeling then.

So fair a fancy few would weave
  In these years!   Yet I feel,
If someone said on Christmas eve,
  "Come: see the oxen kneel

In the lonely barton by yonder coomb
  Our childhood used to know,"
I should go with him in the gloom,
  Hoping it might be so.

            THOMAS HARDY.
        From "Moments of Vision".

A reference to the same legend is found in the
Rev. Francis Kilvert's "Diary" for 1878.   He
notes that one of his parishioners, Priscilla Price,
speaking of the blowing of the Holy Thorn and
the kneeling and weeping of the oxen on old
Christmas Eve said:—

    "I have known old James Meredith 40 years
and I have never known him far from the truth,

and I said to him one day, 'James, tell me the truth, did you ever see the oxen kneel on old Christmas Eve at the Weston?' And he said, 'No, I never saw them kneel at the Weston, but when I was at Hinton at Staunton-on-Wye I saw them. I was watching them on old Christmas Eve, and at 12 o'clock the oxen that were standing knelt down upon their knees and those that were lying down rose up on their knees and there they stayed kneeling and moaning, the tears running down their faces "

*

IX

The Philosophy of Life

*

There is all Africa and her prodigies in me.
—SIR T. BROWNE.

A man may dwell so long upon a thought that it may take him prisoner.—1ST MARQUIS OF HALIFAX.

It is shocking, it is scandalous to enjoy life as I do.
—MONCKTON MILNES.

The fly that sips treacle is lost in the sweets.—JOHN GAY.

A good leg will fall; a straight back will stoop; a black beard will turn white; a curled pate will grow bald; a fair face will wither; a full eye will wax hollow: but a good heart, Kate, is the sun and the moon; or rather the sun and not the moon; for it shines bright and never changes, but keeps his course truly.

SHAKESPEARE.
From "Henry V".

We see a little, presume a great deal and so jump to a conclusion.—JOHN LOCKE.

Every man, by consulting his own breast, may easily know whether he is or is not a patriot. But it is not so easy for the bystanders.—BISHOP BERKELEY.

A man will love his country the better for (owning) a pig.—ARTHUR YOUNG.

The happy life should be three parts practical.
—J. S. MILL.

One of the prettiest spectacles to me is a costermonger's donkey going blithely at the trot. Our maxim should be—Merry in harness while we have to serve.—G. MEREDITH.

Every man soon falls behind that does not aspire to keep up with the foremost in the race.—SCOTT.

Judge a man's wisdom by his hopes.—EMERSON.

To know the universe itself as a road, as many roads, as roads for travelling souls.—WALT WHITMAN.

The art of loving is to know how to enjoy a little and to endure much.—HAZLITT.

Nothing is more unpleasant than a virtuous person with a mean mind.—WALTER BAGEHOT.

Fanaticism consists in redoubling your effort when you have forgotten your aim.—SANTAYANA.

I hope our young men will not grow up such *dodgers* as these old men are.—DR. BENJAMIN JOWETT.

The business of life is to go forward.—DR. JOHNSON.

Everything comes out of the dirt—everything: everything comes out of the people, everyday people, the people as you find them and leave them: people, people, just people.—WALT WHITMAN.

Life is like playing a violin solo in public and learning the instrument as one plays it.—S. BUTLER.

Damn braces: bless relaxes.—WILLIAM BLAKE.

Many men swallow their being cheated, but no man could ever endure to chew it.—1ST LORD HALIFAX.

It is better that the drones be fed than the Bees be starved.—FULLER.

It is most important in this World to be pushing, but it is fatal to seem so.—DR. JOWETT.

S' adapter aux illusions courantes.—AMIEL.

> This is the curse of life! that not
>   A nobler, calmer train
> Of wiser thought and feeling blot
>   Our passions from our brain;
>
> But each day brings its petty dust
>   Our soon-choked souls to fill,
> And we forget because we must
>   And not because we will.
>   M. ARNOLD.
>   From "Absence".

"Mr. Johnson! would you advise me to marry?"
"I would advise no man to marry, Sir, who is not likely to propagate understanding."

JOHNSON.

Every man has all the centuries in him.—JOHN MORLEY.

I wish my temper had changed with the years; but to be romantic even yet is a mistake and I feel it keenly.

DISRAELI (at seventy-four).

Old age flowing free, with the delicious near-by assurance of Death.—WALT WHITMAN.

In 70 or 80 years a man may have a deep gust of the world, know what it is, what it can afford and what it is to have been a man.—SIR T. BROWNE.

I never felt life to be so precious as now when it is ebbing away.—M. PATTISON.

The power of books in generating virtue is probably much greater than in generating vice.—S. GODWIN.

I really think that old age is the best part of life, because you see things more truly and impersonally and less under the influence of party or interest or the world (having nothing to fear and nothing to hope for except rest with God) than you did in the days of youth.—DR. JOWETT.

265

THE LOWEST TREES HAVE TOPS

The lowest trees have tops, the ant her gall,
  The fly her spleen, the little spark his heat;
And slender hairs cast shadows, though but small,
  And bees have stings, although they be not great;
Seas have their source, and so have shallow springs;
And love is love in beggars and in kings!

Where waters smoothest run, deep are the fords;
  The dial stirs, yet none perceives it move;
The firmest faith is in the fewest words;
  The turtles cannot sing, and yet they love;
True hearts have eyes and ears, no tongues to speak;
They hear, and see, and sigh, and then they break.

ANON. (1603).

*

GOOD COUNSEL

Pitch thy behaviour low, thy projects high;
So shalt thou humble and magnanimous be:
Sink not in spirit; who aimeth at the sky
Shoots higher much than he that means a tree.
  A grain of glory mixed with humbleness
  Cures both a fever and lethargicness.

Scorn no man's love, though of a mean degree;
Love is a present for a mighty king;
Much less make any one thine enemy.
As guns destroy, so may a little sling.
  The cunning workman never doth refuse
  The meanest tool that he may chance to
  use . . .

Sum up at night what thou hast done by day,
And in the morning what thou hast to do.
Dress and undress thy soul; mark the decay
And growth of it; if, with thy watch, that too
    Be down, then wind up both; since we shall be
    Most surely judged, make thy accounts agree.

In brief, acquit thee bravely; play the man.
Look not on pleasures as they come, but go.
Defer not the least virtue; life's poor span
Make not an ell by trifling in thy woe.
    If thou do ill, the joy fades, not the pains;
    If well, the pain doth fade, the joy remains.
            GEORGE HERBERT (1593–1633).

*

REVISITING THE OLD SCHOOL

Sir Henry Wotton yearly went to Oxford. But
the summer before his death he changed that for
a journey to Winchester College, to which school
he was first removed from Bocton. And as he
returned from Winchester towards Eton College
he said to a friend, companion in that journey,
"How useful was that advice of a holy Monk, who
persuaded his friend to perform his customary
devotions in a constant place, because in that
place we usually meet with those very thoughts
which possessed us at our last being there! And
I find it thus far experimentally true, that at my
now being in that School and seeing that very

place where I sat when I was a boy, occasioned me to remember those very thoughts of my youth which then possessed me: sweet thoughts indeed that promised my growing years numerous pleasures without mixtures of cares, and those to be enjoyed when time—which I therefore thought slow-paced—had changed my Youth into manhood. But age and experience have taught me that those were but empty hopes, for I have always found it true, as my Saviour did foretell, 'sufficient for the day is the evil thereof.' Nevertheless, I saw there a succession of boys, using the same recreations, and questionless possessed with the same thoughts that then possessed me. Thus one generation succeeds another, both in their lives, recreations, hopes, fears and death."

ISAAC WALTON (1593–1683).
From "Life of Sir Henry Wotton".

*

THE HAPPY MAN

All our trouble is from within us; and if a dish of lettice and a clear fountain can cool all my heats, so that I shall have neither thirst nor pride, lust nor revenge, envy nor ambition, I am lodg'd in the bosome of felicity and indeed no men sleep so soundly as they that lay their head upon Nature's lap.

He therefore that hath the fewest desires and the most quiet passions, whose wants are soon provided for and whose possessions cannot be disturbed with violent fears, he that dwells next door to satisfaction and can carry his needs and lay them down where he please, this man is the happy man, and this is not to be done in great designes and swelling fortunes.

JEREMY TAYLOR (1613–1667).

*

MAGNA EST VERITAS

Give me the liberty to know, to utter, and to argue freely according to conscience, above all liberties. Though all the winds of doctrine were let loose to play upon the earth, so Truth be in the field, we do injuriously to misdoubt her strength. Let her and Falsehood grapple! Who ever knew Truth put to the worse in a free and open encounter? Who knows not that Truth is strong next to the Almighty? She needs no policies, no stratagems, nor licensings to make her victorious: those are the shifts and defences that Errors use against her power. Give her but room and do not bind her when she sleeps.

When God shakes a kingdom it is not untrue that many false teachers are busiest, but yet more true it is that God then raises to his own work men of rare abilities and more than common industry to gain some new steps in the discovery of Truth.

JOHN MILTON (1608–1674).

RENAN EXHORTS NATURE TO PERSEVERE

We may as well allow the destinies of this planet to work themselves out without undue concern. We should gain nothing by exclaiming against them and a display of temper would be very much out of place. It is by no means certain that the earth is not falling short of its destiny, as has probably happened in countless worlds; it is even possible that our age may one day be regarded as the culminating point since which humanity has been steadily deteriorating. But the universe does not know the meaning of the word discouragement; it will commence anew the work which has come to naught; each fresh check leaves it young, alert and full of illusions.

Be of good cheer, Nature! Pursue like the deaf and blind star-fish which vegetates in the bed of the ocean, thy obscure task of life! Persevere! Mend for the millionth time the broken meshes of the net! Repair the boring machine which sinks to the last limit of the attainable the well from which living water will be drawn up. Sight and sight again the aim which thou hast failed to hit throughout the ages; try to struggle through the scarcely perceptible opening which leads to another firmament. Thou hast the infinity of time and space to try the experiment. He who can commit blunders with impunity is certain to succeed.

ERNEST RENAN (1823–1892).
From Preface to "Recollections of my Youth".

MIRACLES

Why, who makes much of a miracle?
As to me I know of nothing else but miracles,
Whether I walk the streets of Manhatten,
Or dart my sight over the roofs of houses toward
    the sky,
Or wade with naked feet along the beach just in
    the edge of the water,
Or stand under trees in the woods,
Or talk by day with anyone I love or sleep in the
    bed at night with anyone I love,
Or sit at table at dinner with the rest,
Or look at strangers opposite me riding in the car,
Or watch honey-bees busy around the hive of a
    summer forenoon,
Or animals feeding in the fields.
Or birds, or the wonderfulness of insects in the air,
Or the wonderfulness of the sundown, or of stars
    shining so quiet and bright,
Or the exquisite delicate thin curve of the new
    moon in spring;
These with the rest, one and all, are to me miracles,
The whole referring, yet each distinct and in its
    place.

To me every hour of the light and dark is a
    miracle,
Every cubic inch of space is a miracle,
Every square yard of the surface of the earth is
    spread with the same,
Every foot of the interior swarms with the same.

To me the sea is a continual miracle,
The fishes that swim—the rocks—the motion of
the waves—the ships with men in them,
What stranger miracles are there?

WALT WHITMAN (1819–1892).

*

SELF-DEPENDENCE

Weary of myself and sick of asking
What I am and what I ought to be,
At this vessel's prow I stand, which bears me
Forwards, forwards, o'er the starlit sea.

And a look of passionate desire
O'er the sea, and to the stars I send:
"Ye who from my childhood up have calmed me,
Calm me, ah, compose me to the end!

Ah! once more," I cried, "ye stars, ye waters,
On my heart your mighty charm renew:
Still, still let me, as I gaze upon you,
Feel my soul becoming vast like you!"

From the intense, clear, star-sown vault of heaven,
Over the lit sea's unquiet way,
In the rustling night-air came the answer,
"Would'st thou *be* as these are, *Live* as they.

"Unaffrighted by the silence round them,
Undistracted by the sights they see,
These demand not that the things without them
Yield them love, amusement, sympathy.

272

"And with joy the stars perform their shining,
And the sea its long moon-silvered roll:
For self-poised they live, nor pine with noting
All the fever of some differing soul.

"Bounded by themselves, and unregardful
In what state God's other works may be,
In their own tasks all their powers pouring,
These attain the mighty life you see."

O air-born voice! long since, serenely clear,
A cry like thine in mine own heart I hear:
"Resolve to be thyself—: and know that he,
Who finds himself, loses his misery!"

MATTHEW ARNOLD (1822–1888).

*

REBUS IN ARDUIS

Shall we, with temper spoiled,
Health sapped by living ill,
And judgment all embroiled
By sadness and self-will,
Shall *we* judge what for man is not true bliss or is?

Is it so small a thing
To have enjoyed the sun,
To have lived light in the spring,
To have loved, to have thought, to have done,
To have advanced true friends and beat down
baffling foes—

273

That we must feign a bliss
Of doubtful future date,
And, while we dream on this,
Lose all our present state,
And relegate to worlds yet distant our repose?

Not much, I know, you prize
What pleasures may be had,
Who look on life with eyes
Estranged, like mine, and sad:
And yet the village churl feels the truth more than
  you,

Who's loth to leave this life
Which to him little yields—
His hard-tasked sunburnt wife,
His often laboured fields,
The boors with whom he talked, the country spots
  he knew.

But thou because thou hear'st
Men scoff at Heaven and Fate,
Because the Gods thou fear'st
Fail to make blest thy state,
Tremblest, and wilt not dare to trust the joys there
  are!

I say: Fear not! Life still
Leaves human effort scope.
But since life teems with ill,
Nurse no extravagant hope:

274

Because thou must not dream, thou need'st not
then despair.

> MATTHEW ARNOLD (1822-1888).
> The concluding stanzas of "Empedocles
> on Etna".

*

THE IVORY TOWER

I very well recall the emergence of the feeling
which the phrase—The Ivory Tower—is used to
express. Every sensitive high-school boy, I dare
say, has known it, the first half-pleasurable, half-
painful discovery that there is an enclosure of
exquisite things in which one may find refuge
from the realm of banality or hardness or futility
or brutality which encompasses him, or which
perhaps he unendurably feels to encompass him.

For me, as for many, poetry and music were the
first realms of gold in which I discovered the
goodly states and countries of the mind and senses
and spirit. The world closes in upon us in our
infancy: it oppresses us in our adolescence. And
then comes the delicious discovery of a world
elsewhere in which one can live. The high school
with its stale routine and stale smells, the cur-
riculum with its hateful algebra and its regimented
classes, was still there. The starched collars in
which the children of my generation were imprisoned were still there. But there were the
doves and the "murmuring of innumerable bees"

in poetry and the heard melodies of music. There were a few friends to walk with along the beach and with whom one exchanged misquotations in the moonlight. . . . Or one found the Rubaiyat and murmured with sweet sadness about

> A book of verses underneath a bough,
> A jug of wine, a loaf of bread and Thou
> Singing beside me in the wilderness

or thought of the days when one would be gone and they would turn down an empty glass.

IRWIN EDMAN.

From "Philosopher's Holiday".

*

THE REAL GOLDEN MOMENTS

When you think of the youth that you have lost, the times when it seems to you now that life was most poignantly good may not be the ones when everything seemed at the time to go well with your plans, and the world, as they say, to be at your feet; rather some few unaccountable moments when nothing took place that was out of the way and yet some word of a friend's, or a look on the face of the sky, the taste of a glass of spring water, the plash of laughter and oars heard across midsummer meadows at night raised the soul of enjoyment within you to strangely higher powers of itself. That spirit bloweth and is still: it will not rise for our whistling nor keep a time-table; no wine that we know can give us anything more than a fugitive caricature of its ecstasies. When it has blown free we remember it always, and know, without proof, that while the rapture was there we were not drunk, but wise; that for a moment some intervening darkness had thinned and we were seeing further than we can see now into the heart of life.

C. E. MONTAGUE.
From "Disenchantment".

*

A WISE BISHOP'S APHORISMS

We live in a perfect bacchanalia of nonsense. The great question of the future is the discipline of liberty.

Character is revealed in crises. The great marks of character are teachableness and a capacity for growth.

No people do such harm as those who go about doing good.

We cannot improve the World further than we improve ourselves.

Nothing is so pernicious as mere diffusion. What you need is a definite object and perseverance.

Paradoxes are useful to attract attention to ideas.

The duty of a politician is to educate the people, not to obey them.

In the Middle Ages poverty was respected for itself; there was an aristocracy of poverty. We are the poorer by its loss.

DR. MANDELL CREIGHTON (1843–1901)
(Bishop of London).

*

"TO THE MAKING OF MAN"

Before the beginning of years
   There came to the making of man
Time, with a gift of Fears
   Grief with a glass that ran:
Pleasure with pain for leaven
   Summer with flowers that fell:
Remembrance fallen from heaven
   And madness risen from hell:
Strength without hands to smite;
   Love that endures for a breath:
Night the shadow of Light
   And Life the shadow of Death.

ALGERNON CHARLES SWINBURNE (1837–1909).
From "Atalanta in Calydon".

*

OLD LOVES ARE BEST

Those that have loved longest love best. A single blaze of kindness may by a single blast of coldness be extinguished, but that fondness which

278

length of time has connected with many circumstances and occasions, though it may for a while be suppressed by disgust or resentment, with or without a cause, is hourly revived by accidental recollection. To those who have lived long together, everything heard and everything seen recalls some pleasure communicated, or some benefit conferred, some petty quarrel or some slight endearment. Esteem of great powers or amiable qualities newly discovered, may embroider a day or week, but a friendship of twenty years is interwoven with the texture of life: a friend may be often found and lost, but *an old friend* never can be found and nature has provided that he cannot easily be lost.

DR. JOHNSON (1709-1784).

*

THE VALUE OF THE STUDY OF HISTORY

The study of history can give no mathematical certainty, but it can create a sober temper, which is the basis of all true wisdom. It can give a sense of the largeness of problems, of their complexity, of the danger of over-haste, of the limits of man's power over his surroundings. The study of history rightly pursued ought to be the most useful means of forming a capacity for dealing with affairs. It shows us great ideas prevailing at all times: it shows us repeated failure to give these ideas effect: it shows the conditions under which these ideas influenced political action: it shows us seeming triumphs which ended in disaster; it enables us to judge of the qualities which led to permanent achievements: it points out the nature and limits of man's foresight. These are the important lessons of history, and they are lessons which may be learned from any period and from any field of man's activity. For my own part I think that they are best learned in periods which do not challenge direct comparisons with the present. We are calmer and more impartial when the conditions of the problem are somewhat remote, when there is no danger of awakening our own feelings of partisanship.

DR. CREIGHTON (1843–1901).
From his Inaugural Lecture as Regius Professor of History at Cambridge (1884).

*

THE SYSTEM OR THE INDIVIDUAL

I do not believe that civilisation has yet foundered, but I am certain that there is an active force of evil which, unless we fight it, will rapidly reduce our civilisation to a desert of the soul. That evil force is at work in a period of human history in which change has been so sudden as to bring grave confusion of thought, to give more favourable conditions for the Devil's work. It is, of course, true that the world never stands still, but there are times when the flywheel races and you and I live in such a time to-day.

Your world has been influenced, whether you acknowledge it or not, by what I must take leave to call the inhuman conception of the so-called Economic man. There has been a tendency for great thinkers, who have analysed the social and moral values on which the human community has been built, to stress the need for finding the perfect system. There has been a tendency to explain all history and humanity in economic instead of human terms. Christianity, on the other hand, has rather made its end the perfection of the individual, in the conviction that here, too, lay the secret of life for all society. And this emphasis upon the ideal system, instead of the ideal individual, has not helped the development of the human character. Yet, fundamentally, men remain to-day much the same men as they were yesterday. They may be better informed: but they are not necessarily wiser. They wish to emancipate themselves from artificial conventions, but they are not more free from the dangers and pitfalls which caused those conventions to be accepted.

LORD HALIFAX (Feb. 1940).
From "The Challenge to Liberty", delivered in the Sheldonian Theatre, Oxford.

*

MEN AND WOMEN IN LOVE

You say you want women to like you, well, don't tell them so; don't make too much of them; don't let them order you about as they please. Women, though they do not seem to know it themselves, like far better to obey than to be obeyed. They pretend to be our equals, but they know jolly well themselves that they are not— luckily for them, for if they were our equals we should like them far less.

I think on the whole much better of women than of men, but I do not tell it to them. They have far more courage; they face disease and death better than we do; they have more pity and less vanity. Their instinct is on the whole a safer guide through their life than our intelligence: they do not make fools of themselves as often as we do.

Love means to a woman far more than it means to a man: it means everything. It is less a question of senses than man understands. A woman can fall in love with an ugly man, even an old man, if he rouses her imagination. A man cannot fall in love with a woman unless she rouses his sexual instinct, which, contrary to nature's intention, survives in modern man his sexual power. There is, therefore, no age limit for falling in love. Richelieu was irresistible at the age of eighty, when he could hardly stand on his legs, and Goethe was seventy when he lost his head for Ulrike von Levetzow.

Love itself is short lived like the flower. With man it dies its natural death in marriage; with woman it often survives to the last, transformed in a purely maternal tenderness for the fallen hero of her dreams. Women cannot understand that man is by nature polygamous. He may be tamed to enforced submission to our recent code of social morals, but his indestructible instinct is only dormant. He remains the same animal his Creator made him, ready to carry on business as usual, regardless of undue delay.

AXEL MÜNTHE.

From "The Story of San Michele".

*

WANTED, A NATIVE CIVILISATION

It so happens that just at a time when everything shakeable is being shaken, when all authorities and all traditions are being thrown into the melting pot, just when more than at other times we crave for some wise and strong leadership, we are suffering from one of those mysterious eclipses of genius which often follow periods of great energy and activity. In every department of life the place of the Victorian giants is filled (it seems to me) by pygmies. As in the days of Eli, the word of the Lord is precious—there is no open vision.

This state of things will pass: we shall have great men again before long: and they will have to address themselves to the great problem which is at the bottom of all lesser departmental problems —the desire of the progressive nations of the North and West to beat out for themselves a really native civilisation, which hitherto they have never enjoyed. We are still the barbarians who broke up the Roman Empire and took over what we could lift of their Culture. Our religious books come from Palestine: our "humaner" letters from Athens and Rome: our whole mental furniture, except our science, is a queer assortment of miscellaneous antiques, which we wear as incongruously as an African chief decks himself in European clothes. And beneath all is our own native moral ideal, our secular religion which we have evolved for ourselves, which we believe in and live by—the Northern European code of honour—the ideal of a gentleman.

It is a queer state of things, and we shall not see our way out till we have more genius among us than can at present be discerned. Meanwhile we have our cocksure little guides, some of whom say to us, "That is primitive, therefore it is good", and others, "This is up-to-date, therefore it is better". Not very wise persons, any of them, I fear.

Dean Inge (1911).
From "Speculum Animæ".

*

284

THE PRICELESS POSSESSION OF LAUGHTER

Laughter may be claimed to be one of the possessions of men to which they should jealously cling. It brings gaiety into what is always tending to grow a dull world, and of which at times the onlooker is disposed to say what Walpole said of the doings of the fashionable æsthetes at Bath, "there never was anything so entertaining or so dull." It supplies diversion in Youth and it may with a few, as it did with Heine and R. L. Stevenson, remain a bright comrade on the sick bed. It is the manna on which good fellowship loves to feed. And, so many sided is it, it may be recommended as a planer for moral ridges, and it may add the last touch to the character picture which every man is engaged in painting. It will graciously accompany us when we visit the nursery and try our cumbrous hand in the art of entertaining childhood: and will not forsake us—if we care for its company—when we betake ourselves to the graver occupations.

PROF. SULLY (1842–1923).

From "An Essay on Laughter".

*

THE RIPENESS AND FULNESS OF AGE

The debt of our civilisation to the ancient Greeks is beyond all calculation. Their adoration of the youthful human form, in contrast to the

Eastern idealisation of venerable age, has put a kind of blight on human life: our progress as we grow older in wisdom and humanity is thought of in terms of the physical decay which accompanies that luminous advance. We feel ashamed, instead of feeling proud, like the Chinese, of our accumulating years: we are always trying in vain to seem younger than we really are: and in our western world it is by no means a compliment to attribute to others a greater age than their appearance might suggest. When I think of my brother and sister at Harvard fifty years ago—endowed it may be with the grace of Youth, but full otherwise of ignorance and folly—I cannot but prize more highly our present state. Our bones are ripening, it is true, for their ultimate repose, but how small a price after all is that to pay for the knowledge we have acquired of the world and men, for the splendid panorama of literature and the arts which years of travel and study have unrolled before us, and above all for those adequate conceptions in whose possession, according to Spinoza's wisdom, true felicity consists.

LOGAN PEARSALL SMITH.
"Unforgotten Years".

*

THE END OF THE PASSAGE

What if some little pain the passage have
That makes frail flesh to fear the bitter wave;

Is not short pain well borne, that brings long
    ease,
And lays the soul to sleep in quiet grave?
Sleep after toil, port after stormy seas,
Ease after war, death after life, doth greatly please.

           EDMUND SPENSER (1552-1599).

*

CHANGE IS THE LAW OF LIFE

If the very law of life is a law of change; if
every blossom of beauty has its root in fallen
leaves; if love and thought and hope would faint
beneath the constant light, and need for their
freshening the darkness and the dews; if it is in
losing the transient that we gain the eternal; then
let us shrink no more from sorrow, and sigh no
more for rest; but have a genial welcome for
vicissitude, and make quiet friends with loss and
death. Through storm and calm fresh be our
courage and quick our eye for the various service
that may await us! Nay, when God Himself
turns us not hither and thither, when He sends us
no changes for us to receive and consecrate, be it
ours to create them for ourselves, by flinging
ourselves into generous enterprises and worthy
sacrifice; by the stirrings of sleepless aspiration,
and all the spontaneous vicissitudes of holy and
progressive souls; keeping always the moral spaces
round us pure and fresh by the constant thought
of truth and the frequent deed of love.

And then, when for us too death closes the great series of mortal changes, the past will lie behind us green and sweet as Eden, and the future before us in the light of eternal peace. Tranquil and fearless we shall resign ourselves to God, to conduct us through that ancient and invisible way which has been sanctified by the feet of all the faithful, and illuminated by the passage of the Man of griefs.

JAMES MARTINEAU (1805–1900).

*

READY FOR EITHER FATE

The Grave shall not be vilipended. To the perfectly healthy mind (mine) it appeals with a double suggestion—the satisfaction of one's unbounded curiosity about *what next* and the alternative of honest extinction—a great luxury, looked at rightly.

* * * *

Well, I am quite ready for either Extinction or Extension, whichever and whenever. Only, if the latter, all I stipulate for is absolute good, on the terms that the Master shall manage it and that we shall all be safeguarded against the rack of this tough world.

WILLIAM DE MORGAN (1907).

*

288

LIFE A DREAM WE WAKE FROM

How I wish that I could write a word to put heart into an old friend—so old a friend!—face to face with Death. I grieve to have nothing to say, that I am at liberty to say, beyond that my own belief is fixed, that this life is an instalment of a larger and longer one.

I know—or think—your enquiry to mean, "Has this belief been founded on mere reason or on some confirmatory experience?" My answer is that some small experience I have had of apparent communication with folk on the other side *must* have had *some* weight in turning the scale so decidedly. But it may have been very small. I suspect that the lifelong faith of the strongest consecutive reasoner I ever knew—my father—had more to do with it than anything else.

If the few things that I have met with, that have any value, could be told without involving others than myself, I would gladly write them to you. But they would amount to very little, all said and done.

Perhaps we shall die and after all be none the wiser as to what Death means and Life. But it does not recommend itself to my understanding. Intense curiosity, and a hope that this life is a dream we wake from, rather than Death a sleep we fall into—these are my mental conditions

WILLIAM DE MORGAN (1914).

From a letter to May Morris, published in Mrs. Stirling's "William de Morgan and His Wife".

SHARP SPIKES WHERE FLOWERS WERE

This place of withered recollections is like an old life to be lived again without sunshine. I cross and recross it. Sharp spikes where flowers were. Death is death, as you say, but I get to her by consulting her thoughts and wishes—and so she lives in me. This, if one has the strength of soul, brings a spirit to us: I feel the blow as I get more distant from it. While she lingered I could not hope for it to last, and now I could crave any of the latest signs of her breathing—a weakness of my flesh. When the mind shall be steadier, I shall have her calmly present—past all tears. . . .

GEORGE MEREDITH (1828–1909).
From a Letter to John Morley.

*

SO LIVE THAT WHEN . . .

So live that when thy summons comes to join
The innumerable caravan that moves
To the pale realms of shade, where each shall take
His chamber in the silent halls of death,
Thou go not, like the quarry-slave at night
Scourged to his dungeon; but sustained and soothed
By an unfaltering trust, approach thy grave
Like one who wraps the drapery of his couch
About him and lies down to pleasant dreams.

WILLIAM CULLEN BRYANT (1794–1878).
From "Thanatopsis".

SOME RULES OF LIFE BY MARCUS AURELIUS

Let it be thy earnest and incessant care as a Romane and a man to performe whatsoever it is that thou art about, with true and unfained gravity, naturall affection, freedome and justice: and as for all other cares, and imaginations, how thou mayest ease thy minde of them. Which thou shalt doe; if thou shalt goe about every action as thy last action, free from all vanitie, all passionate and wilfull aberration from reason, and from all hypocrisie, and selfe-love, and dislike of those things, which by the fates or appointment of God have hapned unto thee.

From "The Golden Book".
(Trans. Meric Casaubon, 1634.)

*

AS AT A BANQUET

Remember to order your behaviour in life as at a banquet. When a dish that is being served reaches you, stretch out your hand and take a modest helping. If the servant passes you by do not seek to detain him. Do not be eager to anticipate it: wait till it comes round. Deal so with your children, your wife, your office and with wealth and one day you will be fit to take part in the banquets of the Gods. But if you refrain from touching what is set before you and despise it, you will be fit to share not their banquets only but their rule.

EPICTETUS.

*

ALWAYS THE OPEN DOOR

Above all remember that the door stands open. Be not more fearful than children who when they tire of a game, say, "I will play no more" and go. So, when you find yourself in the like plight, say "I will play no more" and go. But if you stay, utter no laments!

Is the room smoky? I stay if the nuisance is but slight: if it is great, I go. Remember this and do not forget it—the door stands open.

EPICTETUS.

*

"LINQUENDA TELLUS ET DOMUS"

When I die, I must depart not only from sensual delights, but from the more manly pleasures of my studies, knowledge and converse with many wise and godly men and from all my pleasure in reading, hearing, public and private exercise of religion, etc. I must leave my library and turn over those pleasant books no more: I must no more come among the living, nor see the faces of my faithful friends, nor be seen of man: houses and cities and fields and countries, gardens and walks will be nothing to me. I shall no more hear of the affairs of the world, of man, or wars, or other news, nor see what becomes of that beloved interest of wisdom, piety and peace, which I desire may prosper.

RICHARD BAXTER (1615-1691).
From "Dying Thoughts".

*

DEATH WITHOUT TRAPPINGS

Take away but the pomps of death, the disguises and solemn bug-bears, the tinsell and the actings by candle-light, and proper and phantastic ceremonies, the minstrels and the noise-makers, the swoonings and the shriekings, the nurses and the physicians, the kindred and the watchers and then to die is easie, ready and quitted from its troublesome circumstances. It is the same harmless thing that a poor shepherd suffered yesterday or a maid servant to-day.

JEREMY TAYLOR (1613-1667).

*

RENAN DESIRES A CALM AND SUDDEN DEATH

All that I have to ask of the good genius which has so often guided, advised and consoled me is a calm and sudden death at my appointed hour, be it near or distant. The Stoics maintained that one could have led a happy life in the belly of the bull of Phalaris. This is going too far. Suffering degrades, humiliates and leads to blasphemy. The only acceptable death is the noble death which is not a pathological accident but a premeditated and precious end before the Everlasting. Death upon the battle field is the grandest of all: but there are others which are as illustrious—forms of death which are very preferable to a long illness which kills you by inches and demolishes you bit by bit.

God's will be done! I have little chance of adding much to my store of knowledge; I have a pretty accurate idea of the amount of truth which the human mind can, in the present state of its development, discern. I should be very grieved to have to go through one of those periods of enfeeblement during which the man, once endued with strength and virtue, is but the shadow and ruin of his former self and, often to the delight of the ignorant, sets himself to demolish the life which he has so laboriously constructed. Such an old age is the worst gift which the gods can give to man. If such a fate be in store for me, I hasten to protest beforehand against the weaknesses which a softened brain might lead me to say or sign.

It is Renan, sane in body and mind, as I am now—not the Renan half destroyed by death and no longer himself, as I shall be if my decomposition is gradual—whom I wish to be believed and listened to. I disavow the blasphemies to which in my last hour I might give way against the Almighty.

ERNEST RENAN (1823–1892).
From "Recollections of my Youth".

*

"NOTHING TO REGRET IN THE GOING"

We too have looked at the world and through men, and to us the word consolation is but a common scribble, for there is none under a deep affliction that can come from without, nor from the dearest of friends. What I most wish for you I know you to have, fortitude to meet a crisis, and its greater task, to endure. We have come to the time of life when the landscape surrounding —*haec data pœna diu viventibus*—the tombstones of our beloved and the narrowing of our powers, throws a not unpleasant beam on the black gateway, as we take it to be in the earlier days. And those young ones, whom Nature smites with the loss of us, she will soon bring into her activities, if they are the healthy creatures we wish them to be. I find nothing to regret in the going, at my age, and only a laughing snarl when I look about on the deprivations, which make the going easy. So I see things in your mind as well.

G. MEREDITH (1828–1909).
From a Letter to Sir Leslie Stephen.

*

THE GODS DON'T CARE

Ego genus esse semper dico et dixi Caelitum,
Sed non eos curare opinor quid agat humanum genus,
Nam si curent, bene bonis sit malis male, quod
    nunc abest.

                    ENNIUS.

[I always say and have always said that there
is a race of heavenly beings, but I do not think
that they concern themselves with the doings of
mankind; for if they did, the good would get the
good things of life and the bad the bad, and that
is not so to-day.]

      *   *   *   *

Hoc etiam faciunt ubi discubuere tenentque
Pocula saepe homines et inumbrant ora coronis
Ex animo ut dicunt, "Brevis est hic fructus homullis;
Iam fuerit neque post unquam revocare licelit."

[This men often do when they lie at ease and
hold their wine cups, and crown their brows with
garlands and say, "Brief is this enjoyment for us poor
men; 't will soon be past and gone beyond recall."]

      *   *   *   *

           Sic cum transierint mei
           Nullo cum strepitu dies,
           Plebeius moriar senex:
           Illi mors gravis incubat
           Qui notus nimis omnibus
           Ignotus moritur sibi.

                    SENECA.

[So when without racket and fuss my days have

passed, let me die—a plain old man of the people!
Death lies a heavy load on him who, to the public
too well known, dies to himself unknown.]

*

CATO'S LAST SOLILOQUY

It must be so—Plato, thou reasonest well—
Else whence this pleasing hope, this fond desire,
This longing after immortality?
Or whence this secret dread, and inward horror
Of falling into nought? Why shrinks the soul
Back on herself and startles at destruction?
'Tis the divinity that stirs within us:
'Tis Heaven itself that points out an hereafter,
And intimates eternity to man.
Eternity! thou pleasing, dreadful thought!
Through what variety of untried being,
Through what new scenes and changes must we
   pass!

The wide, th' unbounded prospect lies before me;
But shadows, clouds and darkness rest upon it.
Here will I hold. If there's a Power above us
(And that there is all Nature cries aloud
Through all her works) He must delight in virtue;
And that which He delights in must be happy.
But when? or where? This world was made for
   Cæsar.
I'm weary of conjectures. This must end 'em.
         (laying his hand on his sword.)

Thus am I doubly armed: my death and life,
My bane and antidote are both before me.
This in a moment brings me to an end:
But this informs me I shall never die.
The soul, secure in her existence, smiles
At the drawn dagger and defies its point.
The stars shall fade away, the sun himself
Grow dim with age, and nature sink in years:
But thou shalt flourish in immortal youth,
Unhurt amongst the war of elements,
The wrecks of matter and the crash of worlds.

SENECA from "Cato".

Translated by Dr. Bland for the "Spectator", 1714.

*

AN EPITAPH

Below lies one whose name was traced in sand.
He died, not knowing what it was to live:
Died, while the first sweet consciousness of
    manhood
And maiden thought electrified his soul,
Faint beatings in the calyx of the rose.
Bewildered reader! pass without a sigh
In a proud sorrow! There is life with God,
In other kingdom of a sweeter air.
In Eden every flower is blown. Amen.

DAVID GRAY (1838–1861).

*

X

Authors and Their Ways

*

I don't think Byron wholesome exactly, but a drop or so—Eh!—G. MEREDITH.

If I could get materials I really would write a short life of that wonderful woman (Jane Austen) and raise a little money to put up a monument to her in Winchester Cathedral.—T. B. MACAULAY (1858).

As if it could matter the value of a brass farthing to any human being who was the author of "Junius".—T. CARLYLE.

I have some peculiar notions about money. . . . I have not that horror of being under obligation which is thought an essential refinement in money matters.—LEIGH HUNT.

The truth must be told about Carlyle. He is a man of one idea, but what that idea is no one is able to discover.
FITZJAMES STEPHEN.

One extenuating circumstance attends Yorick's works, that they are too gross to be inflaming.
S. RICHARDSON on Sterne's "Sentimental Journey".

Shortly before his death Herbert Spencer had the eighteen volumes of the Synthetic Philosophy piled on his lap and wondered as he felt their cold weight whether he would not have done better could he have a grandchild in their stead.

Mr. Walter Pater's style is, to me, like the face of some old woman who has been to Madame Rachel and had herself enamelled. The bloom is nothing but powder and paint and the odour is cherry-blossom. Mr. Matthew Arnold's odour is as the faint sickliness of the hawthorn.
S. BUTLER.

What a power there always is in any bit brought in from Shakespeare or Milton among other things! How it shines like a jewel! I think Milton reads best in this way: he is too fine for a continuance.—HAZLITT.

He loved the birds and green places, and the wind on the heath, and saw the brightness of the skirts of God.
On W. H. HUDSON'S grave.

I should like to live in a small house just outside a pleasant English town all the days of my life, making myself useful in a humble way, reading my books and playing a rubber of whist at night.—ED. FITZGERALD.

I shall always reflect with pleasure on Sir Walter Scott's having been the first creation of my reign.
GEORGE IV (to Sir Walter Scott on making him a Baronet).

O RARE BEN JONSON

Ah Ben!
Say how, or when
Shall we thy guests
Meet at those lyric feasts,
Made at the *Sun*,
The *Dog*, the *Triple Tun*?
Where we such clusters had
As made us nobly wild, not mad:
And yet each verse of thine
Outdid the meat, outdid the frolic wine.

R. HERRICK (1591-1674).

*

A SELF-PORTRAIT

Perhaps I may allow the Dean
Had too much satire in his vein:

And seemed determined not to starve it:
Because no age could more deserve it.
Yet, malice never was his air:
He lashed the vice but spared the mare,
No individual could resent
Where thousands equally were meant.
His satire points at no defect,
But what all mortals may correct;
For he abhorred that senseless tribe,
Who call it humour when they gibe:
He spared a hump or crooked nose,
Whose owners set not up for beaux.
True genuine dullness moved his pity
Unless it offered to be witty.
Those who their ignorance confessed
He ne'er offended with a jest:
But laughed to hear an idiot quote
A verse from Horace, learned by rote.
He knew a hundred pleasant stories,
With all the turns of Whigs and Tories.
Was cheerful to his dying day
And friends would let him have his way.
He gave the little wealth he had
To build a house for fools and mad,
And shewed by one satiric touch
No nation wanted it so much:
That kingdom he hath left his debtor,
I wish it soon may have a better.

JONATHAN SWIFT (1667–1745).

*

"EVERYONE CALLS HIM PAPA"

I have digressed from Parsons Green, Fulham. I wished you there, because those who only know Mr. Richardson as an author do not know the most amiable part of his character. His Villa is fitted up in the same style his books are writ. Every minute detail attended to, yet everyone with a view to its being useful or pleasing. Not an inch in his garden unimproved or unadorned; his very Poultry made happy by fifty little neat contrivances; his House prepared not for his family only but for every friend, high or low, to whom Air and Recess may be of Benefit. One always sees there a succession of Young Women and exceedingly elegant, well behaved, sensible young women, who improve and entertain his Daughters, at the same time that their health is mended or their distress assisted by being there and everyone (in the book style again) calls him Papa. Walking round all the Offices with him I could see every domestic Countenance brightening up, as he came near them, with unaffected Joy, while he asked everyone *en passant* some kind question.

CATHERINE TALBOT (1754).

*

"THERE IS DEATH IN THAT HAND"

A loose, slack, not well dressed youth met Mr. —— and myself in a lane near Highgate. —— knew him and spoke. It was Keats. He was introduced to me and stayed a minute or so. After he had left us a little way, he came back and said: "Let me carry away the memory, Coleridge, of having pressed your hand!" "There is death in that hand," I said to ——, when Keats was gone: yet this was, I think, before the consumption had shewed itself distinctly."

S. T. COLERIDGE (1772-1834).

* * * *

The last time I saw Keats was at Hampstead, lying in a white bed with a book, hectic, and on his back, irritable at his weakness, and wounded at the way he had been used. He seemed to be going out of life with a contempt for this world and no hopes of the other. I told him to be calm, but he muttered that if he did not soon get better he would destroy himself. I tried to reason against such violence, but it was no use; he grew angry, and I went away deeply affected.

R. B. HAYDON (1786-1846).

*

COLERIDGE'S ADDICTION TO OPIUM

For ten years the anguish of my spirit has been indescribable, the sense of my danger staring, but the consciousness of my guilt worse—far worse than all. I have prayed with drops of agony on my brow, trembling not only before the justice of my Maker but even before the mercy of my

Redeemer. "I gave thee so many talents, what hast thou done with them?"

Secondly, overwhelmed as I am with a sense of my direful infirmity, I have never attempted to disguise or conceal the cause. On the contrary, not only to friends have I stated the whole case with tears and the very bitterness of shame, but in two instances I have warned young men, mere acquaintances, who had spoken of taking laudanum, of the direful consequences, by an awful exposition of its tremendous effects on myself.

Thirdly, though before God I cannot lift up my eyelids and only do not despair of His mercy, because to despair would be adding crime to crime, yet to my fellow countrymen I can say that I was reduced into the accursed habit ignorantly. I had been almost bed-ridden for many months with swelling on my knees. In a medical journal I unhappily met with an account of a cure performed in a similar case by rubbing in laudanum, at the same time taking a given dose internally. It acted like a charm, like a miracle. I recovered the use of my limbs, of my appetite, of my spirits and this continued for near a fortnight. At length the unusual stimulus subsided, the complaint returned, the supposed remedy was recurred to—but I cannot go through the dreary history.

S. T. C.

From a letter to Cottle in 1814.

*

SHELLEY'S FUNERAL PYRE

The remains of Shelley and Mr. Williams were burnt after the good ancient fashion, and gathered into coffers . . . The ceremony of the burning was alike beautiful and distressing. Trelawny, who had been the chief person concerned in ascertaining the fate of his friends, completed his kindness by taking the most active part on this last mournful occasion. He and his friend, Captain Shenley, were first upon the ground, attended by proper assistants. Lord Byron and myself arrived shortly afterwards. His lordship got out of his carriage, but wandered away from the spectacle, and did not see it. I remained inside the carriage, now looking on, now drawing back with feelings that were not to be witnessed.

None of the mourners, however, refused themselves the little comfort of supposing that lovers of books and antiquity, like Shelley and his companion—Shelley in particular with his Greek enthusiasm—would not have been sorry to foresee this part of their fate. The mortal part of him, too, was saved from corruption; not the least extraordinary part of his history. Among the materials for burning, as many of the gracefuller and more classical articles as could be procured— frankincense, wine, etc.—were not forgotten; and to these Keats's volume was added.

The beauty of the flame arising from the funeral pile was extraordinary. The weather was beautifully fine. The Mediterranean, now soft and lucid, kissed the shore as if to make peace with it. The yellow sand and blue sky were intensely contrasted with one another: marble mountains touched the air with coolness; and the flame of the fire bore away towards heaven in vigorous amplitude, waving and quivering with a brightness of inconceivable beauty. It seemed as though it contained the glassy essence of vitality. You might have expected a seraphic countenance to look out of it, turning once more before it departed, to thank the friends that had done their duty.

LEIGH HUNT (1784-1859).
From "Autobiography".

*

HORACE WALPOLE'S DISLIKE OF JOHNSON

Often, indeed, Johnson made the most brutal speeches to living persons; for though he was good-natured at bottom, he was very ill-natured at top. He loved to dispute, to show his superiority. If his opponents were weak, he told them they were fools; if they vanquished him, he was scurrilous—to nobody more than to Boswell himself, who was contemptible for flattering him so grossly, and for enduring the coarse things he was continually vomiting on Boswell's own country, Scotland.

I expected, amongst the excommunicated, to find myself, but am very gently treated. I never

would be in the least acquainted with Johnson; or,
as Boswell calls it, I had not a just value for him;
which the biographer imputes to my resentment
for the doctor's putting bad arguments (purposely,
out of Jacobitism) into the speeches which he
wrote fifty years ago for my father, in the *Gentleman's Magazine*; which I did not read then, or
ever knew Johnson wrote till Johnson died, nor
have looked at since. Johnson's blind Toryism
and known brutality kept me aloof; nor did I ever
exchange a syllable with him: nay, I do not think I
ever was in the room with him six times in my days.

Boswell came to me, said Dr. Johnson was
writing the *Lives of the Poets*, and wished I would
give him anecdotes of Mr. Gray. I said, very
coldly, I had given what I knew to Mr. Mason.
Boswell hummed and hawed and then dropped,
"I suppose you know Dr. Johnson does not admire
Mr. Gray." Putting as much contempt as I could
into my look and tone, I said, "Dr. Johnson
don't!—humph!"—and with that monosyllable
ended our interview.

After the doctor's death, Burke, Sir Joshua
Reynolds, and Boswell sent an ambling circular-
letter to me, begging subscriptions for a monument
for him—the two last, I think, impertinently; as
they could not but know my opinion, and could
not suppose I would contribute to a monument
for one who had endeavoured, poor soul! to
degrade my friend's superlative poetry. I would
not deign to write an answer; but sent down word

by my footman, as I would have done to parish officers with a brief, that I would not subscribe.

HORACE WALPOLE (1791).

*

DAVID HUME'S DIALOGUE WITH CHARON

Mr. Hume's magnanimity and firmness were such that his most affectionate friends knew that they hazarded nothing in talking and writing to him as a dying man, and that so far from being hurt by this frankness he was rather pleased and flattered by it. . . . "When I lie down in the evening," he said, "I feel myself weaker than when I rose in the morning, and when I rise in the morning weaker than when I lay down in the evening. I am sensible that some of my vital parts are affected, so that I must soon die."

"Well," said I, "if it must be so, you have at least the satisfaction of leaving all your friends, your brother's family in particular, in great prosperity!"

He said that he felt that satisfaction so sensibly that when he was reading, a few days before, Lucian's "Dialogues of the Dead" amongst all the excuses which are alleged to Charon he could not find one that fitted him; he had no house to finish, he had no daughter to provide for: he had no enemies upon whom he wished to revenge himself. "I could not well imagine," he said, "what excuse I could make to Charon in order to obtain a little delay. I have done everything of consequence which I ever meant to do, and I could at no time expect to leave my relations and friends in a better situation than that in which I am now likely to leave them. I, therefore, have every reason to die contented."

He then diverted himself with inventing several jocular excuses which he supposed he might make to Charon and with imagining the very surly answers which it might suit the character of Charon to return to them. "Upon further consideration," said he, "I thought I might say to him, 'Good Charon, I have been correcting my works for a new edition. Allow me a little time to see how the public receives the alterations'! But Charon would answer: 'When you have seen the effect of these you will be for making other alterations. There will be no end of such excuses: so, honest friend, please step into the boat'!

"But I might still urge, 'Have a little patience, good Charon, I have been endeavouring to open the eyes of the public. If I live a few years longer, I may have the satisfaction of seeing the downfall of the prevailing system of superstition.' But Charon would then lose all temper and decency. 'You loitering rogue, that will not happen these many hundred years. Do you fancy I will grant you a leave for so long a term? Get into the boat this instant, you lazy, loitering rogue.'"

DAVID HUME (1711–1776).
From "My Own Life".

A PORTRAIT OF COBBETT

What Mr. Cobbett has written is no rule to him what he is to write. He learns something every day and every week he takes the field to maintain the opinions of the last six days against friend or foe. . . . He is not pledged to repeat himself. Every new *Register* is a kind of new Prospectus. He releases himself from all ties and shackles on his understanding: he has no mortgages on his brain: his notions are free and unencumbered. . . . He takes both sides of a question and maintains one as sturdily as the other. If nobody else can argue against him, he is a very good match for himself. He writes better in favour of Reform than anybody else: he used to write better against it. Wherever he is there is the tug of war, the weight of the argument, the strength of abuse. . . .

Fresh theories give him fresh courage. He is like a young and lusty bridegroom that divorces a favourite speculation every morning and marries a new one every night. He is not wedded to his notions, not he. He has not one Mrs. Cobbett among all his opinions. He makes the most of the last thought that has come in his way, seizes fast hold of it, rumples it about in all directions with strong rough hands, has his will of it, takes a surfeit and throws it away. . . .

Mr. Cobbett is great in attack, not in defence: he cannot fight an uphill battle. He will not bear the least punishing. If anyone turns upon him (which few people like to do) he immediately turns tail. Like an overgrown schoolboy, he is so used to have it all his own way that he cannot submit to anything like competition or a struggle for the mastery: he must lay on all the blows and take none. . . . Whenever he has been set upon, he has slunk out of the controversy.

Mr. Cobbett speaks almost as well as he writes. The only time I ever saw him he seemed to me a very pleasant man: easy of access, affable, clear-headed, simple and mild in his manner, deliberate and unruffled in his speech, though some of his expressions were not very qualified. His figure is tall and portly: he has a good sensible face, rather full, with little grey eyes, a hard square forehead, a ruddy complexion, with hair grey or powdered, and had on a scarlet broadcloth waist-coat, with the flaps of the pockets hanging down, as was the custom for gentlemen farmers in the last century or, as we see it in the pictures of Members of Parliament in the reign of George I. I certainly did not think less favourably of him for seeing him.

W. HAZLITT (1778-1830).

*

THE YOUTHFUL BURNS

In my seventeenth year to give my manners a brush I went to a country dancing school. My father had an unaccountable antipathy against these meetings, and my going was, what to this moment I repent, in opposition to his wishes. My father was subject to strong passions: from that instance of disobedience in me, he took a sort of dislike to me and it was, I believe, one cause of the dissipation which marked my succeeding years. I say dissipation, comparatively with the strictness and sobriety and regularity of Presbyterian country life: for though the Will o' the Wisp meteors of thoughtless whim were almost the sole lights of my path, yet early ingrained piety and virtue kept me for several years afterwards within the line of innocence.

The great misfortune of my life was to want an aim. I saw that my father's situation entailed on me perpetual labour. The only two openings by which I could enter the temple of Fortune were the gate of niggardly economising or the path of little chicaning bargain-making. The former is so contracted an aperture I could never squeeze myself into it: the last I always hated: there was contamination in the very entrance. . . .

But far beyond all other impulses of my heart was *un penchant à l'adorable moitié du genre humain*. My heart was completely tinder and was eternally lighted up by some goddess or other, and as in every other warfare in this world my fortune was various. Sometimes I was received with favour; sometimes I was mortified with a repulse. At the plough, scythe or reap-hook I feared no competitor and thus I set absolute want at defiance, and as I never cared further for my labours than when I was in actual exercise, I spent the evenings in the way after my own heart.

A country lad seldom carries on a love adventure without an assisting confidant. I possessed a curiosity, zeal and intrepid dexterity that recommended me as a proper second on these occasions, and I dare say I felt as much pleasure in being in the secret of half the loves of the parish of Tarbolton as ever did statesman in knowing the intrigues of half the courts of Europe.

ROBERT BURNS (1759–1796).

*

HAZLITT'S INFATUATION

Hazlitt's intellect was completely subdued by an insane passion. He was for a time unable to think or talk of anything else. He abandoned criticism and books as idle matters and fatigued every person whom he met by expressions of his love, of her deceit and of his own vehement disappointment. This was when he lived in Southampton Buildings, Holborn.

Upon one occasion I know that he told the story of his attachment to five different persons on the same day and each time entered into minute details. "I am a cursed fool," he said to me. "I saw I—— going into Wills' Coffee House yday morning: he spoke to me. I followed him into the house and while he lunched I told him the whole story. Then I wandered into the Regent's Park where I met one of M——'s sons. I walked with him some time and on his using some civil expressions, by Jove, Sir, I told him the whole story!" (Here he mentioned another instance which I forget.)

"Well, sir" (he went on), "I then went and called on Haydon, but he was out. There was only his man there, but by Jove! I could not help myself. It all came out, the whole cursed story. Afterwards I went to look at some lodgings in Pimlico. The landlady at the place, after some explanations as to rent, etc., said to me very kindly, "I am afraid you are not well, Sir." "No, ma'am," said I, "I am not well": and on enquiring further the devil take me if I did not let out the whole story from beginning to end."

I used to see this girl, Sarah Walker, at his lodgings and could not account for the extravagant passion of her admirer. She was the daughter of the lodging house keeper. Her face was round and small, and her eyes were motionless, glassy and without any speculation (apparently) in them. Her movements in walking were very remarkable, for I never observed her to make a step. She went onwards in a sort of wavy, sinuous manner like the movements of a snake. She was silent, or uttered monosyllables only, and was very demure. Her steady unmoving gaze upon the person she was addressing was exceedingly unpleasant.

To this girl Hazlitt gave all his valuable time, all his wealth of thought, and all the loving frenzy of his heart. For a time I think that he was on this point substantially insane—certainly beyond self-control. To him she was a being full of witchery, full of grace and with all the capacity of tenderness. The retiring coquetry which had also brought others to her invested her in his sight with all the attractions of a divinity.

BRYAN WALLER PROCTER (1787–1874).
("Barry Cornwall".)

*

"THAT OLD MAHOMETAN BLACKGUARD"

One day in the spring of 1873 when I was walking with Carlyle I spoke to him of this little book. ("The Rubaiyat of Omar Khayyam") expressing my admiration of it. He had never heard of it. He asked me whose work it was and I told him what I had heard, that the translation was made by a Rev. Edward Fitzgerald, who lived somewhere in Norfolk, and spent much of his time in his boat. "The Reverend Fitzgerald!" said he in reply, "why, he is no more Reverend than I am. He's a very old friend of mine. I am surprised, if the book is as good as you tell me it is, that my old friend has never mentioned it to me," and then he went on to give me a further account of Fitzgerald. I told Carlyle I would send him the book and did so the next day.

315

Two or three days later, when we were walking together again, he said, "I've read that little book you sent me, and I think my old friend Fitzgerald might have spent his time to much better purpose than in busying himself with the verses of that old Mahometan Blackguard." I could not prevail on him even to do credit to the noble English in which Fitzgerald had rendered the audacious quatrains of the Persian poet: he held the whole thing as worse than a mere waste of labour.

CHARLES ELIOT NORTON.
From a letter in "Memorials of
Edward Burne-Jones".

*

MACAULAY AS A BOOK-BUYER

The first shop I opened in London—wrote Mr. Salkeld, a London bookseller, to Macaulay's biographer, Sir George Trevelyan—was in the Featherstone Buildings, a little thoroughfare off Holborn. I was unpacking some cases of books one morning, and, because there was no other place available, I was unpacking them in the roadway. Up came a grave and pleasant gentleman, very well set up and neatly dressed, who stopped, and looked on, as if he were fully at home in that kind of neighbourhood, and also with the job I was engaged on. It was a long time afterwards that I heard he was Lord Macaulay; and the customer who told me became Lord Justice Fry.

"May I look at these books?" the stranger asked. I said, "Certainly," and went and got a chair for him; but I was in so small a way then that I had to borrow it. He sat down and went through the lot, quickly but thoroughly, and made a big selection of historical tracts of the period just after the Civil War. He asked what he was to pay, and I said a shilling apiece. He seemed astonished, and I was prepared to hear him grumble, when he said, "I am very pleased to have come across them, and to find you are so reasonable in your terms." He came again and again, and each time took several pounds' worth away with him, carrying them himself, and never allowing me to make a parcel except so far as to string them up.

From Sir G. O. Trevelyan's
"Life of Lord Macaulay".

*

MACAULAY'S LOVE OF TRINITY

Of all his places of sojourn during his joyous and shining pilgrimage through the world, Trinity, and Trinity alone, had any share with his home in Macaulay's affection and loyalty. To the last he regarded it as an ancient Greek, or a mediæval Italian, felt towards his native city. As long as he had place and standing there, he never left it willingly or returned to it without delight. The only step in his course about the wisdom of which

he sometimes expressed misgiving was his preference of a London to a Cambridge life. The only
dignity that in his later days he was known to
covet was an honorary fellowship, which would
have allowed him again to look through his window
upon the college grass-plots, and to sleep within
sound of the splashing of the fountain; again to
breakfast on commons, and dine beneath the
portraits of Newton and Bacon on the dais of the
hall; again to ramble by moonlight round Neville's
cloister, discoursing the picturesque but somewhat
esoteric philosophy which it pleased him to call
by the name of metaphysics.

From the door of his rooms, along the wall of
the Chapel, there runs a flagged pathway which
affords an acceptable relief from the rugged
pebbles that surround it. Here as a Bachelor of
Arts he would walk, book in hand, morning after
morning throughout the Long Vacation, reading
with the same eagerness and the same rapidity
whether the volume was the most abstruse of
treatises, the loftiest of poems, or the flimsiest of
novels. That was the spot where in his failing
years he specially loved to renew the feelings of
the past; and some there are who can never
revisit it without the fancy that there, if anywhere,
his dear shade must linger.

Sir G. O. Trevelyan (1838–1928).

*

A SCHOLAR'S DEVOTION TO HIS BOOKS

Mark Pattison (Rector of Lincoln College, Oxford) had a quite human fondness for his books: nothing annoyed him so much as to hear one of them fall, and dusting them, which he reduced to a science, seemed to give him real pleasure. In his last illness the sight of many of his favourites depressed him greatly. "Ah," he would say, "I am to leave my books." And sometimes, "They have been more to me than my friends." He would ask for them one after the other, till he was literally covered almost to his shoulders as he lay and the floor around was strewn with them. He used to say that the sight of books was necessary to him at his work: and once reading how Schiller always kept rotten apples in his study, because their scent was beneficial to him, he pointed to some shelves above his head, where he kept his oldest and most prized editions, and said, "There are my rotten apples."

MRS. PATTISON.

* *

DICKENS AT DONCASTER

On their way home, Dickens and Wilkie Collins were at Doncaster and this was Dickens' first experience of the St. Leger and its saturnalia. The impressions received from the race-week were not favourable.

It was noise and turmoil all day long and a gathering of vagabonds from all parts of the racing earth. Every bad face that had ever caught wickedness from an innocent horse had its representative in the streets: and as Dickens, like Gulliver looking down upon his fellow men coming from the horse-country, looked down into Doncaster High Street from his inn window, he seemed to see everywhere a notorious personage who had just poisoned his betting companion. "Everywhere I see the late Mr. Palmer* with his betting book in his hand. Mr. Palmer sits next me at the theatre: Mr. Palmer goes before me down the street: Mr. Palmer follows me into the chemist's shop where I go to buy rose-water after breakfast and says to the chemist, 'Give me soom sal volatile or soom damned thing o' that soort in watter—my head's bad.' And I look on the back of his bad head repeated in long long lines on the race course, and in the betting stand, and outside the betting rooms in the town and I vow to God that I can see nothing in it but cruelty, covetousness, calculation, insensibility and low wickedness."

JOHN FORSTER (1812–1876).
From the "Life of Charles Dickens".

* Mr. Palmer was the Rugeley murderer, recently hanged for poisoning with arsenic a friend with whom he had gone to the Doncaster races.

*

W. M. THACKERAY

When one, whose nervous English verse
    Public and party hate defied,
Who bore and bandied many a curse
    Of angry times—when Dryden died,

Our royal abbey's Bishop-Dean
    Waited for no suggestive prayer,
But ere one day closed o'er the scene
    Craved, as a boon, to lay him there.

The wayward faith, the faulty life,
    Vanished before a nation's pain,
Panther and Hind forgot their strife
    And rival statesmen thronged the fane.

O gentle censor of our age!
    Prime master of our ampler tongue!
Whose word of wit and generous page
    Were never wroth except with wrong—

Fielding—without the manner's dross,
    Scott—with a spirit's larger room,
What Prelate deems thy grave his loss,
    What Halifax erects thy tomb?

But maybe he—who could so draw
    The hidden great, the humble wise—
Yielding with them to God's good law,
    Makes the Pantheon where he lies.

LORD HOUGHTON (1809–1885).

On the proposal to bury Thackeray
in Westminster Abbey 1864.

SWINBURNE RECITES POETRY

The dinner—at Balliol—passed off pleasantly.
Swinburne showed himself an intelligent, though
by no means a brilliant talker; and as soon as we
had returned to the drawing-room, where we drank
a cup of coffee standing, Jowett, who had some
engagement, abruptly left us to finish the evening
by ourselves. On Swinburne the effect of the
Master's disappearance was magical. His manner
and aspect began to exhibit a change like that of
the moon when a dim cloud drifts away from it.

Of what we discussed at starting I have not the
least remembrance, but before very long Swinburne was on the subject of poetry. His observa-
tions at first consisted of general criticisms.
Then he began to indulge in quotations from
various poems—none of them, I think, from his
own; but however this may have been, the music
seemed to intoxicate him. The words began to
thrill me with the spell of his own recitation of
them. Here at last I realised the veritable genius
who had made the English language a new
instrument of passion. Here at last was the singer
for whose songs my ears were shells which still
murmured with such lines as I had first furtively
read by the gas-light of the Brighton theatre.

My own appreciation as a listener more and more
encouraged him. If he began a quotation sitting,
he would start from his chair to finish it. Finally
he abandoned the restraints of a chair altogether.
He began, with gesticulating arms, to pace the

322

room from one end to the other, reciting passage after passage, and appealing to me, who managed to keep pace with him, for applause. "The most beautiful lines that Tennyson ever wrote," he exclaimed, "were these from 'Maud':

"And like silent lightning under the stars
        She seemed to divide in a dream from a
            band of the blest."

"Yes," he went on, "and what did the dream-Maud tell her lover when she had got him? That the salvation of the world depended on the Crimean War and the prosecution of Lord Palmerston's policy." Finally he strayed into quotations from Sydney Dobell, a writer now hardly remembered, with one of which, describing a girl bathing, he made the Master's academic rafters ring:

She with her body bright sprinkles the waters
        white,
Which flee from her fair form, and flee in vain,
Dyed with the dear unutterable sight
And circles out her beauties to the circling main.

He was almost shouting these words when another sound became audible—that of an opening door, followed by Jowett's voice, which said in high pitched syllables, "You'd both of you better go to bed now."

W. H. MALLOCK.

*

323

SALA AND HIS CRITICS

Charles Austin was a frequent contributor to the *Saturday Review*, in which he once wrote a very slashing article castigating the young and aggressive *Daily Telegraph*. In those days our leading columns were rather too full of quotations from the classics: and of course our critics insinuated that all our classical quotations were taken from Lemprière or from the mottoes appended to the armorial bearings in "Burke's Peerage". . . .

Calmly reviewing in this the late evening of my life what I have done in letters and journalism, I have arrived at two very carefully decided conclusions. First, that the *Saturday Review* was in many respects quite justified in reviling me, and next that the animadversions of that able journal did me a great deal more good than harm. . . . I was earning at the time when it was wont most fiercely to attack me, say in 1863, about £2,000 a year and I cannot remember, save when I was prostrated with sickness, to have earned since then a smaller sum.

Nor did the *Saturday* prevent me from acquiring a certain amount of popularity. Celebrated I never was and celebrated I never wanted to be, yet I have been as well known for many years past as Horniman's Tea or Thorley's Food for Cattle, or any much advertised soap that you care to know of. The *Saturday* was equally mistaken as unjust in asserting that I was destitute of humour and of learning: but it was quite right in accusing me of writing in a turgid, inflated and bombastic manner.

Style, the French philosopher has said, is the Man: and my style, from the English point of view, is and has always been incurably vicious. I was brilliantly educated: but half my education was imparted to me at a French public school and at the academy at Turnham Green, and the remainder I have acquired by rigid study which will not be relaxed till I grow blind or die. During the six years of my connection with Dickens on *Household Words* I had to subdue my tendency to use words derived from the Latin instead of the Anglo-Saxon. . . .

But when I joined the staff of the *Daily Telegraph* and had a free hand in writing at least three thousand words every day, I soon relapsed into that style which so roused the ire of the *Saturday*. Out came, or rather streamed, the long-tailed words, the hyperboles, the rhodomontade, the similes and the quotations dragged in by the head or the heels. I knew, perhaps, but little: but I made as much as I could of what I knew. I was impatient, dogmatical, illogical and from time to time aggressive and abusive.

* * *

How little people know about one another to be sure! There was brilliant whole-souled Matthew Arnold, who was so very fond of snarling and sneering at the journalists whom he called "the young lions of the *Daily Telegraph*." Bless us and save us! When he was jibing, some of the writers whom he assailed were growing middle-aged lions, and those of us at least who yet contrive to roar daily in the columns of the *Daily Telegraph* —Edwin Arnold, Francis Lawley and myself— are rather ancient lions. Many years afterwards I met Matthew Arnold at the house of Mr. George Russell, now Under-Secretary of State for India, and we had much merriment about the young lions.

G. A. SALA (1828–1896).

From "Life and Adventures".

*

SIR RICHARD BURTON'S ODD FOIBLES

Sir Richard Burton was intensely simple in his tastes. I used to busy myself, Martha-like, about making his room extremely comfortable: but the moment I put anything pretty in it, it used to be put in the passage. He liked large plain deal tables, about six feet long and three or four feet broad, with no table cloth. He would tie a red bandanna on the leg for a penwiper. He liked hard wooden writing chairs, and to have a great many of these tables—one for each separate work: a small iron bedstead, with iron wove mattress, no sheets but plenty of English white soft warm blankets. He would have no night-light: but would never have blinds nor shutters drawn, that he might see daylight as soon as possible, and the last of the twilight.

His bookshelves were all of plain deal and each category upon which he was working was kept separate. He would not have his books and papers touched and preferred dust and cobwebs to their being moved. His three private rooms contained only books, swords, pistols and guns, scientific instruments, a few medicines, and plenty of clothes.

He loved his old clothes. He would order rows of greatcoats and ulsters, and then go out in a little thin coat to keep himself hardy. He had a great love for boots, and sometimes had as many as a hundred pairs in the house. I used to implore to be allowed to give his old hats away to the cabmen, and he only laughed immensely at my getting so ashamed of them: but he always had loads of new clothes and wore the old ones for preference.

As some people know when there is a cat in the room, he could not sit in the room with honey and knew even if it was kept in the most secret drawer or cup-board. . . . His great treat of all was a sucking pig, three weeks old, roasted well with the crackle, stuffing and apple-sauce: and this was always ordered on our wedding day and on his birthday. . . . His favourite wine was port—he used to call it "the prince of wines", but he was not allowed it during the last three years and a half.

LADY BURTON.
From "Life of Sir Richard Burton".

*

A GLORIOUS SUNSHINY DAY

Here is a glorious sunshiny day; all the morning I have read about Nero in Tacitus, lying at full length on a bench in the garden; a nightingale singing, and some red anemones eyeing the sun manfully not far off. A funny mixture, all this; Nero and the delicacy of Spring; all very human, however. Then at half-past one lunch on Cambridge cream cheese; then a ride over hill and dale; then spudding up some weeds from the grass; and then, coming in, I sit down to write to you, my sister winding red worsted from the back of a chair, and the most delightful little girl in the world chattering incessantly. You think I live in Epicurean ease; but this happens to be a jolly day; one isn't always well, or tolerably good; the weather is not always clear, nor nightingales singing, nor Tacitus full of pleasant atrocity. But such as life is, I believe I have got hold of a good end of it.

EDWARD FITZGERALD (1809–1883).

*

A PEACEFUL COURT IN TRINITY

The windows of my study look on the tranquil court of an ancient college, where the sundial marks the silent passage of the hours, and in the long summer days the fountain plashes drowsily amid flowers and grass: where as the evening shadows deepen the lights come out in the blazoned windows of the Elizabethan Hall and from the chapel the sweet voices of the choir, blent with pealing music of the organ, float on the peaceful air, telling of man's eternal aspirations after truth and goodness and immortality.

Here, if anywhere, remote from the tumult and bustle of the world with its pomps and vanities and ambitions, the student may hope to hear the still voice of truth, to penetrate through the little transitory question of the hour to the realities which abide or rather which we fondly think must abide while the generations come and go. I cannot be too thankful that I have been allowed to spend so many quiet and happy years in such a scene.

J. G. FRASER.

From the Preface to "Pausanias' Description of Greece".

*

BURNE-JONES AT BROWNING'S BURIAL

I broke off work and went to Browning's funeral—under protest—for I hate that beautiful heaven (Westminster Abbey) to be turned into a stonemason's yard for anyone. No one is good enough to spoil that divine citadel, and I am sick of dead bodies and want them burnt and scattered to winds. It wasn't impressive—no, not a bit. People said to me, "How impressive!" and I said, "Yes, indeed!" one has to in the world—but it wasn't, it was stupid. No candles, no incense, no copes, no nothing that was nice. . . .

I would have given something for a banner or two, and much I would have given if a chorister had come out of the triforium and rent the air with a trumpet. How flat these English are—most people are. And when a coffin covered with a pall is carried on the shoulders of six men, it looks like a great beetle. And what Paul said was partly so grand that it is the last word that need be said, and partly so poor and flat that I wondered anyone could take the pains to say it.

But I spent the time looking at the roof and its groining and the diapered walls and wanted a service one day in praise of the church, and wondered who had built it and why his name was forgotten and thought how only the church mattered at all and I wanted to push people, and wasn't in a holy frame of mind, I assure you. And why couldn't they leave him in Royal Venice?

SIR E. BURNE-JONES (1889).
From Lady Burne-Jones' "Memorials of
Edward Burne-Jones".

330

A COUNTERBLAST TO TOBACCO

If fellows must smoke, let them retire into a remote smoking-den, wash, be shampooed and change all their clothes, before they dare to mix in general society. Of course, the smoking tribe will call me a milksop, an old "crank", with abnormal olfactories and so forth. Well! I remember when I was a bowler to our eleven of Non-Smokers, we won in an innings, and no wonder. That is fifty-five years ago, but I can bowl a good ball still. I have been a member of the Alpine Club and two famous Smoking Clubs: and I founded one of them, not to smoke but to talk. I have been about in London society and in London clubs any time these fifty years.

So far from being abnormal in my sense of smell, I will not deny that the scent of a very fine Havannah in the open air on a frosty night, smoked by a pleasant friend a few yards off me, is not so offensive. It is the nasty cigarette, the stinking pipe, the rotten garbage of cheap stuff, the stale, clammy reek where smoke has been every night, which is intolerable. If I am a "crank" I can only say that fifty years ago gentlemen, as a rule, must have been "cranks", for they used to regard a man who habitually smoked everywhere and anywhere, in mixed society and in association with ladies, as a dirty brute.

As to women smoking, I cannot bring myself to speak. I cannot get over the feeling that they do not as they should do. I will just end with the words of two illustrious men. William Morris wrote: "Tobacco seems to me a more dangerous intoxicant than liquors". John Ruskin scorns the men "who would put the filth of tobacco into the first breeze of a May morning". Yes! and into the golden curls of a child.

FREDERIC HARRISON (1905).

*

A POET WELCOMES DEATH

On the day before his death Tennyson talked to the doctor about death: "What a shadow this life is, and how men cling to what is after all but a small part of the great world's life!" Then the doctor told him (for his interest was always keen "in the lot of lowly men") of an incident that had happened lately. "A villager, ninety years old, was dying and had so much pined to see his old bed-ridden wife once more that they carried her to where he lay. He pressed his shrunken hand upon her hand and in a husky voice he said to her, 'Come soon', and soon after passed away himself." My father murmured, "True Faith", and the tears were in his voice. Suddenly he gathered himself together, and spoke one word about himself to the doctor, "Death?" The doctor bowed and he said, "That's well".

HALLAM, LORD TENNYSON.
From his "Memoirs" of his father.

*

HENLEY'S "UNCONQUERABLE SOUL"

The place* chosen for the memorial of W. E. Henley, in the heart of the great city he loved well and sang of nobly, strikes the mind as the fulfilment of this English poet's highest material aspiration, and cannot but be in full accord with the wishes of his admirers. He had the poet's passion for nature, and by reason of it the poet's fervent devotion to humanity. Light of the skies playing upon smoky vapour, city scenery, city crowds, stirred in him those raptures which are the founts of spirited verse.

Rightly could he speak of his "unconquerable soul". It was a soul that had to do perpetual battle with an undermined and struggling body, and this joyfully, and as far as could be possible, buoyantly; for all his nature sprang up to hail the divinity of life. From a bed of sickness that might seem a hopeless imprisonment he gave out impressions of a daily hospital round and his own moods without a shadow of despair to darken the poetic vision; but when he was restored to companionship with his fellows one involuntary touch occurs in his verse to tell of the suffering he had passed through. He rejoiced in the smell of the streets. There we have the lover of life rising from the depths.

Such was the man. As critic he had the rare combination of enthusiasm and wakeful judgment. Pretentiousness felt his whip smartly. The

* The crypt of St. Paul's Cathedral.

accepted imbecile had to bear the weight of his epigram. But merit under a cloud or just emerging he sparkled on or lifted to the public view. He was one of the main supports of good literature in our time. His inspiriting heartiness and inciting counsels gathered about him a troop of young writers who are proud in acknowledging their debt to him for the first of the steps they made on the road to distinction. Deploring we have lost him, we may marvel that we had him with us so long. What remains is the example of a valiant man, the memory of him in poetry that will endure.

G. MEREDITH (1828–1909).
(From a letter to Lord Plymouth.)

*

CHATEAUBRIAND

M. de Chateaubriand at the beginning of 1837 was paralysed: Madame Récamier was blind. Everyday at three o'clock they carried M. de Chateaubriand close to the sofa of Madame Récamier. It was touching and sad. The woman who no longer could see sought the man who could no longer feel. Their two hands met. God be blessed! Hearts can go on loving when they almost cease to beat.

VICTOR HUGO (1820–1885).
From "Choses Vues".

334

XI

London Pride and Prejudice

*

Then in town let me live, and in town let me die
For I own I can't relish the country, not I.
If I *must* have a villa in summer to dwell
O give me the sweet shady side of Pall Mall!
                                        CAPT. MORRIS.

And I have seen the Park and the paleass of Saint Gimses
and the King's and the Queen's magisterial passing, and
the sweet young princesses and the hillifents and the pye-
bald ass, and the rest of the royal family.
                                        A SMOLLETT CHARACTER.

No man fond of letters leaves London without regret.
                                        DR. JOHNSON.

Of all London he liked Fleet Street most. "This is the
place where I should like to live," he used to say.
        HALLAM, LORD TENNYSON, of his father the poet.

Samuel Butler used to say that "the finest view in
Europe" was the view of St. Paul's from the north side of
Fleet Street as you walk from Fetter Lane to Ludgate
Circus.

Two eminent Victorians were passing one day through
the vault-like passage under the railway at Charing Cross,
where liquorish fumes from the cellared arches on either
side sometimes oppress the stagnant air. Lord Kil-
bracken's sensitive lungs coughed indignant protest.
"Oh! I like the smell of beer," cheerfully replied his

335

companion—Matthew Arnold, the apostle of Sweetness and Light.

As Pitt's coffin descended into the earth (at the Abbey) the eagle face of Chatham seemed to look down with consternation into the dark home which was receiving all that remained of so much power and glory.—MACAULAY.

It is easy to sit in arm-chairs at a Club in Pall Mall and rail on the stupidity and brutality of those in High Suffolk.
ED. FITZGERALD.

Felt the exquisite enjoyment, tossing nightly off, oh Heavens!
Brandies at the Cider Cellars, kidneys smoking hot at Evans'!
From the "Bon Gaultier Ballads".

Think what ruin it is for men of any sensitive faculty to live in such a city as London is now!—J. RUSKIN.

"I should like to have a good spin" (on his bicycle) "down Regent Street."—Last words of ROBERT BUCHANAN, the poet (1901).

LONDON THE FLOWER OF CITIES

London, thou art of townes "A per se"
Sovereign of cities, seemliest in sight,
Of high renoun, riches and royaltie.
Of lordis, barons, and many a goodly knyght;
Of most delectable lusty ladies bright;
Of famous prelates, in habits clericall;
Of merchauntis full of substaunce and of myght;
London, thou art the flour of Cities all.
Gemme of all joy, jasper of jocunditie,
Most myghty carbuncle of vertue and valour:

Strong Troy in vigour and in strenuytie;
Of royal cities rose and geraflour;
Empress of townes, exalt in honour;
In beawtie berying the crone imperiall;
Swete paradise precelling in pleasure:
London, thou art the flour of Cities all.

WILLIAM DUNBAR (1465–1520).

*

A COURT MARRIAGE

Yesterday, being St. John's Day, the marriage of Sir Philip Herbert and the Lady Susan Vere was performed at Whitehall, with all the honour could be done a great favourite. The King (James I) gave the bride, and she in her tresses and trinkets bridled it so handsomely that the King said if he were not married he would not give her but keep her himself. The marriage dinner was kept in the great chamber and at night there was a masque in the hall. The presents of plate and other things given by the noblemen are valued at £2,500: but that which made it a good marriage was a gift of the King's of £500 land for the bride's jointure. No ceremony was omitted of bride cakes, points, garters and gloves; and at night there was sewing into the sheet, casting of the bride's left hose, with many other pretty sorceries. They were lodged in the Council Chamber where in the morning the King, in his shirt and night-

gown, gave them a *reveilee matin* before they were
up and spent a good time in or upon the bed.

From "A Jacobean Journal".

Ed. G. B. Harrison.

*

TREASURE HUNTING IN THE ABBEY

Davy Ramsey, his Majesty's clockmaker, had
been informed that there was a great quantity of
treasure buried in the cloister of Westminster
Abbey. He acquaints Dean Williams therewith,
who was also then Bishop of Lincoln: and the
Dean gave him liberty to search after it, with this
proviso that if any was discovered, his Church
should have a share in it. Davy Ramsey finds out
one John Scott, who pretended the use of the
Mosaical rods, to assist him herein. I was
desired to join with him, unto which I consented.

One winter's night, Davy Ramsey, with several
gentlemen, myself and Scott, entered the cloisters:
he played the hazel-wand round the cloister: upon
the west side the rods turned over one another, an
argument that the treasure was there. The
labourers digged at least six feet deep, and then
we met with a coffin, but as it was not heavy, we
did not open it, which we afterwards much
repented. From the cloisters we went into the
abbey church where upon a sudden (there being
no wind when we began) so fierce, so high, so
blustering a wind did rise that we verily believed

the west end of the church would have fallen upon us. Our rods would not move at all: the candles and torches, all but one, were extinguished, or burned very dimly. John Scott, my partner, was amazed, grew pale, knew not what to think or do, until I gave directions and command to dismiss the demons, which when done all was quiet again, and each man returned unto his lodging late about 12 o'clock at night. I could never since be induced to join with any in such like acting.

The true miscarriage of the business was by reason of so many being present at the operation: for there was about thirty, some laughing, others deriding us; so that if we had not dismissed the demons, I believe most part of the abbey church had been blown down. Secrecy and intelligent operators, with a strong confidence and knowledge of what they are doing, are best for this work.

WILLIAM LILLY, the Astrologer (1634).

*

THE BIRD WITH THE WHITE BREAST

As I passed by St. Dunstan's in Fleet Street the last Saturday, I stepped into a lapidary, or stone-cutter's shop, to treat with the master for a stone to be put upon my father's grave, and casting my eyes up and down, I spied a huge marble with a large inscription on it, which ran thus to my best remembrance:

Here lies John Oxenham, a goodly young man in whose chamber, as he was struggling with the pangs of death, a bird with a white breast was seen fluttering about his bed and so vanished.

Here lies also Mary Oxenham, the sister of the said John, who died the next day and the said apparition was seen in the room.

Then another sister is spoken of, then:—

Here lies hard by James Oxenham, the son of the said John, who died a child in his cradle a little after, and such a bird was seen fluttering about his head, a little before he expired, which vanished afterwards.

At the bottom of the stone there is:—

Here lies Elizabeth Oxenham, the mother of the said John, who died sixteen years since when such a bird with a white breast was seen about her bed before her death.

To all these there be diverse witnesses, both squires and ladies, whose names are engraved upon the stone. This stone is to be sent to a town hard by Exeter, where this happened.

JAMES HOWELL (1632).

[Charles Kingsley made use of this story in "Westward Ho!"]

*

DR. DONNE'S MEMORIAL IN ST. PAUL'S

A monument being resolved upon, Dr. Donne sent for a carver to make for him in wood the figure of an urn, giving him directions for the compass and height of it, and to bring with it a board of the just height of his body. "These being got, then without delay a chosen painter was got to be in readiness to draw his picture, which was taken as followeth: Several charcoal fires being first made in his large study, he brought with him into that place his winding sheet in his hand, and having put off all his clothes, had that sheet put on him, and so tied with knots at his head and feet, and his hands so placed as dead bodies are usually fitted, to be shrowded and put into their coffin or grave. Upon this urn he thus stood, with his eyes shut and with so much of the sheet turned aside as might shew his lean, pale and death-like face, which was purposely turned towards the East, from whence he expected the second coming of his and our Saviour Jesus." In this posture he was drawn at his just height, and when the picture was fully finished, he caused it to be set by his bed-side, where it continued and became his hourly object till his death and was then given to his dearest friend and executor, Dr. Henry King, then Chief Residentiary of St. Paul's, who caused him to be thus carved in one entire piece of white marble, as it now stands, in that Church.

ISAAC WALTON (1593-1683).

From the Life of Dr. Donne.

[This memorial was one of the very few which survived the destruction of St. Paul's Cathedral in the Great Fire. It slid down into the crypt uninjured.]

A CASEMENT OPENS IN LOTHBURY

Passing through Tokenhouse, in Lothbury, of a sudden a casement violently opened just over my head, and a woman gave three frightful screeches, and then cried, "Oh, death, death, death," in a most inimitable tone, and which struck me with horror and a chillness in my very blood. There was nobody to be seen in the whole street, neither did any window open, for people had no curiosity now in any case, nor could anybody help one another, so I went on to pass into Bell Alley.

Just in Bell Alley, on the right hand of the passage, there was a more terrible cry than that, though it was not so directed out at the window; but the whole family was in a terrible fright, and I could hear women and children run screaming about the rooms like distracted, when a garret window opened and somebody from a window on the other side of the alley called and asked, "What is the matter?" Upon which from the first window it was answered, "O Lord! my old master has hanged himself." The other asked again, "Is he quite dead?" And the first answered, "Ay, ay, quite dead, quite dead, and cold." This person was a merchant and a deputy alderman, and very rich.

DANIEL DEFOE (1661?–1731).
From the "History of the Great Plague".

*

AT THE BURIAL OF GEORGE II

When we came to the chapel of Henry the Seventh all solemnity and decorum ceased—no order was observed, people sat or stood where they could or would, the Yeomen of the Guard were crying out for help, oppressed by the immense weight of the coffin; the Bishop read sadly and blundered in the prayers: the fine chapter *Man that is born of a woman* was chanted not read and the anthem, besides being immeasurably tedious, would have served as well for a nuptial.

The real serious part was the figure of the Duke of Cumberland, heightened by a thousand melancholy circumstances. He had a dark brown adonis (wig) and a cloak of black cloth with a train of five yards. Attending the funeral of a father, how little reason so ever he had to love him, could not be pleasant. His leg extremely bad, yet forced to stand upon it near two hours; his face bloated and distorted with his late paralytic stroke, which has affected too one of his eyes, and placed over the mouth of the vault into which he must in all probability himself so soon descend —think how unpleasant a situation! He bore it all with a firm and unaffected countenance.

This grave scene was fully contrasted by the burlesque Duke of Newcastle. He fell into a fit of crying the moment he came into the Chapel and flung himself back in a stall, the Archbishop hovering over him with a smelling bottle—but in two minutes his curiosity got the better of his hypocrisy and he ran about the Chapel with his glass to spy who was or was not there, spying with one hand and mopping his eyes with t'other. Then returned the fear of catching cold and the Duke of Cumberland, who was sinking with heat, felt himself weighed down and turning round found it was the Duke of Newcastle standing upon his train to avoid the chill of the marble.

It was very theatric to look down into the vault where the coffin lay, attended by mourners with lights. Clavering, the Groom of the Bedchamber, refused to sit up with the body and was dismissed by the King's order.

HORACE WALPOLE (1760).

*

A FATAL DUEL IN HYDE PARK

Before this comes to your hands, you will have heard of the most terrible accident that has almost ever happened. This morning at eight, my man brought me word that duke Hamilton had fought with lord Mohun, and killed him, and was brought home wounded. I immediately sent him to the duke's house in St. James' Square; but the porter could hardly answer for tears, and a great rabble was about the house. In short, they fought at seven this morning: the dog Mohun was killed on the spot; and while the duke was over him, Mohun shortening his sword stabbed him in at the shoulder to the heart.

The Duke was helped towards the cake-house by the ring in Hyde Park (where they fought), and died on the grass, before he could reach the house; and was brought home in his coach by eight, while the poor duchess was asleep. Macartney and one Hamilton were the seconds, who fought likewise, and are both fled. I am told that a footman of lord Mohun's stabbed duke Hamilton, and some say Macartney did so too. Mohun gave the affront, and yet sent the challenge.

I am infinitely concerned for the poor duke, who was a frank, honest, good-natured man. I loved him very well, and I think he loved me better. He had the greatest mind in the world to have me go with him to France, but durst not tell it me; and those he did tell said I could not be spared, which was true.

They have removed the poor duchess to a lodging in the neighbourhood, where I have been with her for two hours, and am just come away. I never saw so melancholy a scene; for indeed all reasons for real grief belong to her; nor is it possible for anybody to be a greater loser in all regards. She has moved my very soul. The lodging was inconvenient, and they would have moved her to another; but I would not suffer it, because it had no room backward, and she must have been tortured with the noise of the Grub street screamers mentioning her husband's murder in her ears.

DEAN SWIFT (1712).

*

LONDON BREAD IN 1750

The bread I eat in London is a deleterious paste, mixed up with chalk, alum and bone ashes; insipid to the taste and destructive to the constitution. The good people are not ignorant of this adulteration: but they prefer it to wholesome bread, because it is whiter than the meal of corn: thus they sacrifice their taste and their health and the lives of their tender infants to a most absurd gratification of a misjudging eye: and the miller or the baker is obliged to poison them and their families in order to live by his profession. The same monstrous depravity appears in their veal, which is bleached by repeated bleedings, till there is not a drop of juice left in the body and the poor animal is paralytic before it dies: so void of all taste, nourishment and savour that a man might dine as comfortably on a white fricasee of kid-skin gloves or chip hats from Leghorn.

T. SMOLLETT (1721–1771).
From "Humphry Clinker".

*

346

"IN A GARRET IN EXETER STREET"

The secret that Dr. Johnson was the author of the Parliamentary debates for the year 1745 in *The Gentleman's Magazine* was avowed by himself on the following occasion. Mr. Wedderburne, now Lord Loughborough, Dr. Johnson, Dr. Francis, the translator of Horace, the present writer and others dined with the late Mr. Foote. An important debate, towards the end of Sir Robt. Walpole's administration being mentioned, Dr. Francis observed that Mr. Pitt's speech on that occasion was the best he had ever read. He added that he had employed eight years of his life in the study of Demosthenes and finished a translation of that celebrated author with all the decorations of style and language within the reach of his capacity, but he had met with nothing equal to the speech above mentioned.

Many of the company remembered the debate and some passages were cited with the approbation and applause of all present. During the ardour of conversation Dr. Johnson remained silent. As soon as the warmth of praise subsided he opened with these words: "That speech I wrote in a garret in Exeter Street." The company was struck with astonishment.

After staring at each other in silent amaze Dr. Francis asked how that speech could be written by him. "Sir," said Johnson, "I wrote it in Exeter Street. I never had been in the gallery of the House of Commons but once. Cave* had interest with the door-keepers. He and the persons employed under him gained admittance: they brought away the subject of discussion, the names of the speakers, the side they took and the order in which they rose, together with notes of the arguments advanced in the course of the debate. The whole was afterwards communicated to me and I composed the speeches in the tone which they now have in the parliamentary debates."

To this discovery Dr. Francis made answer, "Then, Sir, you have exceeded Demosthenes himself: for to say that you have exceeded Francis' Demosthenes would be saying nothing." The rest of the company bestowed lavish encomium on Johnson: one in particular praised his impartiality, observing that he had dealt out reason and eloquence with an equal hand to both parties. "That is not quite true," said Johnson, "I saved appearance tolerably well, but I took care that the Whig dogs should not have the best of it."

ARTHUR MURPHY (1727–1805).

*

GENTLEMEN AT PLAY!

We now sallied forth like a pack in full cry, with all the loud expressions of mirth and riot and proceeded to old 77 (St. James' Street) which being shut-up we swore like troopers and broke

* Cave was the proprietor of the *Gentleman's Magazine*.

348

the parlour windows in a rage. We next cut the traces of a hackney coach and led the horses into a mews, where we tied them up, coachee being asleep inside the whole time. We then proceeded to old Ham-a-dry-ed, the bacon's man, called out Fire and got the old man down to the door in his shirt, when Lavender ran away with his nightcap and threw it into the water in St. James' Square, whilst the Baronet put it in right and left at his sconce and told him to hide his d——d ugly masard. This induced him to come out and call the Watch.

After giving a view halloa we ran off, with the Charleys in full cry after us, when Sir G. W., who had purposely provided himself with a long cord, gave me one end and ran to the opposite side of Jermyn Street with the other in his hand, holding it about two feet from the pavement. The old Scouts came up in droves and we had 'em down in a moment, for every mother's son of the guardians were caught in the trap and rolled over each other, slap into the Kennel. Never was such a prime bit of gig! One old buck got his jaw-bone broken: another staved in two of his crazy timbers, that is to say, broke a couple of ribs: a third bled from the nose like a pig: a fourth squinted admirably from a pair of painted peepers.

Their numbers however increasing, we divided our forces and marched in opposite directions; one party sallied along Bond Street, hailed up a snoosy Charley in his box and bolted with his lantern; the others were not fortunate, for A's deputy cushion-thumper and the Baronet's brother got safely lodged in St. James' Watch House.

PIERCE EGAN (1772–1849).

*

LEIGH HUNT IN THE MARSHALSEA

I papered the walls of my room with a trellis of roses; I had the ceiling coloured with clouds and sky; the barred windows I screened with Venetian blinds; and when my bookcases were set up with their busts, and flowers and a pianoforte made their appearance, perhaps there was not a handsomer room on that side of the water. I took a pleasure, when a stranger knocked at the door, to see him come in and stare about him. The surprise on issuing from the Borough, and passing through the avenues of a gaol, was dramatic. Charles Lamb declared there was no other such room, except in a fairy tale.

But I possessed another surprise; which was a garden. There was a little yard outside the room, railed off from another belonging to the neighbouring ward. This yard I shut in with green palings, adorned it with a trellis, bordered it with a thick bed of earth, from a nursery, and even contrived to have a grass plot. The earth I filled with flowers and young trees. There was an apple-tree, from which we managed to get a pudding the second year. As to my flowers, they

350

were allowed to be perfect. Thomas Moore, who came to see me with Lord Byron, told me he had seen no such heart's-ease.

LEIGH HUNT (1784–1859).

*

DANDIES IN HYDE PARK

Patting the crest of his well-managed steed
Proud of his action, D'Orsay vaunts the breed:
A coat of chocolate, a vest of snow,
Well brushed his whiskers, as his boots below:
A short-napped beaver, prodigal in brim,
With trousers tightened to a well turned limb;
O'er play, o'er dress extends his wide domain,
And Crockford trembles when he calls a main:
No joys for him can vulgar pleasures yield,
Good taste his forte, he sticks to Chesterfield:
Surrounding dandies vainly ape his dress
By him George Wombwell sinks to nothingness:
His fate is destined round Hyde Park to prance,
For ne'er again he'll view the shores of France,
He left his name behind in tradesmen's books,
The boast of tailors and the pride of cooks.
W——'s* pale Countess, of her lineage proud,
Urges her phaeton thro' the admiring crowd;
Diana's self could scarcely match the team
That fairy body and those steeds of cream!
Whilst on his switch-tailed bay, with wandering eye
Attenuated W——n* canters by:
His character how difficult to know,

* The Earl and Countess of Wilton.

351

A compound of psalm tunes and Tally-ho!
A forward rider half inclined to preach
Tho' not disposed to *practise* as to *teach,*
An amorous lover, with the *saintly twist,*
And now a *sportsman,* now an *organist.*

PAT-ROCLUS.

From "The Chaunt of Achilles".

From the "New Sporting Magazine".

Sept. 1838.

[Pat-roclus was the pseudonym of Bernal Osborne. 1808–1882.]

*

SALOOP

Now albeit Mr. Read boasteth, not without reason, that his is the only Salopian House: yet, be it known to thee, reader—if thou art one that keepest what was called good hours, thou art haply ignorant of the fact—he hath a race of industrious imitators who from stalls and under open sky dispense the same savoury mess to humbler customers, at that dead time of the dawn when (as extremes must) the rake, reeling home from his midnight cups, and the hard handed artisan, leaving his bed to resume the premature labours of the day, jostle, not infrequently, to the manifest disconcerting of the former for the honours of the pavement. . . . The rake who wisheth to dissipate his o'ernight vapours in more grateful coffee, curses the ungenial fume, as he

352

passeth, but the artisan stops to taste and blesses the fragrant breakfast.

This is saloop, the precious herb-woman's darling—the delight of the early gardener, who transports his smoking cabbages by break of day from Hammersmith to Covent Garden's famed piazzas—the delight and oh! I fear too often the envy of the unpennied sweep.

CHARLES LAMB (1775–1834).

[The Saloop stalls were the predecessors of the coffee stalls. Saloop was an infusion of sassafras chips boiled down to a kind of tea and mixed with milk and sugar. Originally, salep or salop was a medicinal drink made from the root of the "Orchis mascula" and imported from the Indies.]

*

THE HEART OF CITY LIFE

I got into the heart of City life. I saw and felt London at last. I got into the Strand: I went up Cornhill: I mixed with the life passing along. I dared the perils of the crossings. To do this, to do it utterly alone, gave me perhaps an irrational but real pleasure. . . . I have seen the West End, the parks, the fine squares: but I love the City far better. The City seems so much more in earnest: its business, its rush, its roar are such serious things, sights and sounds. The City is getting its living—the West End but enjoying its pleasure. At the West End you may be amused, but in the City you are deeply excited.

CHARLOTTE BRONTË (1816–1855).

*

A DINNER AT BLACKWALL

A dinner I ordered this very day at Lovegrove's at Blackwall—where, if you have never dined, so much the worse for you—will illustrate my doctrines on dinner-giving better than a long abstract discourse. The party will consist of seven men beside myself. Eight I hold to be the golden number. The dinner is to consist of turtle, followed by no other fish but whitebait: which is to be followed by no other meat but grouse, which are to be succeeded by apple fritters and jelly, pastry on such occasions being quite out of place. With the turtle, of course, there will be punch: with the whitebait, champagne: with the grouse, claret: the two former I have ordered to be particularly well-iced, and they will all be placed in succession upon the table, so that we can help ourselves as we please. I shall permit no other wines, unless perchance a bottle or two of port, if particularly wanted, as I hold variety of wine a great mistake.

With respect to the adjuncts I shall take care there is cayenne, with lemons cut in halves not quarters, within reach of every one for the turtle: and that brown bread and butter in abundance is set upon the table for the whitebait. The dinner will be followed by ices and a good dessert, after which coffee and one liqueur each and no more, so that the present may be enjoyed rationally, without inducing retrospective regrets. If the master of a feast wishes his party to succeed, he must know how to command and not let his guests run riot according each to his own wild fancy.

Such is my idea of a dinner, which I hope you will approve; *and I cannot help thinking that if Parliament were to grant me £10,000 a year in trust to entertain a series of worthy guests, it would promote trade and increase the revenue more than any hugger-mugger measure ever devised.*

Later:

The turtle and whitebait were excellent: the grouse not quite of equal merit: and the apple fritters so much relished that they were entirely cleared and the jelly left untouched. The only wines were champagne and claret and they both gave great satisfaction. As soon as the liqueurs were handed round once, I ordered them out of the room and the only heresy committed was by one of the guests asking for a glass of bottled porter, which I had not the presence of mind instantly to forbid. There was an opinion broached that some flounders, water-zoutched, between the turtle and the whitebait, would have been an improvement—and perhaps they would.

THOMAS WALKER.

From "The Original", 1835.

A LONDON FOG

Implacable November weather. As much mud in the streets, as if the water had but newly retired from the face of the earth and it would not be wonderful to meet a Megalosaurus, forty feet long or so, waddling like an elephantine lizard up Holborn Hill. Smoke lowering down from chimney pots, making a soft black drizzle, with flakes of soot in it as big as full grown snow-flakes —gone into mourning, one might imagine, for the death of the sun. Dogs undistinguishable in mire. Horses, scarcely better, splashed to the very blinkers. Foot passengers, jostling one another's umbrellas, in a general infection of ill temper and losing their foothold at street corners, where tens of thousands of other foot passengers have been slipping and sliding since the day broke (if this day ever broke) adding new deposits to the crust upon crust of mud, sticking at those points tenaciously to the pavement and accumulating at compound interest. Fog everywhere. Fog up the river, fog down the river, where it rolls defiled among the tiers of shipping and the waterside pollutions of a great (and dirty) city. Fog on the Essex marshes. Fog on the Kentish heights. Fog creeping into the cabooses of collier-brigs; fog lying out on the yards, and hovering in the rigging of great ships; fog drooping on the gunwales of barges and small boats. Chance people on the bridges, peering over the parapets into a nether sea of fog, with fog all round them, as if they were in a balloon, and hanging in the misty clouds.

Gas, looming through the fog in divers places in the streets, much as the sun may, from the spongy fields, be seen to loom by husbandmen and ploughmen. Most of the shops lighted too, hours before their times—as the gas seems to know, for it has a haggard and unwilling look.

CH. DICKENS (1812–1870).
From "Bleak House".

*

A DRAMATIC CRITIC OF THE OLD SCHOOL

There never was such a companion as Blanchard. He made the dreary task of playgoing a pleasure for many a long year. Who would mind going up to Sadlers Wells to see a new play when E. L. B. was there to act as guide and counsellor and take us off to some hostelry, where he ever had a story to tell about the merit of a particular tap of ale, or the advantage on a cold winter night of "white rum at the Angel" or the stomachic properties of "shrub"? Wherever he led we were bound to follow. Whether it was to Highbury Barn, or to the Surrey, or to the Grecian, or any of the outlying theatres, there was always some old inn at hand, with a history attached to it, or some refreshment better than any in the world.

Who that ever accompanied "the old man garrulous" can forget those simple dinners at the

Old Edinburgh Castle, near St. Mary's in the Strand, where John the waiter attended to our wants: or Carr's, near St. Clement Danes, where once on a time you could get a pint of extra-ordinary Beaune for a shilling: or the Old Scotch Stores, in Oxford Street, where under the consoling eye of "Curtis", the head-waiter, we have cracked many a bottle of old port in a cosy mahogany box by a warm winter fire?

It seems to me that the days of cheery conviviality departed with the abolition of the old coffee-house and the advent of the flashy restaurant bar. No one loved the old coffee-house life better than E. L. B. He remembered the days when the inn parlour was the debating club of the district and has often told me that as a lad he wrote all his best work—plays, stories, poems, guide-books, miscellaneous essays—in the quiet box of an inn parlour after a frugal meal and over a consoling "churchwarden".

CLEMENT SCOTT (1841–1904).

[Blanchard was Clement Scott's predecessor as dramatic critic of *The Daily Telegraph*.]

*

A FIRST NIGHT AT THE LYCEUM

It was a splendid first night and everyone was on the tip-toe of excitement. Royalty was there and eager eyes looked towards the well-known box, with a ledge of flowers and a brilliant mass of depending ribbons. . . .

All forms and features of art were there. Painters assembled to congratulate Sir Edward Burne-Jones on his welcome wandering from the studio to the stage. Musicians came once more to cheer Sir Arthur Sullivan. Doctors were present, the best friends, the truest kindest counsellors of the representatives of every phase of art. Judges and lawyers came. Literature in all its branches: journalism in all its various states sent the "fine flower" of its nobility to the well-organised court of art—the Lyceum Theatre.

As to old play-goers, steady, loyal, consistent old play-goers, who shall count them? Some there were who knew the Lyceum and its history long before Henry Irving and Ellen Terry were names to venerate. One, at least, had sat in this very theatre, which has remained the same except in decoration and modern detail, during every change of stress and circumstance and on every important first night, whether it was under Charles Dillon, or Charles Fechter, or E. T. Smith, ever since the year 1848, when Madame Vestris was playing in Planché's extravaganzas and Charles Mathews was acting "Used Up". Prominent in the stalls was a retired actress, who had been in this very theatre Fechter's incomparable heroine in "The Duke's Motto" and "Bel Demonio" and who is to devote her daughter to the stage next Thursday.

But enough of recollections started by that memorable Lyceum audience. They would fill a bulky volume.

CLEMENT SCOTT in *The Daily Telegraph* on the first night of "King Arthur", Jan. 12, 1895.

*

THE WHIRLPOOL AT OLD LONDON BRIDGE

Stretching below me, the troubled breast of the mighty river, and immediately below, the main whirlpool of the Thames—the maelstrom of the bulwarks of the middle arch—a grisly pool which, with its super-abundance of horror, fascinated me. Who knows but that I should have leapt into its depths?—I have heard of such things—but for a rather startling occurrence which broke the spell.

As I stood upon the bridge, gazing into the jaws of the pool, a small boat shot suddenly through the arch beneath my feet. There were three persons in it: an oarsman in the middle, whilst a man and woman sat in the stern. I shall never forget the thrill of horror which went through me at this sudden apparition. What! a boat, a small boat, passing beneath that arch into yonder roaring gulf! Yes, yes, down through that awful water-way, with more than the swiftness of an arrow, shot the boat or skiff, right into the jaws of the pool. A monstrous breaker curls over the prow—there is no hope. The boat is swamped and all drowned in that strangling vortex. No! the boat, which appeared to have the buoyancy of a feather, skipped over the threatening horror, and the next moment was out of danger, the boatman—a true boatman of Cockaigne that—elevating one of his sculls in sign of triumph, the man hallooing, and the woman, a true English-woman that—of a certain class—waving her shawl.

GEORGE BORROW (1805–1881).

From "Lavengro".

*

THE DELIGHTS OF THE TEMPLE

Not far removed from Mt. Olympus, but some-what nearer to the blessed regions of the West is the most favoured abode of Themis. We sped by the rich tide which now passes from the towers of Cæsar to Barry's halls of eloquence: and again back, with new offerings of a city's tribute from the palaces of peers to the mart of merchants. Here stand those quiet walls which Law has delighted to honour by its presence. What a world within a world is this Temple! How quiet are its "entangled walks", as someone lately has called them, and yet how close to the densest concourse of humanity! How gravely respectable its sober alleys, though removed but by a single step from the profanity of the Strand and the low iniquity of Fleet Street. Old St. Dunstan's with its bell-smiting bludgeoners has been removed:* the ancient shops with their faces full of pleasant history are passing away one by one: the Bar itself is to go—its doom has been pronounced; rumour tells me of some huge building that is to appear in these latitudes dedicated to law, subversive of the Courts of Westminster and antagonistic to the Rolls and Lincoln's Inn. But nothing yet threatens the silent beauty of the Temple. It is the mediæval court of the metropolis.

Here on the choicest spot of this choice ground stands a lofty row of chambers, looking obliquely upon the sullied Thames. Before the windows the lawn of the Temple Gardens stretches with that dim yet delicious verdure so refreshing to the eyes of Londoners. If doomed to live within the thickest of London smoke, you would surely say that that would be your chosen spot.

Yes, you, you whom I now address, my dear, middle-aged bachelor friend, can nowhere be so well domiciled as here. No one here will ask whether you are out or at home: alone or with friends. Here no Sabbatarian will investigate your Sundays; no censorious landlady will scrutinise your empty bottle, no valetudinarian neighbour will complain of late hours. If you love books, to what place are books so suitable? The whole spot is redolent of typography. Would you worship the Paphian goddess, the groves of

* This clock has recently been restored.

Cyprus are not more taciturn than those of the Temple. Wit and wine are always here and always together. The revels of the Temple are as those of polished Greece, where the wildest worshipper of Bacchus never forgot the dignity of the God whom he adored. Where can retirement be so complete as here? Where can you be so sure of all the pleasures of society?

ANTHONY TROLLOPE (1815–1882).
From "The Warden".

*

THE DOME OF ST. PAUL'S

I wonder if I am at last beginning to understand and appreciate St. Paul's. We get a wonderful view of the Dome from our upper windows (in Cloth Fair) but what I like best is to come upon it gradually, to stalk St. Paul's by a stealthy approach. Down Little Britain, whence you catch your first sight of the Dome in its splendour and then Canons Row, where the north front is marvellously framed by the tall houses, and then the steps leading to the north porch and the trees. . . .

Learn to watch for the Dome as it appears in different weathers and in different lights! It knows how to frown: it can look all pearly: it can look hard and steely: it can blush like a rose.

H. L. PAGET, Bishop of Chester.
From Mrs. E. K. Paget's "H. L. Paget, Portrait and Frame".

IN THE CHARTERHOUSE GARDEN

It chanced last summer I was advised to spend part of my time sitting in the sunshine. There was plenty of sunshine: the question was where to sit. But I got leave to sit in the garden of the Charterhouse and I never want to sit anywhere else. Just think of it! The place hallowed by the memory of Carthusian martyrs, dishonoured and then recovered by Sutton's wise and considerate foundation: the famous home of a great Public School and still the quiet haven of rest for the brethren.

You will remember how Herkomer came to their chapel when he wanted to paint a beautiful picture of venerable old age: the place where Colonel Newcome made his last answer to the calling of his name. Is it not enough for most of us? There it is, in the very heart of London: the grey walls, the green sward, the rows of ancient mulberry trees, the tinkle of the little fountain: you can sit in the sunshine or watch the brethren playing their croquet or their bowls. And if, perhaps, comfortable seats invite slumber, you ought to sit there and dream dreams worth the dreaming.

H. L. PAGET, Bishop of Chester.
From Mrs. E. K. Paget's "H. L. Paget,
Portrait and Frame".

*

IN BERKELEY SQUARE

Round and round Berkeley Square one night in 1848 walked Lord Malmesbury, afterwards Foreign Secretary, and the exiled Louis Napoleon, later Emperor of the French. They were deep in talk—the subject being whether if Napoleon proposed to Lady Jersey's daughter, Lady Clementina Villiers, she was likely to accept him.

Round the same square one night in 1905 tramped Mr. Haldane and Sir Edward Grey, discussing how best they should break the news to their leader, Lord Rosebery, whose house was in the square, that they had determined to make their peace with Sir Henry Campbell-Bannerman and join the rival "Tabernacle".

*

BURIAL IN THE ABBEY

Burial in Westminster Abbey lies theoretically within the discretion of the Dean. But that discretion is not absolute. It was Archbishop Davidson's opinion that the Dean should always accept a formal request from the Government of the day, thus leaving responsibility with them, it being understood, of course, that the Government would first consult the Dean. On one occasion at least the House of Commons expressly opposed the desire of Queen Victoria and Dean Stanley that a statue should be erected to the Prince Imperial who had lost his life while with the

British forces in Zululand. They held that it would be inconsistent with the national character of the Abbey.

Sometimes a Dean has withstood strong expressions of public opinion. Dean Robinson, for example, declined to offer a grave in the Abbey to George Meredith on the ground that he was not in the highest rank as a man of letters and in a few years time would cease to be "a conspicuous literary figure." It also fell to him to deal with the question whether Herbert Spencer should be commemorated in the Abbey:

"A group of admirers asked the Dean to allow a bust of Herbert Spencer to be erected in the Abbey. Dean Robinson took counsel: but of those whom he consulted the philosophers said that Spencer was no philosopher, though he might be a scientist, while the scientists said that he was no scientist, though he might be a philosopher. The Dean accordingly refused: and was glad to receive a word of commendation from Lord Kelvin, who said to him one day at a party at Buckingham Palace, 'I am glad you did not put that fellow Spencer in the Abbey.'"

When in 1927 Dean Norris offered burial in the Abbey in the case of Lord Oxford and Asquith, it was found that acceptance was precluded by Lord Oxford's own instructions that he should be buried as privately as possible. Archbishop Davidson was not pleased. His view was that "great men belong to the nation and in such matters the individual ought not to override the nation's wishes. If a great man objected to cremation (that being the condition of burial in the Abbey) such a wish might be respected, but he could not agree that the mere wish for a private burial was in such cases a proper wish."

Material taken from Dr. Bell's (Bishop of Chichester) "Life of Archbishop Davidson".

*

XII

Man Proposes

*

"Barkis is willing."
From "David Copperfield".

NAPOLEON TO THE COUNTESS WALEWSKA

Jan. 1807 (?).

I have seen only you; I have admired only you;
I desire only you. A very prompt reply to calm
the impatient ardour of

N.

Have I displeased you? I hoped the opposite.
Or has your first feeling vanished? My passion
grows. You rob me of my rest. Vouchsafe a
little joy, a little happiness, to the poor heart that
would fain worship you! Is it so hard to give me
an answer? You now owe me two.

(Unsigned.)

There are moments in life when high position
is a heavy burden. That is borne in on me at
this moment. . . . If only you would! None

but you can overcome the obstacles which separate us. My friend Duroc will do what he can to make it easy for you. Oh, come, come! All your wishes shall be fulfilled! Your country will even be dearer to me, if you have compassion on my heart.

N.

*

"I CANNOT BREATHE WITHOUT YOU"
MY DEAREST GIRL,

This moment I have set myself to copy some verses out fair. I cannot proceed with any degree of content. I must write you a line or two and see if that will assist in dismissing you from my Mind for ever so short a time. Upon my Soul I can think of nothing else. The time is passed when I had power to advise and warn you against the unpromising morning of my Life. My love has made me selfish. I cannot exist without you. I am forgetful of everything but seeing you again— my Life seems to stop there—I see no further. You have absorb'd me. I have a sensation at the present moment as though I was dissolving—I should be exquisitely miserable without the hope of soon seeing you. I should be afraid to separate myself far from you. My sweet Fanny, will your heart never change? My love, will it? I have no limit now to my love. . . .

Your note came in just here. I cannot be happier away from you. 'Tis richer than an

Argosy of Pearls. Do not threat me even in jest. I have been astonished that Men could die Martyrs for religion—I have shudder'd at it. I shudder no more—I could be martyr'd for my Religion—Love is my religion—I could die for that. I could die for you. My Creed is Love and you are its only tenet. You have ravish'd me away by a Power I cannot resist; and yet I could resist till I saw you; and even since I have seen you I have endeavoured often to reason against the reasons of my Love. I can do that no more— the pain would be too great. My love is selfish. I cannot breathe without you.

Yours for ever,

JOHN KEATS (1795–1821).

Letter to Fanny Brawne.

*

"YOU ARE ALWAYS NEW"

SWEETEST FANNY,

You fear, sometimes, I do not love you so much as you wish? My dear Girl, I love you ever and ever and without reserve. The more I have known the more I have loved. In every way— even my jealousies have been agonies of Love; in the hottest fit I ever had I would have died for you. I have vexed you too much. But for Love! Can I help it? You are always new. The last of your kisses was ever the sweetest: the last smile the brightest: the last movement the gracefullest.

371

When you passed my window yesterday I was filled with as much admiration as if I had then seen you for the first time.

You uttered a half complaint once that I only loved your beauty. Have I nothing else then to love in you but that? Do not I see a heart naturally furnished with wings imprison itself with me? No ill prospect has been able to turn your thoughts a moment from me. This perhaps should be as much a subject of sorrow as of joy— but I will not talk of that. Even if you did not love me I could not help an entire devotion to you: how much more deeply then must I feel for you, knowing you love me.

My mind has been the most discontented and restless one that ever was put into a body too small for it. I never felt my mind repose upon anything with complete and undistracted enjoyment —upon no person but you! When you are in the room my thoughts never fly out of the window: you always concentrate my whole senses. The anxiety shown about our loves in your last note is an immense pleasure to me: however, you must not allow such speculations to molest you any more: nor will I any more believe you can have the least pique against me.

Brown is gone out, but here is Mrs. Wylie— when she is gone, I shall be awake for you.

Remembrances to your mother.

Your affectionate

J. KEATS (1795–1821).

A TIRED SCIENTIST CANNOT CON-CENTRATE ON A LOVE LETTER

Royal Institution: Thursday
evening. (December, 1820.)

MY DEAR SARAH,

It is astonishing how much the state of the body influences the powers of the mind. I have been thinking all the morning of the very delightful and interesting letter I would send you this evening, and now I am so tired, and yet have so much to do, that my thoughts are quite giddy, and run round your image without any power of themselves to stop and admire it. I want to say a thousand kind and, believe me, heartfelt things to you, but am not master of words fit for the purpose; and still, as I ponder and think on you, chlorides, trials, oil, Davy, steel, miscellanea, mercury, and fifty other professional fancies swim before me and drive me further and further into the quandary of stupidness.

From your affectionate
MICHAEL (FARADAY) (1791–1867).

*

POE'S FIRST LETTER TO HELEN

I have pressed your letter again and again to my lips, sweetest Helen—bathing it in tears of joy or of a divine despair. But I, who so lately vaunted in your presence the power of words— of what avail are mere words to me now? Could

I believe the efficacy of prayers to the God of
Heaven, I would indeed kneel, humbly kneel, at
this the most earnest epoch of my life—kneel in
entreaty for words—but for words that should
disclose to you—that might enable me to lay bare
to you my whole heart. All thoughts, all passions
seem now merged in that one consuming desire to
make you see that for which there is no human
voice, the unalterable fervour of my love for you:
for so well do I know your poet nature that I feel
sure that if you could but look down into the
depths of my soul with your pure spiritual eyes,
you could not refuse to speak to me what alas!
you still resolutely leave unspoken—You would
love me if only for the greatness of my love. Is
it not something in this cold dreary world to be
loved? . . .

Could I have but held you close to my heart
and whispered to you the strange secrets of its
passionate history, then indeed you would have
seen that it was not and never could have been in
the power of any other than yourself to move me
as I am now moved—to oppress me with this
ineffable emotion, to surround and bathe me in
this electric light, illumining and enkindling my
whole nature, filling my soul with glory, with
wonder and with awe. During our walk in the
cemetery I said to you, while the bitter, bitter
tears sprang into my eyes, "Helen, I love now—
now—for the first and only time. . . ."

I saw that you were *Helen—my* Helen—the

374

Helen of a thousand dreams. . . . She whom the great Giver of all good had preordained to be mine—mine only—if not now, alas! then hereafter and for ever in the Heavens. . . .

Do you not—I ask it of your reason, *darling*, not less than of your heart—do you not perceive that it is my diviner nature, my spiritual being which burns and pants to commingle with your own? Has the soul age, Helen? Can Immortality regard Time? Can that which began never and shall never end consider a few wretched years of its incarnate life? Ah! I could *almost* be angry with you for the unwarranted wrong you offer to the sacred reality of my affection? . . .

Write soon—soon—oh soon!—but not much. Do not weary or agitate yourself for *my* sake. Say to me those coveted words that would turn Earth into Heaven.

E. A. POE (1809–1849).

And all my days are trances
And all my nightly dreams
Are where thy grey eye glances
And where thy footstep gleams—
In what ethereal dances
By what Eternal streams!

E. A. POE (1835).

*

CARLYLE ENTREATS JANE WELSH TO MAKE UP HER MIND

On the whole I begin to entertain a certain degree of contempt for the destiny which has so long persecuted me. I will be a man in spite of it. Yet it lies with you whether I shall be a *right* man or only a hard and bitter stoic. What say you? Decide for yourself and me. Consent if you dare trust me and let us live and die together. Yet fear not to deny me if your judgment so determines. It will be a sharp pang that tears away from me for ever the hope which now for years has been the solace of my existence: but better to endure it and all its consequences than to witness and to cause the forfeit of your happiness.

At times I confess when I hear you speak of your gay cousins and contrast with their brilliant equipments my own simple exterior and scanty prospects and humble but to me most dear and honorably-minded kinsmen, whom I were the veriest dog if I ceased to love and venerate and cherish for their true affection and for the rugged sterling worth of their character—when I think of all this I could almost counsel you to cast me utterly away and to connect yourself with one whose friends and station are more analogous to your own.

But anon in some moment of self love, I say proudly there is a spirit in *me* which is worthy of this maiden and which shall be worthy of her. I will teach her, I will guide her, I will make her happy. Together we will share the joys and sorrows of existence.

Speak then. . . . Think well of me, of yourself, of our circumstances and determine. Dare you trust your fate with mine, as I trust mine with you? Judge if I wait your answer with impatience. I know you will not keep me waiting. . . . May God bless you and direct you! Decide how you will.

THOMAS CARLYLE (1825).

Jane Welsh replied four days later.

I love you and I should be the most ungrateful and injudicious of mortals if I did not. But I am not *in love* with you: that is to say, my love for you is not a passion which overclouds my judgment and absorbs all my regard for myself and others. It is a simple, honest, serene affection, made up of admiration and sympathy and better perhaps to found affection on than any other. In short it is a love which *influences*, does not *make*, the destiny of a life. . . .

And now let me ask you, have you any *certain* livelihood to maintain me in the manner I have been used to live in? any fixed place in the rank of society I have been born and bred in? No. You have projects for attaining both, capabilities for attaining both, and much more, but as yet you have not attained them. Use the noble gifts which God has given you! You have prudence—though, by the way, this last proceeding is no great proof of it. Devise then how you may gain yourself a moderate but *settled* income. Think of some more promising plan than farming the most barren spot in the county of Dumfriesshire! What a thing that would be to be sure! You and I keeping house at Craigenputtock! I would as soon think of building myself a nest on the Bass Rock. . . . For my part I could not spend a month at it with an angel.

Think of something else then. Apply your industry to carry it into effect: your talents to gild over the inequality of our births—and then we will talk of marrying. If all this was realised, I *think* I should have good sense enough to abate something of my romantic ideal and to content myself with stopping short of this side idolatry. At all events I will marry no one else. This is all the promise I can or will make. . . .

Write instantly and tell me you are content to leave the event to time and destiny, and in the meanwhile to continue my friend and guardian, which you have so long faithfully been, and *nothing more.*

JANE WELSH.

Many years later:

I married for ambition. Carlyle has exceeded all that my wildest hopes ever imagined of him—and I am miserable.

JANE CARLYLE.

LOVE FINDS A WAY

Her consent she finally gave me, seated on the second bench on the right hand side in the Long Walk in Kensington Gardens, leading from Lancaster Gate to the Albert Memorial. My proposal was made under great difficulties, as she was placed between her father and mother and I was next to her father and had to carry on a conversation with him and at the same time communicate with his daughter behind his back.

(Fragment taken from a volume of Victorian Reminiscences).

*

"GLORIFIED AND BEAUTIFIED, YET STILL IDEAL"

You and I, I take it, don't want to scream with the rabble, to feel the pleasure of a gush for the moment, and then sink back to the commonplace level: we want to devote our whole lives to one another, and not to one another irrationally, but to one another glorified and beautified, yet still real: to weave the gossamer of sentiment into the web of common stuff, and make the coarsest threads glitter with its brilliance.

Is it an easy task? Is it one which the coarse mechanical appliance of getting married to-morrow, and settling it somehow, will help us to do best? I should strongly doubt it: our characters are, both of them, many-sided and not simple: the position of marriage involves necessarily a loss of independence of judgment: you cannot estimate a thing so well when it is fixed permanently at a given distance from you: to see it at various distances, in various lights, to weigh the treasure well which you know you are going to sell all you have to buy, but have not bought yet, will not this help you to value to the full its preciousness, will not the longings you have gone through make you esteem the possession more? I don't want us to depend too much on one another. I want you to be you and me to be me, and yet both of us absolutely one: and to do so we must each of us fuse together the ideal and the real, not rush too soon to grasp the real and so sink with the ideal.

> MANDELL CREIGHTON, afterwards Bishop
> of London (1871).
>
> From a letter to his fiancée, Louise
> von Glehn.

*

SARAH BERNHARDT TO VICTORIEN SARDOU

(Undated.)

WONDERFUL BOY,

Where are you to-night? Your letter came only an hour ago—cruel hour—I had hoped you would spend it with me here.

Paris is a morgue without you: before I knew you, it was Paris, and I thought it heaven; but now it is a vast desert of desolation and loneliness. It is like the face of a clock, bereft of its hands.

All the pictures that hung in my memory before I knew you have faded and given place to our radiant moments together.

Now I cannot live apart from you; your words, even though bitter, dispel all the cares of the world and make me happy; my art has been suckled by them and softly rocked in their tender cradle; they are as necessary to me now as sunlight and air.

I am as hungry for them as for food, I am thirsty for them, and my thirst is overwhelming. *Your words are my food, your breath my wine. You are everything to me.*

YOUR SARAH.

*

"ANY ONE OF NINE DAUGHTERS, BUT PREFERABLY JANE"

These and his other visible virtues begot him (Mr. George Herbert) much love from a gentleman of a noble fortune and a near kinsman to his friend the Earl of Danby: namely from Mr. Charles Danvers of Bainton, in the county of Wilts, Esq. This Mr. Danvers, having known him long and familiarly, did so much affect him that he often and publicly declared a desire that

Mr. Herbert would marry any of his nine daughters —for he had so many—but rather his daughter Jane than any other, because Jane was his beloved daughter. And he had often said the same to Mr. Herbert himself, and that if he could like her for a wife and she him for a husband, Jane should have a double blessing, and Mr. Danvers had so often said the like to Jane and so much commended Mr. Herbert to her, that Jane became so much a platonic as to fall in love with Mr. Herbert unseen.

This was a fair preparation for a marriage: but alas! her father died before Mr. Herbert's retirement to Dauntsey: yet some friends to both parties procured their meeting: at which time a mutual affection entered into both their hearts, as a conqueror enters into a surprised city: and love having got such possession, governed and made there such laws and resolutions, as neither party was able to resist: insomuch that she changed her name into Herbert the third day after this first interview.

This haste might in others be thought to be a love-frenzy or worse: but it was not, for they had wooed so like princes as to have select proxies. . . . The suddenness was justifiable by the strictest rules of prudence, and the more because it proved so happy to both parties: for the eternal lover of mankind made them happy in each other's mutual and equal affections and compliance: indeed so happy that there never was any opposition betwixt them, unless it was a contest which should most incline to a compliance with the other's desires.

ISAAC WALTON (1593–1683).
From "Life of Mr. George Herbert".

*

SIR CHARLES GRANDISON BEGS "AN EARLY DAY"

After breakfast, first one, then another, dropped away and left only Sir Charles and me together. Lucy was the last that went and the moment she had withdrawn, while I was thinking to retire to dress, he placed himself by me. "Think me not abrupt, my dearest Miss Byron," said he, "if I take almost the only opportunity that has offered of entering upon a subject that is next my heart."

I found my face glow. I was silent.

"You have given me hope, madam; all your friends encourage that hope. I love, I revere your friends. What I have now to petition for is a confirmation of the hope I have presumed upon. Can you, madam, can you say that the man before you is the man whom you can, whom you do prefer to any other?"

He stopped, expecting my answer.

Although my cheeks were crimson I answered with a calmness that astonished myself: "Sir, I Can—I Do."

He kissed my hand with fervour; dropped down on one knee; again kissed it.

383

"You have laid me, madam, under everlasting obligation; and will you permit me before I rise to beg an early day. . . . Make me soon, madam, the happy 'husband' I hope to be. I prescribe not to you the time; but you are above empty forms. May I presume to hope it will be before the end of a month to come? . . ."

He clasped me in his arms with an ardour that displeased me not, though at the time it startled me. He then thanked me again on one knee. I held out the hand he had not in his, with intent to raise him, for I could not speak. He received it as a token of favour; kissed it with ardour, arose; again pressed my cheek with his lips.

Sir Charles, on my making towards the door that led to the stairs, withdrew with such a grace as shewed he was capable of recollection.

S. RICHARDSON (1689–1761).

From "The History of Sir Charles Grandison".

*

WORDS FAIL RODERICK RANDOM

DEAR MADAM,

Were it possible for the powers of utterance to reveal the soft emotions of my soul: the fond anxiety, the glowing hopes, and chilling fears that rule my heart in turns, I should need no other witness than this paper, to evince the purity and ardour of that flame your charms have kindled in my heart. But alas! expression wrongs my love. I am inspired with conceptions that no language can convey! Your beauty fills me with wonder, your understanding with ravishment, and your goodness with adoration! I am transported with desire, distracted with doubts, and tortured with impatience! Suffer me, then, lovely arbitress of my fate, to approach your person, to breathe in soft murmurs my passion to your ears, to offer the sacrifice of a heart overflowing with the most genuine and disinterested love, to gaze with ecstasy upon the divine object of my wishes, to hear the music of her enchanting tongue, to rejoice in her smiles of approbation—and banish the most intolerable suspence from the bosom of

Your enraptured

R—— R——

T. SMOLLETT (1721–1771).

From "The Adventures of Roderick Random".

*

CAPTAIN WENTWORTH RENEWS HIS SUIT TO ANNE ELLIOT

I can listen no longer in silence. I must speak to you by such means as are within my reach. You pierce my soul. I am half agony, half hope. Tell me not that I am too late, that such precious feelings are gone for ever. I offer myself to you again with a heart even more your own than when you almost broke it, eight and a half years ago.

Dare not say that man forgets sooner than woman, that his love has an earlier death. I have loved none but you. Unjust I may have been, weak and resentful I have been, but never inconstant You alone have brought me to Bath. For you alone I think and plan. Have you not seen this? Can you fail to have understood my wishes? I had not waited even these ten days, could I have read your feelings, as I think you must have penetrated mine. I can hardly wait. I am every instant hearing something which overpowers me. You sink your voice, but I can distinguish the tones of that voice when they would be lost on others. Too good, too excellent creature! You do me justice indeed. You do believe that there is true attachment and constancy among men. Believe it to be most fervent, most undeviating in

F. W.

"I must go uncertain of my fate: but I shall return hither, or follow your party, as soon as possible. A word, a look will be enough to decide whether I enter your father's house this evening or never."

Such a letter was not to be soon recovered from. Half an hour's solitude and reflexion might have tranquillised her: but the two minutes only which now passed before she was interrupted, with all the restraints of her situation, could do nothing towards tranquillity. Every moment rather brought fresh agitation. It was an overpowering happiness. And before she was beyond the first stage of full sensation Charles, Mary and Henrietta all came in.

JANE AUSTEN (1775–1817).

From "Persuasion".

*

SIR PITT CRAWLEY PROPOSES TO BECKY

"She's too ill to see you, sir!" Rebecca said, tripping down to Sir Pitt, who was preparing to ascend.

"So much the better," Sir Pitt answered, "I want to see *you*, Miss Becky. Come along a me into the parlour," and they entered that apartment together.

"I wawnt you back at Queen's Crawley, Miss," the baronet said, fixing his eyes upon her, and taking off his black gloves and his hat with his ·great crape hat-band. His eyes had such a strange look and fixed upon her so steadfastly that Rebecca Sharp began almost to tremble.

"I hope to come soon," she said in a low voice, "as soon as Miss Crawley is better—and return to the dear children."

"You've said so these three months, Becky," replied Sir Pitt, "and still you go hanging on to my sister, who'll fling you off like an old shoe, when she's worn you out. I tell you I *want* you. I'm going back to the Vuneral. Will you come back? Yes or No?"

"I daren't—I don't think—it would be right—
to be alone—with you, Sir," Becky said, seemingly in great agitation.

"I say again, I want you," Sir Pitt said, thump-
ing the table. "I can't git on without you. I
didn't see what it was till you went away. The
house all goes wrong. It's not the same place.
All my accounts has got muddled again. You
must come back. Do come back. Dear Becky,
do come!"

"Come—as what, Sir?" Rebecca gasped out.

"Come back as Lady Crawley, if you like," the
Baronet said, grasping his crape hat. "There!
will that zatusfy you? Come back and be my
wife. Your vit for't. Birth be hanged. You're
as good a lady as ever I see. You've got more
brains in your little vinger than any baronet's
wife in the county. Will you come? Yes or
no?"

"Oh, Sir Pitt!" Rebecca said, very much moved.

"Say yes, Becky," Sir Pitt continued. "I'm
an old man but a good 'un. I am good for twenty
years. I'll make you happy, zee if I don't. You
shall do what you like: spend what you like: and
'av it all your own way. I'll make you a settle-
ment. I'll do everything regular. Look year!"
and the old man fell down on his knees and leered
at her like a satyr.

Rebecca started back a picture of consternation.
In the course of this history we have never seen
her lose her presence of mind: but she did now,

388

and wept some of the most genuine tears that ever
fell from her eyes.

"Oh, Sir Pitt!" she said, "Oh Sir! I—I'm
married already."

W. M. THACKERAY (1811–1863).

From "Vanity Fair".

*

MR. CASAUBON PROPOSES

MY DEAR MISS BROOKE,

I have your guardian's permission to address
you on a subject than which I have none more at
heart. I am not, I trust, mistaken in the recognition of some deeper correspondence than that
of date in the fact that a consciousness of need in
my own life had arisen contemporaneously with
the possibility of my becoming acquainted with
you. For in the first hour of meeting you I had
an impression of your eminent and perhaps
exclusive fitness to supply that need (connected
I may say with such activity of the affections as
even the preoccupations of a work too special to
be abdicated could not uninterruptedly dis-
simulate) and each succeeding opportunity of
observation has given the impression an added
depth by convincing me more emphatically of that
fitness which I had preconceived and thus evoking
more decisively those affections to which I have
referred.

Our conversations have, I think, made sufficently clear to you the tenor of my life and purposes, a tenor unsuited, I am aware, to the commoner order of minds. But I have discovered in you an elevation of thought and a capability of devotedness which I had hitherto not conceived to be compatible either with the early bloom of youth or with those graces of sex that may be said at once to win and to confer distinction, when combined, as they notably are in you, with the mental qualities above indicated. . . . .

Such, my dear Miss Brooke, is the accurate statement of my feelings and I rely on your kind indulgence in venturing now to ask you how far your own are of a nature to confirm my happy presentiments. To be accepted by you as your husband and the earthly guardian of your welfare I should regard as the highest of providential gifts. In return I can at least offer you an affection hitherto unwasted and the faithful consecration of a life which, however short in the sequel, has no backward pages, whereon if you choose to turn them, you will find records such as might justly cause you either bitterness or shame. I await the expression of your sentiments with an anxiety which it would be the part of wisdom (were it possible) to divert by a more arduous labour than usual. But in this order of experience I am still young and in looking forward to an unfavourable possibility I cannot but feel that resignation to solitude will be more difficult after the temporary illumination of hope.

In any case I shall remain yours with sincere devotion.

EDWARD CASAUBON.

Dorothea trembled while she read this letter: then she fell on her knees, buried her face and sobbed. She could not pray: under the rush of solemn emotion in which thoughts became vague and images floated uncertainly, she could but cast herself with a childlike sense of reclining in the lap of a divine consciousness which sustained her own. She remained in that attitude till it was time to dress for dinner.

GEORGE ELIOT (1819–1880).
From "Middlemarch".

*

MR. TOOTS CONTRIVES TO SAY IT

Miss Dombey, I beg your pardon," says Mr. Toots, in a sad fluster, "but if you will allow me to—to——"

The smiling and unconscious look of Florence brings him to a dead stop.

"If you will allow me to—if you would not consider it a liberty, Miss Dombey, if I was to—without any encouragement at all, if I was to hope, you know," says Mr. Toots.

Florence looks at him inquiringly.

"Miss Dombey," says Mr. Toots, who feels that he is in for it now, "I really am in that state of adoration of you that I don't know what to do with myself. I am the most deplorable wretch. If it wasn't at the corner of the Square at present, I should go down on my knees, and beg and entreat of you, without any encouragement at all, just to let me hope that I may——may think it possible that you——"

"Oh, if you please, don't," cries Florence, for the moment quite alarmed and distressed. "Oh pray don't, Mr. Toots. Stop, if you please. Don't say any more. As a kindness and a favour to me, don't."

Mr. Toots is dreadfully abashed, and his mouth opens.

"You have been so good to me," says Florence, "I am so grateful to you. I have such reason to like you for being a good friend to me, and I do like you so much": and here the ingenuous face smiles upon him with the pleasantest look of honesty in the world: "that I am sure you are only going to say good-bye."

"Certainly, Miss Dombey," says Mr. Toots, "I—I—that's exactly what I mean. It is of no consequence."

"Good-bye!" cries Florence.

"Good-bye, Miss Dombey!" stammers Mr. Toots. "I hope you won't think anything about it. It's—it's of no consequence, thank you. It's not of the least consequence in the world."

CHARLES DICKENS (1812–1870).
From "Dombey and Son".

MR. COLLINS PROPOSES TO ELIZABETH

"My reasons for marrying are, first, that I think it a right thing for every clergyman in easy circumstances (like myself) to set the example of matrimony in his parish: secondly, that I am convinced it will add very greatly to my happiness, and, thirdly, which perhaps I ought to have mentioned earlier, that it is the particular advice and recommendation of the very noble lady whom I have the honour of calling patroness.

"Twice has she condescended to give me her opinion (unasked, too!) on this subject, and it was but the very Saturday night before I left Hunsford —between one pool, at quadrille, while Mrs. Jenkinson was arranging Miss de Burgh's footstool—that she said, 'Mr. Collins, you must marry. Choose properly; choose a gentlewoman for *my* sake and for your *own*: let her be an active useful sort of person, not brought up high, but able to make a small income go a good way! This is my advice—Find such a woman as soon as you can; bring her to Hunsford and I will visit her.'

"Thus much for my general intention in favour of matrimony: it remains to be told why my views were directed to Longbourn instead of my own neighbourhood where, I assure you, there are many amiable young women. But the fact is that being, as I am, to inherit this estate after the death of your honoured father (who, however, may live many years longer), I could not satisfy myself without resolving to choose a wife from among his daughters, that the loss to them might be as little as possible when the melancholy event takes place, which, however, as I have said, may not be for several years. This has been my motive, my fair cousin, and I flatter myself it will not sink me in your esteem.

"And now nothing remains for me but to assure you in the most animated language of the violence of my affection. To fortune I am perfectly indifferent, and shall make no demand of that nature on your father, since I am well aware it could not be complied with, and that one thousand pounds in the four per cents, which will not be yours till after your mother's decease, is all you may ever be entitled to. On that head, therefore, I shall be uniformly silent, and you may assure yourself that no ungenerous reproach shall ever pass my lips when we are married."

It was absolutely necessary to interrupt him now.

"You are too hasty, sir," Elizabeth cried. "You forget that I have made no answer. Let me do it without further loss of time. Accept my thanks for the compliment you are paying me: I am very sensible of the honour of your proposals, but it is impossible for me to do otherwise than to decline them."

"I am not now to learn," replied Mr. Collins, with a formal wave of the hand, "that it is usual with young ladies to reject the addresses of the man whom secretly they mean to accept, when he

first applies for their favour; and that sometimes
the refusal is repeated a second or even a third
time. I am, therefore, by no means discouraged
by what you have just said and shall hope to lead
you to the altar before long."

JANE AUSTEN,
From "Pride and Prejudice."

*

"SHALL IT BE A SUCCESSION?"

Ponder, illustrious Statia, on the important
point! Consider what it is to die a maid, when
you may, in a regular way, produce heirs to that
inestimable blessing of life and favour, which the
munificence of the Most High was pleased freely
to bestow and which the first Christian Mediator,
agent and negotiator, republished, confirmed and
sealed with his blood. Marry then in regard to
the gospel and let it be the fine employment of
your life to open gradually the treasures of
revelation to the understandings of the little
Christians you produce!

This I am sure your holy religion requires from
you and if from the sacred oracles we turn to the
book of Nature, is it not in this volume written
that there must be a malignity in the hearts of
those mortals who can remain unconcerned at the
destruction and extirpation of the rest of mankind,
and who want even so much good-will as is
requisite to propage a creature, in a regular and

hallowed way, though they received their own being from the mere benevolence of their own divine Master?

What do you say, illustrious Statia? Shall it be a succession, as you are an upright Christian? and may I hope to have the honour of sharing in the material satisfaction that must attend the discharge of so momentous a duty?

All the smiles sat on the face of Statia, while I was haranguing in this devout manner, and her countenance became a Constellation of wonders. When I had done the beauty said, "I thank you, sir, for the information you have given me. You have altered my way of thinking and I now declare for a succession. Let Father Fleming be sent for and without waiting for my being two and twenty, or minding my father's will, as there is no one to oblige me to it, I will give you my hand."

JOHN AMORY (1691?–1788).

From "The History of John Buncle Esq.".

*

XII

Treasure Trove

*

Some smack of age in you, some relish of the saltness of time.—SHAKESPEARE ("Henry IV").

Nationalism is full of the seeds of future civil convulsion.
SIR HENRY MAINE.

The combination of different nations in one State is as necessary a condition of civilised life as the combination of men in society. . . . It is in the cauldron of the State that the fusion takes place by which the vigour, the knowledge, and the capacity of one portion of mankind may be communicated to another.—LORD ACTON.

The proudest Empire in Europe is but a bauble compared to what America will be, must be, in the course of two centuries, if not one.—GOUVERNEUR MORRIS (1801).

It is the business of the legislature to remedy practical grievances not to run after theoretical perfection.
G. CANNING.

Politics are the sport of circumstance and principle the slave of opportunity.—LORD ROSEBERY.

History is the final remedy for untruth and the sovereign arbiter of opinion.—LORD ACTON.

So little done, so much to do.—CECIL RHODES.

397

Where are those martyred saints—the Five per Cents?
And where, oh where, the devil are the rents?
                                                    BYRON.

"Say what you have to say, don't quote Latin, and sit
down."—WELLINGTON'S advice to Sir George Murray.

What a grand sight it will be when twelve Dukes of
Hamilton rise together here at the Resurrection!
            The keeper of the Ducal Mausoleum to a visitor.

Hurt not this tomb: raze not what thou hast read,
Oh! in thy mercy do not wrong the dead!
                                                    ANON.

Truth like a bastard comes into the world
Never without ill-fame to him that gives her birth.
                                                    JOHN MILTON.

Avoid the ancient insanity of Governments—the mania
of wishing to govern too much.—ROBESPIERRE (1793).

A haggard eye, a moustache, a dull, gloomy, stilted,
disingenuous style of writing, does all the merit of patriotism
lie in these?—SAINT JUST (1793).

Seventy-one is a burden to himself and others—a brittle
elm-tree to have near you.—G. MEREDITH.

It is not the uncontrolled ascendency of popular power,
but of any power, which is formidable.—J. S. MILL.

The hour of the hereditary Peerage and eldest sonship
and immense properties has struck.
                                        MATTHEW ARNOLD (1848).

It is not worth while to travel round the world to count
the cats in Zanzibar.—THOREAU.

*

398

KEEP YOUR "DISTEMPERS" TO YOURSELF

There is one topic peremptorily forbidden to all well-bred, to all rational mortals, namely, their distempers. If you have not slept, or if you have slept; or if you have headache, sciatica, or leprosy, or thunder-stroke, I beseech you by all angels to hold your peace, and not pollute the morning, to which all the housemates bring serene and pleasant thoughts, by corruption and groans.

R. W. EMERSON (1803–1882).

*

RECIPES FOR OLD AGE

Honour thy father and thy mother that thy days may be long in the land which the Lord, thy God, giveth thee.

THE FIFTH COMMANDMENT.

*　　*　　*　　*

Never mix white wines with red.

JEROME CARDAN.

*　　*　　*　　*

Temperance, the bath, the flesh brush and—don't fret!

S. ROGERS.

*　　*　　*　　*

Though I look old, yet am I strong and lusty,
For in my youth I never did apply
Hot and rebellious liquors in my blood,

399

Nor did not with unbashful forehead woo
The means of weakness and debility;
Therefore my age is as a lusty winter,
Frosty but kindly.

SHAKESPEARE.
From "As You Like It".

* * * *

Ampliat ætatis spatium sibi vir bonus; hoc est
Vivere bis vita posse priore frui.

MARTIAL.

[The good man lengthens his space of life: to
be able to enjoy the life you have already lived is
to live twice.]

*

THE NAME AND DIGNITY OF DE VERE

This grave and weighty cause requires great
deliberation, and solid and mature judgment to
determine it, and I wish that all the Judges of
England had heard it. . . . Here is represented
to your Lordships *certamen honoris* and I may
well say *illustris honoris*, illustrious honour. I
heard a great peer of this realm and a learned
say when he lived that no king in Christendom
had such a subject as Oxford. He came in with
the Conqueror, Earl of Gwynes: shortly after the
Conquest made Great Chamberlain of England
above 500 years ago, by Henry I, the Conqueror's
son, brother to Rufus: by Maud the Empress

Earl of Oxford: confirmed and approved by Henry II Alberico Comiti, so Earl before.

This great honour, this high and noble dignity, hath continued ever since in the remarkable surname of De Vere, by so many ages, descents and generations, as no other kingdom can produce such a peer in one and the self same name and title. I find in all this length of time but two attainders of this noble family, and those in stormy and tempestuous times, when the government was unsettled and the kingdom in competition. I have laboured to make a covenant with myself that affection may not press upon judgment, for I suppose there is no man that hath any apprehension of gentry or nobleness, but his affection stands to the continuance of so noble a name and house, and would take hold of a twig or twine-thread to uphold it.

And yet Time hath his revolutions: there must be a period and an end to all temporal things—*finis rerum*—an end of names and dignities, and whatever is terrene, and why not of De Vere? For where is Bohun? Where is Mowbray? Where is Mortimer? Nay, which is more and most of all, where is Plantagenet? They are entombed in the urns and sepulchres of mortality. And yet let the name and dignity of De Vere stand so long as it pleaseth God!

CHIEF JUSTICE CREWE (1558–1646).

[From a judgment in favour of Robert de Vere who claimed the earldom as heir male of Aubrey de Vere. The rival claimant was Lord Willoughby de Eresby, who claimed as heir-general of the last Earl. The line became extinct at the death of Robert de Vere's son in 1702.]

*

INVOKING THE ANGELS

I was very familiar with one Sarah Skelhorn, who had been speculatrix unto one Arthur Gauntlet, about Gray's Inn Lane, a very lewd fellow, professing physick. This Sarah had a perfect sight and indeed the best eyes for that purpose I ever yet did see. She lived a long time, even until her death, with one Mrs. Stockman in the Isle of Purbeck.

Her mistress being one day desirous to accompany her mother, the Lady Beconsfield, unto London, who lived twelve miles from her habitation, caused Sarah to inspect her crystal to see if she, her mother, was gone, yea or not; the angels appeared and shewed her mother opening a trunk and taking out a red waistcoat; whereby she perceived she was not gone. Next day she went to her mother's and there, as she entered the chamber, she was opening a trunk and had a red waistcoat in her hand. Sarah told me oft the angels would for some years follow her, and appear in every room of the house till she was weary of them.

Sarah Skelhorn's call unto the crystal began

"Oh! ye good angels, only and only——". Ellen Evans, daughter of my tutor Evans, called to her crystal thus: *O Micol, O tu Micol, regina pigmæorum, veni!*

It is not every one that these angelical creatures will appear unto, though they may say the call over and over, nor indeed is it given to very many persons to endure their glorious aspects. Many have failed when they were ready to manifest themselves: even persons of undaunted spirits and firm resolution are astonished and tremble, as happened not many years since with me.

A very sober, discreet person of virtuous life and conversation, desirous of seeing something of this nature, went with a friend to my Hurstwood.

The Queen of Fairies was invocated; a gentle murmuring wind came first. After that, amongst the hedges, a smart whirlwind. By and by a strong blast of wind blew upon the face of the friend, and the Queen appeared in a most illustrious glory. "No more, I beseech you," quoth the friend. "My heart fails. I am not able to continue any longer."

Nor was he: his black curling hair stood up and I believe a bullrush would have knocked him to the ground.

These glorious creatures, if well commanded and well observed, do teach the Master anything he desires. *Amant secreta, fugiunt aperta.* The fairies love the southern side of hills, mountains, groves. Neatness and cleanliness in apparel, a strict diet and upright life, fervent prayers unto God conduce much to the assistance of those who are curious in these ways.

WILLIAM LILLY (the Astrologer).

(1602–1681).

*

THE JOURNEYING MOON

In his loneliness and fixedness he yearneth towards the journeying Moon, and the stars that still sojourn, yet still move onward; and everywhere the blue sky belongs to them and is their appointed rest, and their native country and their own natural homes, which they enter unannounced, as lords that are certainly expected, and yet there is a silent joy at their arrival.

> The moving Moon went up the sky,
> And no where did abide:
> Softly she was going up
> And a star or two beside.

S. T. COLERIDGE (1772–1834).
From "The Ancient Mariner".

*

THE GLORY THAT WAS GREECE

The sight of the Acropolis was like a revelation of the Divine, such as that which I experienced when, gazing down the valley of the Jordan from

404

the heights of Casyoun, I first felt the living reality of the Gospel. The whole world then appeared to me barbarian. The East repelled me by its pomp, its ostentation and its impostures. The Romans were merely rough soldiers: the majesty of the noblest Roman of them all, of an Augustus and a Trajan, was but attitudinising compared to the sure and simple nobility of these proud and peaceful citizens. Celts, Germans and Slavs appeared as conscientious but scarcely civilised Scythians.

Our own Middle Ages seemed to me devoid of elegance and style, disfigured by misplaced pride and pedantry. Charlemagne was nothing more than an awkward German stableman: our chevaliers louts at whom Themistocles and Alexander would have laughed. But here you had a whole people of aristocrats, a general public composed entirely of connoisseurs, a democracy which was capable of distinguishing shades of art so delicate that even our most refined judges can scarcely appreciate them. Here you had a public capable of understanding in what consisted the beauty of the Propylæa and the superiority of the sculptures of the Parthenon. This revelation of true and simple grandeur went to my very soul. All that I had hitherto seen seemed to me the awkward effort of a Jesuitical art, a rococo mixture of silly pomp, charlatanism and caricature.

ERNEST RENAN (1823–1892).
From "Recollections of my Youth".

IN A LIBRARY

I go into my library and all history unrolls before me. I breathe the morning air of the world while the scent of Eden's roses yet lingered in it, while it vibrated only to the world's first brood of nightingales and to the laugh of Eve. I see the Pyramids building: I hear the shoutings of the armies of Alexander; I feel the ground shake beneath the march of Cambyses. I sit as in a theatre: the stage is time, the play is the play of the world. What kingly pomp, what processions file past, what cities burn to heaven, what crowds of captives are dragged at the chariot wheels of conquerors! I hear or cry "Bravo" when the great actors come on shaking the stage. I am a Roman Emperor when I look at a Roman coin. I lift Homer and I shout with Achilles in the trenches. The silence of the unpeopled Syrian plains, the outgoings and incomings of the patriarchs, Abraham and Ishmael, Jacob's guile, Esau's face reddened by desert sun-heat, Joseph's splendid funeral procession—all these things I find within the boards of my Old Testament.

What a silence in those old books of a half-peopled world—what bleating of flocks—what green pastoral rest—what indubitable human existence! Across brawling centuries of blood and war, I hear the bleating of Abraham's flocks, the tinkling of the bells of Rebekah's camels. O men and women, so far separated yet so near, so strange yet so well known, by what miraculous

power do I know ye all! Books are the true
Elysian fields where the spirits of the dead converse, and into these fields a mortal may venture
unappalled.

ALEXANDER SMITH (1830–1867).
From "Dreamthorpe".

*

CHEERFUL COUNSEL FROM A GHOST

'Tis late and cold, stir up the fire;
Sit close and draw the table nigher;
Be merry and drink wine that's old,
A hearty medicine 'gainst a cold.
Your beds of wanton down the best,
Where you shall tumble to your rest.
Call for the best the house may ring,
Sack, white, and claret let them bring,
And drink apace, whilst breath you have;
You'll find but cold drink in the grave;
Plover, partridge for your dinner,
And a capon for the sinner,
You shall find ready when you're up,
And your horse shall have his sup.
Welcome, welcome, shall fly round,
And I shall smile, though underground.

JOHN FLETCHER (1579–1625).
From "The Lover's Progress".

*

THE CANDID FRIEND

"Much may be said on both sides."   Hark! I
    hear
A well known voice that murmurs in my ear—
The voice of Candour.   Hail! most solemn sage,
Thou drivelling virtue of this moral age,
Candour, which softens party's headlong rage,
Candour, which spares its foes! nor e'er descends
With bigot zeal to combat for its friends.
Candour, which loves in see-saw strain to tell
Of *acting foolishly*, but *meaning well*:
Too nice to praise by wholesale, or to blame,
Convinced that all men's motives are the same:
And finds with keen, discriminating sight,
BLACK'S not so black, nor WHITE *so very* white.
  Fox, to be sure, was vehement and wrong,
But then Pitt's words, you'll own, were *rather*
    strong:
Both must be blamed, both pardoned: 'twas just so
With Fox and Pitt full forty years ago!
So Walpole, Pulteney—factions in all times
Have had their follies, Ministers their crimes.
  Give me th' avowed, th' erect, the manly foe,
Bold I can meet—perhaps can turn his blow:
But of all plagues, good Heaven, thy wrath can
    send,
Save, save, oh! save me from the *Candid Friend*!
           GEORGE CANNING (1770–1827).

*

UP TO THEIR ANKLES IN CARDS

There is a well authenticated story of Lord Granville's devotion to whist. Intending to set out in the course of the afternoon for Paris he ordered his carriage and four posters to be at Graham's (Hotel) at four. They were kept waiting till ten; when he sent out to say that he should not be ready for another hour or two and that the horses had better be changed. They were changed three times in all at intervals of six hours, before he started. When the party rose they were up to their ankles in cards, and the Ambassador (it was reported) was a loser to the tune of eight or ten thousand pounds.

* * * *

The De Roos affair was a sad blow and a temporary discredit to whist players, for some of them were unluckily seduced into acting on the late Lord Hertford's maxim, "What would you do if you saw a man cheating at cards?" "Bet upon him, to be sure." Lord de Roos' methods of aiding his skill were only available for one hand in four—when he dealt. He then contrived to turn an honour by what is called *sauter le coup* and having marked the higher honours with his nail, he could see to whom they fell.

From "Whist and Whist Players"
Fraser's Magazine. 1869.

*

409

FIVE BAD PROPHECIES

Prussia is a country without bottom and could not maintain a war for six weeks.

DISRAELI (1864).

(Two years before the Austro-Prussian War.)

*   *   *   *

In the next war there will be no neutrals.

PRESIDENT WILSON (1918).

*   *   *   *

If the Americans got their independence the sun of England would set and her glories be eclipsed for ever.

LORD SHELBURNE (1771).

*   *   *   *

It seems possible to hope that war may come to be conducted without intentional injury to non-combatants and with the smallest possible damage to combatants.

CHARLES PEARSON (1893).

*   *   *   *

This great hour which rings in a new era and which is going to lift up humanity to a higher plane of existence for all the ages of the future.

D. LLOYD GEORGE
At Guildhall, Nov. 11, 1918.

*

HENRY THE NINTH OF ENGLAND

From Angharad Lloyd I have heard a story which is worth recording. Her sister, Helen

Lloyd, was (through the interest of Lady Crewe, I believe) governess to the younger daughters of the Duke of Clarence. He, as was his custom, lived with her on terms of familiar intimacy and friendship from the time of her first presentation to the day of his death.

He had expressed a strong preference for his second name of Henry, which he liked much better than that of William. The day after the death of George IV, Miss Helen Lloyd met the King at the house of Lady Sophia Sydney: she asked him familiarly whether he was to be proclaimed as King William or as King Henry. "Helen Lloyd," he replied, "that question has been discussed in the Privy Council, and it has been decided in favour of King William." He added, that the decision had been mainly influenced by the idea of an old prophecy of which he had never heard before, nor had he any evidence that it had ever been made.

The drift of the prophecy was, that as Henry VIII "had pulled down monks and cells, Henry IX would pull down bishops and bells." Helen exclaimed, "I have seen that in an old book at home." The King was astonished and pleased; he desired her to send for the book as soon as possible. Diligent search was made for it, but unhappily it was not discovered till after the King's death. It was found by me.

FRANCES WILLIAMS WYNN (1844).
From "Diaries of a lady of Quality".

The title of the book is as follows:

"A Briefe View of the State of the Church of England as it stood in Queen Elizabeth's and King James his Reigne, to the Yeare 1608. Being a Character and History of the Bishops of those Times, and may serve as an additional Supply to Dr. Goodwin's Catalogue of Bishops. Written for the use of Prince Henry upon occasion of that Proverb—

'Henry VIII pulled down Monks and their Cells,'
Henry IX should pull down Bishops and their Bells.'

By Sir John Harrington of Kilston near Bath, Knight. London, printed for J. Keston, St. Paul's Churchyard, 1653".

*

AT THE PRINCE OF WALES' WEDDING
(1863)

The wedding was certainly the most moving sight I ever saw. The Queen above looking down added such a wonderful chord of deep feeling to all the lighter notes of joyfulness and show. Everyone behaved quite at their best. The Princess of Wales calm, feeling, self-possessed. The Prince with more depth of manner than ever before. Princess Mary's entrance was grand. The little Prince William of Prussia,* between his

* Afterwards the Kaiser Wilhelm II.

two little uncles, to keep him quiet, both of whom
—the Crown Princess told me—he bit on the bare
Highland legs whenever they touched him to keep
him quiet. I had a nice long talk with the Queen.
I was charmed with the Prince of Prussia and the
warmth of his expression as to his wife. "Bishop,"
he said, "with me it has been one long honey-
moon."

S. WILBERFORCE, Bishop of Oxford
(1805–1873).

*

THE REAL PROBLEM IN EDUCATION

We have lost—at any rate in the post-primary
school—our grip on education. It has become a
mass of uncoordinated subjects, a chaos instead
of a cosmos. Its dominating idea, so far as it has
one, is to provide the equipment of knowledge
which an intelligent man should possess. So it
tends to become a collection of isolated subjects—
a world of planets, as the Greeks conceived
planets, stars wandering each on its irregular way,
occasionally dashing into each other. For this
we need to substitute a solar system whose ruling
principle is the making of human beings. Many
things go to their making, but essentially it is the
training of three aspects of man—body, mind and
character. And neither mind nor character can
be made without a spiritual element. That is
just the element which has grown weak, where

it has not perished, in our education, and therefore in our civilization, with disastrous results. Nothing can be done till that element is restored. Its only sources in Western civilisation—it would be different if we were Chinese or Hindus—are Palestine and Greece: and I suggest that we may adapt and adopt as our motto the advice which Apollo gave to the Trojans: "Seek out your ancient mothers". *Antiquas exquirite matres.* Anyhow the problem is there; it is the greatest of our problems; and, unless we solve it, our civilisation will perish.

> SIR RICHARD LIVINGSTONE (1880–   ).
> From "The Future of Education".

*

THE PIGEONS AT THE BRITISH MUSEUM

Seats should be placed here, under the great columns (of the portico) or by the grass, so that one might enjoy the sunshine after books and watch the pigeons. They have no fear of us people, they come to my feet, but the noise of a door heavily swinging to in the great building alarms them: they rise and float around, and return again. The sunlight casts a shadow of the pigeon's head and neck upon his shoulder; he turns his head, and the shadow of his beak falls on his breast. Iridescent gleams of bronze and green and blue play about his neck; blue predominates. His pink feet step so near, the red round his eye is visible. As he rises vertically, forcing his way in a straight line upwards, his wings almost meet above his back and again beneath his body: they are put forth to his full stroke. When his flight inclines and becomes gradually horizontal, the effort is less and the wing tips do not approach so closely.

They have not laboured in mental searching as we have: they have not wasted their time looking among empty straw for the grain which is not there. They have been in the sunlight. Since the days of ancient Greece the doves have remained in the sunshine, by the shady verge of woods, by the sweet waters where the wild dove sips, there alone will thought be found.

RICHARD JEFFERIES (1848–1887).
From "The Life of the Fields".

*

SHEWING THE FAMILY PORTRAITS

If you please to fall back a little (because it is necessary to look at the next three pictures at one view) these are three sisters. She on the right hand, who is so very beautiful, died a maid; the next to her, still handsomer, had the same fate, against her will: this homely thing in the middle had both their portions added to her own, and was stole by a neighbouring gentleman, a man of stratagem and resolution, for he poisoned three mastiffs to come at her, and knocked down two

deer-stealers in carrying her off. Misfortunes
happen in all families. The theft of this romp
and so much money, was no great matter to our
estate.

But the next heir that possessed it was this soft
gentleman whom you see here. Observe the small
buttons, the little boots, the laces, the slashes
about his clothes and above all the posture he is
drawn in (which, to be sure, was his own choosing:)
You see he sits with one hand on a desk, writing,
and looking, as it were, another way, like an easy
writer or a sonneteer. He was one of those who
had too much wit to know how to live in the world:
he was a man of no justice but of great good
manners: he ruined everybody that had anything
to do with him, but never said a rude word in his
life. The most indolent person in the world, he
would sign a deed that passed away half his estate
with his gloves on, but would not put on his hat
before a lady if it were to save his country. He is
said to be the first that made love by squeezing
the hand. He left the estate with ten thousand
pounds debt upon it, but by all hands I have been
informed that he was every way the finest gentleman in the world.

That debt lay heavy on our house for one generation, but it was retrieved by a gift from that honest
man you see there, a citizen of our name, but
nothing at all akin to us. I know Sir Andrew
Freeport has said behind my back that this man
was descended from one of the ten children of the

maid of honour I showed you above, but it was never made out. We winked at the thing, indeed, because money was wanting at that time.

Here I saw my friend a little embarrassed and turned my face to the next portraiture.

SIR R. STEELE (1672–1729).

*

MÉSALLIANCES DURING THE FORTY-FIVE

This has been a lucky season for low people's marrying, for I am told that since the Duke of Shandois' (Chandos) marriage with the inn-keeper's maid near Slough, the Duke of Ancaster has married his kept mistress and the Duke of Rutland will own his with his kept mistress; the Earl of Salisbury has married his steward's niece, Miss Keate, daughter to a barber and shewer of the tombs in Canterbury, and the Earl of Bristol his late wife's maid. And the Duke of Bridgwater his tutor's niece.

From the Earl of Egmont's Diary for
Feb. 4, 1745.

Hist. Mss Commission III (1923) 307.8.

*

LORD MELBOURNE ON MARRIAGE

The general reason against marriage is this— that two minds, however congenial they may be, or however submissive the one may be to the other, can never act like one. By taking a wife a man certainly adds to the list of those who have a right to interfere with and advise him, and he runs the risk of putting in his own way another very strong and perhaps insuperable obstacle to his acting according to his own opinions and inclinations. By marrying you place yourself upon the defensive instead of the offensive in society, which latter is admitted to be in all contentions the most advantageous mode of proceeding.

Before marriage the shape, the figure, the complexion carry all before them: after marriage the mind and character unexpectedly claim their share, and that the largest, of importance. Before I was married, whenever I saw the children and the dogs allowed, or rather caused, to be troublesome in any family I used to lay it all to the fault of the master of it, who might at once put a stop to it if he pleased. Since I have married, I find that this was a very rash and premature judgment.

LORD MELBOURNE (1779–1848).

From his "Commonplace Book".

*

A MARRIAGE ANALYSIS

Personally, I should estimate that in not one per cent. even of romantic marriages are the husband and wife capable of *passion* for each other after three years. So brief is the violence of love! In perhaps thirty-three per cent. passion settles down into a tranquil affection—which is ideal. In fifty per cent. it sinks into sheer indifference, and one becomes used to one's wife or one's husband as to one's other habits. And in the remaining sixteen per cent. it develops into dislike or detestation.

ARNOLD BENNETT (1867–1931).
From "Mental Efficiency".

*

A TALE OF TWO BROTHERS

A union of two brothers from Avington. The Clerke family were grandfather, father and son, successively Clerks of the Privy Seal. William the grandfather had but two sons—both Thomas. Their wives both Amys, the heirs both Henrys and the heirs of the Henrys both Thomases, both their wives inheritrixes and both had two sons and one daughter. Both their daughters issueless; both of Oxford; both of the Temple; both officers to Queen Elizabeth and our noble King James; both justices of the Peace; both agree in arms, the one a knight, the other a captain.

Si quaeras Avingtonium cancellum petas.

(If you would find them seek out the chancel at Avington.)

From a memorial tablet in the north aisle of Winchester Cathedral (1622).

419

BROWSING ON GREAT FOLIOS

I should like to browse on folios and have to deal chiefly with authors that I have scarcely strength to lift, that are as solid as they are heavy and, if dull, are full of matter. It is delightful to repose on the wisdom of the ancients; to have some great name at hand, besides one's own initials always staring me in the face: to travel out of oneself into the Chaldee, Hebrew and Egyptian characters: to hear the palm-trees waving mystically in the margin of the page and the camels moving slowly on in the distance of three thousand years. In that dry desert we gather strength and patience and a strange and unsatiable thirst of knowledge. The ruined monuments of antiquity are also there, and the fragments of buried cities (under which the adder lurks) and cool springs and green sunny spots and the whirlwind, and the lion's roar and the shadow of angelic wings.

W. HAZLITT (1778–1830).

*

WOORARA, THE BAILLIES' CAT

You may perhaps have heard the name of a celebrated Mr. Brodie who wrote on Poisons. He possessed some of the Woorara poison with which the natives poison their arrows and destroy their victims. It was his theory that this poison destroys by affecting the nervous system only, and that after a time its effects on the nerves would cease, as the effects of intoxicating liquors cease, and that the patient might recover if the lungs could be kept in play, if respiration were not suspended during the trance or partial death in which the patient lies.

To prove the truth of this by experiment he fell to work on a cat which he pricked with the point of a lance dipped in Woorara. It was some minutes before the animal became convulsed, and then it lay, to all appearance, dead. Mr. Brodie applied a tube to its mouth and blew air into it from time to time. After lying for some hours apparently lifeless it recovered, shook itself and went about its own affairs as usual. This was tried several times, much to the satisfaction of the philosophical spectators but not quite to the satisfaction of poor Puss, who grew very thin and looked so wretched that Dr. Baillie's son, then a boy, took compassion on this poor subject of experiment and begged Mr. Brodie to let him carry off the cat. With or without consent, he did carry her off and brought her to his aunts, Joanna and Agnes Baillie.

Then puss' prosperous days began. Agnes made a soft bed for her in her own room and by night and day she was the happiest of cats. She was called Woorara, which in time shortened into Woory.

I wish I could wind up Woory's history by assuring you that she was the most attached and grateful of cats, but truth forbids. A few weeks after her arrival at Hampstead, she marched off and was never heard of more. It is supposed she took to evil courses.

MARIE EDGEWORTH (1822).

*

ATOSSA

Cruel, but composed and bland,
Dumb, inscrutable and grand,
So Tiberius might have sat,
Had Tiberius been a cat.

M. ARNOLD.

*

NERO TRIES TO FLY

He has had another wonderful escape—that dog. I begin to think he bears a charmed life. This time the danger was entirely of his own seeking. Imagine his taking it into his head that he could *fly*—like the birds—if he tried, and actually trying it out at the Library window! For a first attempt his success was not so bad: for he fairly cleared the area spikes—and though he *did* plash down on the pavement at the feet of an astonished boy he broke no bones, was only quite *stunned*. He gave us a horrid fright, however.

It was after breakfast and he had been standing

422

at the other window, watching the birds—one of his chief delights—while Elizabeth was dusting out for Mr. C. Lying in my bed I heard through the deal partition Elizabeth scream: "O God! oh Nero!" . . . I sat up in bed aghast—waiting with a feeling as of the Heaven falling till I heard her re-ascending the stairs and then I ran to meet her in my nightshift. She was white as a sheet, ready to faint, could just say: "Oh! take him!" the dog's body lay on her arm! "Is he killed?" I asked with *terrible self-possession*. "Not quite! I think, all *but*."

Mr. C. came down from his bedroom with his chin all over soap and asked, "Has anything happened to Nero?" "Oh, sir! he must have broken *all* his legs: he leapt out at *your* window." "God bless me!" said Mr. C. and returned to his shaving. I sat down on the floor and laid my insensible dog over my knees, but could see no breakage—only a stun. So I took him to bed with me—under the clothes—and in an hour's time he was as brisk and active as ever.

JANE CARLYLE.
Letter to Jeannie Welsh. 1850.

*

DIZZY'S WHITE OVERCOAT

In the crowd to-day [at the Thanksgiving Service at St. Paul's for the recovery of the Prince of Wales in 1872] one of the figures which I was amused in observing was Mr. Disraeli's. He was clad in a garment which, I believe, he greatly affects—a long white coat, designed, possibly, to assist the curious eye in its search for one. He was paying his wife, Lady Beaconsfield, a degree of attention so unusual in public and so very unusual in Church, as to suggest to the cynical observer that it could scarcely always be maintained in the same perfection under the accomplished gentleman's own roof, but I promptly repressed this thought, as altogether unfair to the courteous author of *Coningsby*. Truly in this land of precedent, a statesman profits by being fashionable—fashionable for his novels, or his eccentricity, or his impudence—for something, at any rate, which forms a brilliant contrast to that grim, tremendous earnestness which we all so profoundly admire, which rules, and bores, the British mind. For every opera-glass which was bent on Gladstone to-day in St. Paul's, I am sure that a dozen were turned on Dizzy.

R. C. JEBB (1841–1905).

*

WHEN BARRISTERS GROW BRISK

There is nothing in the world so brisk as the ways and manners of lawyers when in any great case they come to what they know to be the real bone of the limb and kernel of the nut. The doctor is very brisk when after a dozen moderately dyspeptic patients he comes to some unfortunate gentleman whose gastric apparatus is gone altogether. The parson is very brisk when he reaches the minatory clause in his sermon. The Minister is very brisk when he asks the House for a vote, telling his hoped-for followers that this special point is absolutely essential to his Government— unless he can carry this he and all those hanging on to him must vacate their places. The horse-dealer is very brisk when after four or five indifferent lots he bids his man bring out from the stable the last thoroughbred that he bought and the very best that he put his eye on.

But the briskness of none of these is equal to the briskness of the barrister who has just got into his hands for cross-examination him who we may call the centre witness of a great case.

He plumes himself like a bullfinch going to sing. He spreads himself like a peacock on a lawn. He perks himself like a sparrow on a paling. He crows amidst his attorneys and all the satellites of the court like a cock among his hens. He puts his hands this way and that, settling even the sunbeams as they enter lest a mote should disturb his intellect or dull the edge of his subtlety. There is a modesty in his eye, a quiescence in his lips, a repose in his limbs, under which lie half-concealed—not at all concealed from those who have watched him at work—the glance, the tone, the spring, which are to tear that unfortunate witness to pieces, without infringing any one of those conventional rules which have been laid down for the guidance of successful, well-mannered barristers.

ANTHONY TROLLOPE (1815–1882).
From "Ralph the Heir".

*

AN UNFRIENDLY REVIEW

In this work—James Joyce's "Ulysses"—the spiritually offensive and the physically unclean are united . . . in its reading lies not only the description but the commission of sin against the Holy Ghost. Having tasted and rejected the devilish drench, we must earnestly hope that this book be not only placed upon the *Index Expurgatorius* but that its reading and communication be made a reserved case.

From the "Dublin Review".

*

SURVIVAL BY MERIT

Speaking generally the landed gentry are enduring witnesses of past worth and good work done, and until they forfeit our esteem by demerits of their own, they deserve to be respected and honoured. High place is lost so easily that when a family has been of long continuance we may be sure that it has survived by exceptional merit.

Nature rapidly finds out when the wrong sort have stolen into promotion. When a knave makes a fortune his son spends it—one generation sees an end of him. Even among the best there is a quick succession. The marble monument in the church outlasts the living one. There are no Plantagenets now. The Lacies and the de Courcies drop out. The Nelsons and the Wellesleys step into their places. Warriors, lawyers, politicians press perpetually to the front. The worn out material is for ever being replaced with new. Each family thus raised is on its trial. Those who survive remain as links between the present and the past, and carry on unbroken the continuity of our national existence.

In such families the old expression "Noblesse Oblige" is a genuine force. In a chapel attached to the church of Chenies in Hertfordshire lies the honoured dust of the generations of the house of Russell. There is Lord William, carried there from the scaffold at Lincoln's Inn. There is Lady Rachel. There are the successive Earls and Dukes of Bedford, who, wise or unwise, have been always true to the people's side through three centuries of political struggle. At one end of the chapel are the monuments of the first Lord Russell, King Henry's Minister at the Reformation, and of the first Lady Russell, from whom all the rest are descended. There she lies, a stern austere lady, as you can see in the lines of her marble countenance, evidently an exact likeness, modelled from her features. I could not but feel, as I stood in that chapel, what a thing it would be to know that in death one had to be carried into the presence of that terrible ancestress and that august array of her descendants, and to be examined whether one had been worthy of the race to which one belonged.

J. A. FROUDE (1818–1894).
From "Short Studies". On the use of a
Landed Gentry.

*

A MAJORITY OF ONE FOR REFORM

It must have been impossible, as you may conceive, in the lobbies, crowded as they were, to form any exact estimate of the voting. First we heard that they were three hundred and three; then that number rose to three hundred and ten; then went down to three hundred and seven. Alexander Baring told me that he had counted, and that they were three hundred and four. We were all breathless with anxiety, when Charles Wood, who stood near the door, jumped up on a bench and cried out, "They are only three hundred and one."

We set up a shout that you might have heard to Charing Cross, waving our hats, stamping against the floor, and clapping our hands. The tellers scarcely got through the crowd: for the House was thronged up to the table, and all the

floor was fluctuating with heads like the pit of a
theatre. But you might have heard a pin drop
as Duncannon read the numbers. Then again the
shouts broke out, and many of us shed tears. I
could scarcely refrain. And the jaw of Peel fell;
and the face of Twiss was as the face of a damned
soul; and Herries looked like Judas taking his
necktie off for the last operation.

T. B. MACAULAY (1831).

*

A PHILOSOPHER'S BAGATELLE

Benjamin Franklin and his wife and Helvétius,
the French philosopher, and his wife, had been
intimate friends. Helvétius died in 1771; Mrs.
Franklin in 1773. The survivors maintained their
friendship, and soon Franklin paid his addresses
to the handsome widow. She declined the
honour, however, and he then composed the
following "bagatelle".

Mortified at the barbarous resolution pronounced by you so positively yesterday evening,
that you would remain single the rest of your
life, as a compliment due to the memory of
your husband, I retired to my chamber.
Throwing myself upon my bed I dreamed that
I was dead and was transported to the Elysian
Fields. I was asked whether I wanted to see
any person in particular, to which I replied that
I wanted to see my old friend Helvétius.

I was conducted to him and he received me with good courtesy. "I have taken to myself another wife," he said, "who has a great fund of wit and good sense, and her whole study is to please me. She is at this moment gone to fetch the best nectar and ambrosia to regale me: stay here awhile and you will see her."

"I perceive," said I, "that your former friend is more faithful to you than you are to her and she has had several good offers, but has refused them all. I will confess to you that I loved her extremely, but she was cruel to me and rejected me peremptorily for your sake." "I pity you sincerely," said he, "for she is an excellent woman, handsome and amiable. . . ."

As he finished speaking, the new Madame Helvétius entered with the nectar and I recognised her immediately as my former friend, Mrs. Franklin! I reclaimed her, but she answered me coldly: "I was a good wife to you for forty-nine years and four months, nearly half a century: let that content you. I have formed a new connection here, which will last to eternity."

Indignant at this refusal of my Eurydice, I immediately resolved to quit those ungrateful shades and return to this good world again, to behold the sun and you! Here I am: *let us avenge ourselves.*"

BENJAMIN FRANKLIN.

*

THE TIME TO DRINK PORT

Port could never have attained its unshakeable popularity if it had not a sort of natural affinity with the English climate and the English character. It is a wine that lends itself to ritual, a thing always held in high honour in a country which has banished it from its church. But it has more than its ritual to recommend it. It is hard to find words of praise for the east wind, but it does make a glass of Vintage Port more grateful and comforting. And when in October the nip is coming in the evening air, and the logs are once more crackling on the hearth, what pleasanter occupation could there be than the slow and critical consumption of a bottle of Old Port?

With bed the next halting place, no work to be done, nothing to distract the mind from kindly memories of friends that are gone except good natured gossip about those who are still with us, with good apples and nuts to give the teeth something to bite on and supply a proper contrast of flavour—unless this be sought in a good plain seed cake—this surely is the English autumn at its best.

But Port must be allowed its vagaries. It has never forgotten that its first popularity in England was due to that Champagne-drinking monarch, King Louis XIV: and it will not brook the society of the sparkling wine without exacting a severe retribution from the drinker's head. With Claret it has no quarrel: Burgundy it can tolerate: but if asked its own views as to the best prelude to itself, I am sure it would reply, "Beer, honest English draught beer."

Those who like Port in the middle of the day would be better advised to stick to Wood Port, which seems for some reason to be more digestible. Probably the access of air to the wine in cask has robbed it of much of its heaviness. But in the same way I would counsel Vintage Port for evening drinking. The resulting somnolence is then a blessing rather than a disadvantage: its majesty is more appropriate to the meal that is meant rather to soothe and comfort than to strengthen and energise.

MAURICE HEALY (1887–   ).
From "Stay me with Flagons".

*

THE STRICT LIMITS OF DRINKING

That it is good to be drunk once a month is a common flattery of sensuality, supporting itself upon Physick and the healthful effects of inebriation. This indeed seems plainly affirmed by Avicenna, a physician of great authority, and whose religion, as it prohibits wine, could less extenuate ebriety. But Averroes, a man of his own faith, was of another belief, restraining his ebriety into hilarity and in effect making no more thereof than Seneca commendeth and was allowable in Cato, that is to say, a sober incalescence and regulated æstuation from wine, or what may be conceived between Joseph and his brethren, when the text expresseth they were merry, or drank largely, and whereby indeed the commodities set down by Avicenna, that is, alleviation of spirits, resolution of superfluities, provocation of sweat and urine may also ensue. But as for dementation, sopition of reason and the diviner particle of reason from drink, though American religion approve and Pagan piety of old hath practised it, even at their sacrifices, Christian morality and the doctrine of Christ will not allow. And surely that religion which excuseth the fact of Noah, in the aged surprisal of six-hundred years, and unexpected inebriation from the unknown effects of wine will neither acquit ebriosity nor ebriety, in their known and intended perversions.

SIR THOMAS BROWNE, KNIGHT, M.D.
(1605–1682).
From "Pseudodoxia Epidemica".
(1672)

*

TABLE PLEASURES

When a man is invited to dinner, he is disappointed if he does not get something good.

DR. JOHNSON.

*   *   *   *

I am very glad that my Lord has begun to drink old Hock. I own I wish him to double his quantity of Hock for dinner. Let him drink 2 glasses of plain Hock and 2 glasses of red Port every day over and above the Madeira which he drinks unmixed with water and over and above the Port which is taken in Sago.

DR. ADDINGTON of Lord Chatham.

* * * *

Some people tell you you should never drink claret after strawberries. They are wrong.

W. MAGINN.

* * * *

Madeira and Burgundy carry combined intensity and complexity of vinous delights further than any other wines.

PROF. SAINTSBURY.

* * *

"A good soup, a small turbot, a neck of venison, ducklings with green peas, a chicken with asparagus and an apricot tart is a dinner for an Emperor."

1ST EARL OF DUDLEY.

* * * *

"He was a good man, an excellent man. He had the best melted butter I ever tasted in my life."

From a eulogy of BARON HULLOCK.

* * * *

The first Duke of Cambridge, on being shewn the menu for the Duke of Rutland's birthday

434

dinner at Belvoir Castle, was asked whether he fancied any addition. "Yes," replied His Royal Highness, "a roast pig and an apple pudding."

A. HAYWARD.

*   *   *   *

A little Pipkin with a bit
Of Mutton, or of Veale in it,
Set on my Table (Trouble-free)
More than a Feast contenth me.

R. HERRICK.

*

NELSON'S UNUSED COFFIN

Part of the *Orient's* mainmast* was picked up by the *Swiftsure*. Capt. Hallowell ordered his carpenter to make a coffin of it; the iron as well as wood was taken from the same ship; it was finished as well and handsomely as the workmen's skill and materials would permit and Hallowell then sent it to the Admiral with the following letter:

Sir: I have taken the liberty of presenting you with a coffin made from the main-mast of *l'Orient*, that when you have finished your military career in this world, you may be buried

---

* *L'Orient*, the French flagship, was blown up during the Battle of the Nile. [Nelson was actually buried in a sumptuous sarcophagus prepared by Cardinal Wolsey for his own use. On Wolsey's fall from power it was taken by Henry VIII's order to Windsor Castle.]

in one of your trophies. But that that period may be far distant is the earnest wish of your sincere friend,

BENJAMIN HALLOWELL.

An offering so strange and yet so suited to the occasion, was received by Nelson in the spirit in which it was sent. As if he felt it good for him, now that he was at the summit of his wishes, to have death before his eyes, he ordered the coffin to be placed upright in his cabin. Such a piece of furniture, however, was more suitable to his own feelings than to those of his guests and attendants, and an old favourite servant entreated him so earnestly to have it removed, that at length he asked to have the coffin carried below; but he gave strict orders that it should be safely stored and reserved for the purpose for which its brave and worthy donor had designed it.

JOHN CAMPBELL (1708–1775).
From "Lives of the British Admirals".

*

JUDGMENT ON A BIGAMIST

Prisoner at the bar, you have been convicted before me of what the law regards as a very grave and serious offence, that of going through the marriage ceremony a second time while your wife was still alive. You plead in mitigation of your conduct that she was given to dissipation and drunkenness, that she proved herself a curse to your household while she remained mistress of it, and that she had latterly deserted you; but I am not permitted to recognize any such plea.

You had entered into a solemn engagement to take her "for better, for worse", and if you got infinitely more of the latter, as you appear to have done, it was your duty patiently to submit. You say you took another person to be your wife because you were left with several young children, who required the care and protection of some one who might act as a substitute for the parent who had deserted them; but the law makes no allowances for bigamists with large families. Had you taken the other female to live with you as your concubine you would never have been interfered with by the law. But your crime consists in having—to use your own language— preferred to make an honest woman of her.

Another of your irrational excuses is that your wife had committed adultery, and so you thought you were relieved from treating her with any further consideration; but you were mistaken. The law in its wisdom points out a means by which you might rid yourself from further association with a woman who had dishonoured you; but you did not think proper to adopt it.

I will tell you what that process is. You ought first to have brought an action against your wife's seducer if you could discover him; that might have cost you money, and you say you are a poor working man, but that is not the fault of the law. You would then be obliged to prove by evidence your wife's criminality in a court of justice, and thus obtain a verdict with damages against the defendant, who was not unlikely to turn out to be a pauper. But so jealous is the law (which you ought to be aware is the perfection of reason) of the sanctity of the marriage tie, that in accomplishing all this you would only have fulfilled the lighter portions of your duty.

You must then have gone, with your verdict in your hand, and petitioned the House of Lords for a divorce. It would cost you perhaps five or six hundred pounds, and you do not seem to be worth as many pence. But it is the boast of the law that it is impartial, and makes no difference between the rich and the poor. The wealthiest man in the kingdom would have had to pay no less than that sum for the same luxury; so that you would have no reason to complain. You would, of course, have to prove your case over again, and at the end of a year, or possibly two, you might obtain a decree which would enable you legally to do what you have thought proper to do without it.

You have thus wilfully rejected the boon the legislature offered you, and it is my duty to pass upon you such sentence as I think your offence deserves, and that sentence is, that you be imprisoned for one day, and inasmuch as the present

Assize is three days old the result is that you will be immediately discharged.

MR. JUSTICE MAULE (1788–1858).

[This judgment was largely instrumental in securing a reform of the Divorce Laws in 1857.]

*

A GOLDEN MEMORY

Again and again recurs to me the memory of one particular "long journey" in my first summer at Oxford, when we went below Sandford lock, beyond Nuneham Courtney; then got out of the boat, moored it to the bank, and sprawled in the sunshine among the grass and buttercups of a meadow that ran down to the water's edge. The coach and the captain, hugging their knees, conferred apart in low tones: the coach's horse cropped away contentedly at the grass: number three, to the admiration of the rest of us, rehearsed his one social accomplishment of walking on his hands. Nothing in all this, except the beauty of the place, the perfection of the weather, and our own feelings: it was but a few minutes before we got into the shell again, turned it round, and began to paddle homewards: but the memory of it has come back to me a thousand times.

E. C. BENTLEY (1875–   ).
From "Those Days".

*

BE TO HIS FAULTS A LITTLE KIND

You live in a time which hath rendered some kind of frailties so habitual that they lay claim to large grains of allowance. The world in this is somewhat unequal and our sex seemeth to play the tyrant in distinguishing partially for ourselves by making that in the utmost degree criminal in the woman which in a man passeth under a much gentler censure. The root and the excuse of this injustice is the preservation of families from any mixture which may bring a blemish to them, and whilst the point of honour continues to be so placed, it seems unavoidable to give your sex the greater share of the penalty. . . .

Next to the danger of *committing* the fault yourself the greatest is that of *seeing* it in your husband. Do not seem to look or hear that way. If he is a man of sense he will reclaim himself: the folly of it is of itself sufficient to cure him: if he is not so, he will be provoked but not reformed. To expostulate in these cases looketh like declaring war and preparing reprisals, which to a thinking husband would be a dangerous reflexion. Besides, it is so coarse a reason which will be assigned for a lady's too great warmth upon such an occasion that modesty no less than prudence ought to restrain her, since such an indecent complaint makes a wife much more ridiculous than the injury that provoketh her to it. But it is yet worse and more unskilful to blaze it in the world, expecting it should rise up in arms to take her part: she will find it can have no other effect than that she will be served up in all companies as the reigning jest.

Be assured that in these cases your discretion and silence will be the most prevailing reproof. An affected ignorance, which is seldom a virtue, is a great one here, and when your husband seeth how unwilling you are to be uneasie there is no stronger argument to persuade him not to be unjust to you. Besides, it will naturally make him more yielding in other things. . . . There is nothing so glorious to a wife as a victory so gained. A man so reclaimed is for ever after subjected to her virtue: and her bearing for a time is more than rewarded by a triumph that will continue as long as her life.

GEORGE SAVILE, MARQUIS OF HALIFAX,

(1633–1695).

*

THE TUMULUS ON THE DOWNS

Sweetly the summer air came up to the tumulus, the grass sighed softly, the butterflies went by, sometimes alighting on the green dome. Two thousand years. Summer after summer the blue butterflies had visited the mound, the thyme had flowered, the wind sighed in the grass. The azure morning had spread its arms over the low tomb: the full glowing moon burned on it: the purple of sunset rosied the sward. Stars, ruddy

441

in the vapour of the southern horizon, beamed at midnight through the mystic summer night, which is dusky and yet full of light. White mists swept up and hid it: dews rested on the turf: tender harebells drooped: the wings of the finches fanned the air; finches whose colours faded from the wings how many centuries ago! Brown autumn dwelt in the woods beneath: the rime of winter whitened the beech clump on the ridge: again the buds came on the wind-blown hawthorn bushes, and in the evening the proud constellation of Orion covered the east.

Two thousand times. Two thousand times the woods grew green and ring-doves built their nests. Day and night for two thousand years—light and shadow sweeping over the mound—two thousand years of labour by day and sleep by night. Mystery gleaming in the stars, pouring down in the sunshine, speaking in the night, the wonder of the sun and of far space, for twenty centuries round about this low and green grown dome. Yet all that mystery and wonder is nothing to the Thought that lies therein, to the spirit that I feel so close.

Realising that spirit, recognising my own inner consciousness—the psyche—so clearly, I cannot understand time. It is eternity now; I am in the midst of it. It is about me in the sunshine: I am in it, as the butterfly floats in the light-laden air. Nothing has to come: it is now. Now is eternity: now is the immortal life. Here this moment, by this tumulus, on earth, now: I exist in it. The years, the centuries, the cycles are absolutely nothing: it is only a moment since this tumulus was raised: in a thousand years more it will still be only a moment. To the soul there is no past and no future: all is and will be ever, in now. For artificial purposes time is mutually agreed on; but there is really no such thing. The shadow goes on upon the dial; the index moves round upon the clock, and what is the difference? None whatever. If the clock had never been set going, what would have been the difference? There may be time for the clock, the clock may make time for itself, there is none for me.

RICHARD JEFFERIES.

From "The Story of My Heart" (1883).

*

NOBLE VICTORIAN HEADS

It was a good rule of Thomas Carlyle to set a portrait of the man whom he was describing in front of him on his writing table. It was a practice which would greatly diminish the output of literary impertinence.

Let those who are disposed to follow the present evil fashion of disparaging the great Victorians make a collection of their heads in photographs or engravings and compare them with those of their own favourites. Let them set up in a row good portraits of Tennyson, Charles Darwin, Gladstone, Manning, Newman, Martineau, Lord

Lawrence, Burne-Jones and, if they like, a dozen lesser luminaries, and ask themselves candidly whether men of this stature are any longer among us. I will not speculate on the causes which from time to time throw up a large number of great men in a single generation. I will only ask you to agree with me that since the golden age of Greece (assuming that we can trust the portrait busts of the famous Greeks) no age can boast so many magnificent types of the human countenance as the reign of Queen Victoria. We, perhaps, being epigoni ourselves, are more at home among our fellow pygmies. Let us agree with Ovid, if we will,

> *Prisca juvent alios: ego me nunc denique natum*
> *Gratulor: haec ætas moribus apta meis.*

But let us have the decency to uncover before the great men of the last century: and if we cannot appreciate them, let us reflect that the fault may possibly be in ourselves.

DEAN INGE (1860–   ).
From "Outspoken Essays".

*

FULL SAIL AT NIGHT

One night, while we were in the tropics, I went out to the end of the flying-jib-boom, upon some duty, and, having finished it, turned round, and lay over the boom for a long time, admiring the beauty of the sight before me. Being so far out from the deck, I could look at the ship, as at a separate vessel—and there rose up from the water, supported only by the small black hull. a pyramid of canvas, spreading out far beyond the hull, and towering up almost, as it seemed in the indistinct night air, to the clouds.

The sea was as still as an inland lake; the light trade wind was gently and steadily breathing from astern; the dark blue sky was studded with the tropical stars; there was no sound but the rippling of the water under the stern; and the sails were spread out, wide and high; the two lower studding-sails stretching, on each side, far beyond the deck; the top-mast studding-sails, like wings to the top-sails; the top-gallant studding-sails spreading fearlessly out above them; still higher, the two royal studding-sails, looking like two kites flying from the same string; and highest of all, the little sky-sail, the apex of the pyramid, seeming actually to touch the stars, and to be out of reach of human hand. So quiet, too, was the sea, and so steady the breeze, that if these sails had been sculptured marble, they could not have been more motionless. Not a ripple upon the surface of the canvas; not even a quivering of the extreme edges of the sail—so perfectly were they distended by the breeze.

I was so lost in the sight, that I forgot the presence of the man who came out with me, until he said (for he too, rough old man-of-war's-man as he was, had been gazing at the show), half to himself, still looking at the marble sails—"How quietly they do their work!"

R. H. DANA.

From "Two Years before the Mast".

*

A COLLOQUY WITH DEATH

"Do you wish to send for a priest; there is still time? They always send for a priest when they see me coming."

"It is no use sending for the priest, he can do nothing for me now. It is too late for me to repent and too early for him to condemn, and I suppose it matters little to you either way."

"I do not care; good men or bad men are all the same to me."

". . . I repent little I have done. I retract nothing. I have lived according to my instinct and I believe my instinct was sound. I have made a fool of myself often enough when I tried to be guided by my reason. It was because my reason was at fault, and I have already been punished for it. I wish to thank those who have been kind to me. . . . I wish to ask forgiveness from those to whom I have given pain. That is all, the rest concerns God and myself, not the priest whom I do not accept as my judge."

"I do not like your priests. It is they who have taught men to fear my approach with their menace of eternity and their flaming hell. It is they who have torn the wings from my shoulders and disfigured my friendly face and turned me into a hideous skeleton to wander from house to house, scythe in hand, like a thief in the night and to dance their *danse macabre* in the frescoes on their cloister walls, hand in hand with their saints and their damned. I have nothing to do either with their heaven or with their hell. I am a Natural Law."

"I heard a golden oriole sing in the garden yesterday and just as the sun went down, a little warbler came and sang to me under the window; shall I ever hear him again?"

"Where there are angels there are birds."

"I wish a friendly voice could read the 'Phaedo' to me once more."

"The voice was mortal, the words are immortal. You shall hear them again."

"Shall I ever hear again the sounds of Mozart's Requiem, my beloved Schubert, and the titan chords of Beethoven?"

"It was only an echo from Heaven you overheard."

"I am ready. Strike, friend!"

"I am not going to strike. I am going to put you to sleep."

"Shall I awake?"

No answer came to my question.

"Shall I dream?"

"Yes, it is all a dream."

*   *   *   *   *

"Who are you, beautiful boy? Are you Hypnos, the Angel of Sleep?"

He stood there close by my side with flower-crowned locks and dream-heavy forehead, beautiful as the Genius of Love.

"I am his brother, born of the same Mother, Night. Thanatos is my name. I am the Angel of Death. It is thy life that is flickering out in the light of the torch I tread under my foot."

AXEL MÜNTHE.

From "The Story of San Michele".

*

THE DEATH OF OLD JOLYON

With his lunch they brought him a telegram, running thus: "Your letter received. Coming down this afternoon. Will be with you at four-thirty. Irene."

. . . Coming down! His heart beat fast and then did not seem to beat at all. At three o'clock he got up and dressed deliberately, noiselessly. He opened his door cautiously and went downstairs. In the hall the dog Balthasar lay solitary and followed by him old Jolyon passed into his study and out into the burning afternoon.

He meant to go down and meet her in the coppice, but felt at once he could not manage that in this heat. He sat down instead under the oak tree by the swing and the dog Balthasar, who also felt the heat, lay down beside him. He sat there smiling. What a revel of bright minutes!

What a hum of insects and cooing pigeons! It was the quintessence of a summer day. Lovely! And he was happy—happy as a sand boy, whatever that might be. She was coming: she had not given him up. He had everything in life he wanted—except a little more breath and less weight—just here.

He would see her, when she emerged from the farmery, come swaying just a little, a violet grey figure passing over the daisies and dandelions and "soldiers" on the lawn, the soldiers with their flowery crowns. He would not move, but she would come up to him and say "Dear Uncle Jolyon" and sit in the swing and let him look at her and tell her that he had not been very well, but was all right now: and that dog would lick her hand. That dog knew his master was fond of her: that dog was a good dog.

It was quite shady under the tree: the sun could not get at him, only make the rest of the world bright so that he could see the Grand Stand at Epsom away out there, very far, and the cows cropping the clover in the field and swishing at the flies with their tails.

He smelled the scent of limes and lavender. Ah! that was why there was such a racket of bees. They were excited—busy, as his heart was busy and excited. Drowsy, too, drowsy and drugged on honey and happiness: as his heart was drugged and drowsy. Summer—summer—they seemed saying: great bees and little bees and the flies too!

The stable clock struck four: in half an hour she would be here. He would have just one little nap, because he had had so little sleep of late: and then he would be fresh for her, fresh for youth and beauty, coming towards him across the sunlit lawn—lady in grey. And settling back in his chair he closed his eyes.

Some thistledown came on what little air there was and pitched on his moustache more white than itself. He did not know: but his breathing stirred it, caught there. A ray of sunlight struck through and lodged on his boot. A bumble-bee alighted and strolled on the crown of his Panama hat. And the delicious surge of slumber reached the brain beneath that hat and the head swayed forward and rested on his breast. Summer—summer! So went the hum.

The stable clock struck the quarter past. The dog Balthasar stretched and looked up at his master. The thistledown no longer moved. The dog placed his chin over the sunlit foot. It did not stir. The dog withdrew his chin quickly, rose, and leaped on old Jolyan's lap, looked in his face, whined: then, leaping down, sat on his haunches, gazing up And suddenly he uttered a long, long howl. But the thistledown was still as death, and the face of his old master.

Summer—summer—summer! The soundless footsteps on the grass——

JOHN GALSWORTHY (1867–1933).
From "Indian Summer of a Forsyte".

Index of Subjects

A. J. Balfour (Lord Balfour) .   *Lord Tweedsmuir*   177
Act lively: neglect no means .   *O. Cromwell*   59
Agnostic to Broad Churchman .   *T. H. Huxley*   129
Almost "an odd incident" .   *Archbishop Davidson*   187
Always the Open Door .   *Epictetus*   292
Anne Hyde, Duchess of York .   *John Evelyn*   86
Any excuse for not attending Church . *Dean Swift*   123
" Any one of nine daughters, but preferably Jane "
           I. Walton   381
As at a Banquet .   .   *Epictetus*   291
Atlantic Meeting, The .   *W. S. Churchill*   44
At the Burial of George II .   *H. Walpole*   343
At the Prince of Wales' Wedding . *S. Wilberforce*   412

Bad Habit of Persecution, The .   *Lord Acton*   139
Be to his faults a little kind . *1st Marquis of Halifax*   440
Betty .   *Hon. G. Grantley-Berkeley*   231
Bird with the White Breast, The . *James Howell*   339
Birthday Party at the Macreadys', A   *Jane Carlyle*   106
Bolingbroke's tribute to his wife . *Lord Bolingbroke*   90
Boswell and Voltaire Talk Religion   *James Boswell*   128
Budding Lord Chancellors at Play   *E. C. Bentley*   187
Burial in the Abbey .   .   *Dr. Bell*   365
Burne-Jones at Browning's Burial . *E. Burne-Jones*   329

Captain Wentworth renews his Suit   *Jane Austen*   385
Carlyle entreats Jane Welsh to make up her mind
           T. Carlyle   376
Casement Opens in Lothbury, A .   *D. Defoe*   342
Cato's Last Soliloquy .   .   .   *Seneca*   297
Change is the Law of Life .   *J. Martineau*   287
Character Sketch, A .   .   *Margot Asquith*   109

451

INDEX OF SUBJECTS

Charles Darwin's Self-Analysis	.	C. Darwin	171
Chateaubriand . . .	.	. V. Hugo	334
Christianity Will Find a Way	.	W. E. Gladstone	135
Cob-man at Waterloo, The .	.	R. B. Haydon	72
Coleridge's Addiction to Opium	.	S. T. Coleridge	303
Colloquy with Death, A .	.	Axel Münthe	446
Complete Gamester, The .	.	James Rice	189
Corrupt Lord Chancellor, A .	.	—	185
Cost of the First Battle of Ypres, The			
	Official History of the Great War		82
Counterblast to Tobacco, A .	.	F. Harrison	331
Court Marriage, A .	.	. —	337

David Hume's Dialogue with Charon	.	D. Hume	308
Death of King Harold, The .	Wace the Norman	54
Death of Lord Beaconsfield, The	.	Lord Rowton	173
Death of Old Jolyon, The .	.	J. Galsworthy	448
Death without Trappings .	.	Jeremy Taylor	293
Delights of the Temple, The	.	A. Trollope	361
Dervishes at Omdurman, The	.	G. W. Steevens	77
"Devil" in Lord Brougham, The	.	W. Bagehot	160
Dickens at Doncaster .	.	. J. Forster	319
Dinner at Blackwall, A .	.	. T. Walker	354
Dome of St. Paul's, The .	.	H. L. Paget	363
Dorothy wants a plain gold ring	. Dorothy Osborne	88
Dr. Donne's Memorial in St. Paul's	. I. Walton	340
Dr. Johnson Reflects . .	.	Dr. Johnson	127
Dramatic Critic of the Old School, A	Clement Scott	357

Empress of Fashion, An .	.	Horace Walpole	93
England compared to a Ship of War	. G. Canning	23
Evangelical Asceticism .	Lionel Tollemache	148
"Everyone Calls him Papa" .	.	Catherine Talbot	302
Evolution of a Positivist, The	.	F. Harrison	133

F. E. Smith (Earl of Birkenhead)	Lord Tweedsmuir	179
Faded Beauty, The .	.	Hazlitt and Northcote	96

Famous Leicestershire Whig, A	*W. Gardiner*	154
Fatal Duel in Hyde Park, A	*H. Walpole*	344
Fighting-man and Saint	*Lord Fisher*	79
First great English Soldier, The	*Sir John Fortescue*	55
First Night at the Lyceum, A	*C. Scott*	358
Five Bad Prophecies	—	410
Four Essential Freedoms	*F. D. Roosevelt*	46
Full Sail at Night	*R. H. Dana*	444
Gambler's Daughter, A	*Mary Russell Mitford*	103
Gentlemen at Play	*P. Egan*	348
"Glorified, beautified, yet still real"	*Creighton*	379
Glorious Sunshiny Day, A	*E. FitzGerald*	328
Glory that was Greece, The	*E. Renan*	404
Gods Don't Care, The	*Ennius*	296
Golden Memory, A	*E. C. Bentley*	439
Gracious Service of Moss, The	*J. Ruskin*	227
Happy Man, The	*Jeremy Taylor*	268
"Harry" Cust	*Sir Ronald Storrs*	181
Hazlitt's Infatuation	*Bryan W. Procter*	313
Heart of City Life, The	*C. Bronte*	353
Henry the Ninth of England	*Frances W. Wynn*	410
"I cannot Breathe without You"	*J. Keats*	370
Important Visitors at Dropmore	*Frances William Wynn*	157
"In a Garret in Exeter Street"	*A. Murphy*	347
In a Library	*Alex. Smith*	406
In Berkeley Square	—	365
In the Charterhouse Garden	*H. L. Paget*	364
Inattention at Prayer	*Dr. Donne*	121
Inimitable Mrs. Jordan	*Leigh Hunt*	111
Intervention often necessary	*W. E. Gladstone*	31
Invoking the Angels	*John Lilly*	402
Irish Soldier, The	*Lalor Sheil*	73
Ivory Tower, The	*L. P. Smith*	275

Journeying Moon, The	.	Coleridge	404
Judgment on a Bigamist	.	Mr. Justice Maule	436
Keep your Distempers to Yourself	.	Emerson	396
King Arthur's Last Fight	.	Sir T. Malory	52
Lady Holland in Petulant Mood	.	Thomas Creevey	98
Lane in its Beauty, The	.	Mary R. Mitford	220
Laying the matter before the Lord	.	E. Gosse	144
Leigh Hunt in the Marshalsea	.	Leigh Hunt	350
Leigh Hunt's Mother	.	Leigh Hunt	101
"Let it Roll!"	.	W. S. Churchill	39
Life a Dream we wake from	William de Morgan		289
"Linquenda tellus et domus"	.	Rich. Baxter	292
Little Marjorie Fleming	.	John Brown	97
London Bread in 1750	.	T. Smollett	346
London Fog, A	.	C. Dickens	356
Lord Chief Justice Saunders	.	Roger North	183
Lord Clarendon on Lord Derby	.	S. Wilberforce	162
Lord D'Abernon at Berlin	R. H. Bruce Lockhart		175
Lord Melbourne on Marriage	.	Lord Melbourne	417
Lord Palmerston at Home			
	From "Fraser's Magazine"		162
Love Finds a Way	.		379
Love of Trees, The	.	Alexander Smith	225
Macaulay as a Book Buyer	.	Salkeld	316
Macaulay's Love of Trinity	.	G. O. Trevelyan	317
Magna est Veritas	.	John Milton	269
Majority of One for Reform, A	.	Macaulay	428
Manœuvring with Cherry-stones	R. C. Cumberland		63
Marlborough's Last Days	.	W. S. Churchill	60
Maxims of Lord Fisher	.	Lord Fisher	81
Mddle. Georges	.	Arsène Houssaye	112
Mediocrity was his Merit, His	.	Lord Acton	159
Men and Women in Love	.	Axel Münthe	282
Men that fought at Minden, The	.	T. Bewick	62

Mésalliances during the Forty-Five	*Earl of Egmont*	417
Miss Jenkyns . . .	*Mrs. Gaskell*	105
Miss Julia Dyaway Waltzing	*From "Blackwood"*	100
Mr. Casaubon Proposes .	*G. Eliot*	389
Mr. Collins Proposes to Elizabeth	*Jane Austen*	393
Mr. Jorrocks is Lost . .	*R. Surtees*	196
Mr. Toots contrives to say it .	*C. Dickens*	391
Mr. Walker "Determines to be Well " .	*T. Walker*	192
Mrs. Delany . . .	*Dr. Delany*	107
Mrs. James Analyses Amelia	*Henry Fielding*	95
Mud at Agincourt, The . .	*Michelet*	56
Name and Dignity of De Vere, The	*Crewe, C. J.*	400
Napoleon to the Countess Walewska	*N.*	369
Nature of Religion, The . .	*Whichcote*	124
Nelson uses his Blind Eye .	*John Campbell*	71
Nelson's Three Right Arms .	*S. T. Coleridge*	69
Nelson's Unused Coffin .	*J. Campbell*	435
No Refuge in Littleness .	*G. Canning*	24
Noble Victorian Heads .	*Dean Inge*	443
Not one jot of England's Honour .	*Lord Nelson*	22
Nothing Like Fresh Air .	*R. Jefferies*	224
" Nothing to Regret in the Going "	*G. Meredith*	295
Of one mind on great issues .	*Sir E. Grigg*	47
Old Loves are Best . .	*Dr. Johnson*	278
Oliver dies in a great storm .	*T. Carlyle*	152
On the Transports from the Peninsula		
	Rifleman Harris	65
Only Nucleus for Democracy, The	*Lord Lothian*	49
" Our Solid Stubborn Strength " .	*W. S. Churchill*	42
Owl's Fatal Fascination, The .	*G. A. B. Dewar*	229
Peaceful Court in Trinity, A .	*J. G. Frazer*	329
People Blessed by God, A .	*O. Cromwell*	21
Perseverance Matters Most .	*Baron von Hügel*	143
Philosopher's Bagatelle, A .	*Franklin*	429

Philosophy of Force, The . . *F. D. Roosevelt* 45
Pigeons at the British Museum, The *R. Jefferies* 414
Poe's First Letter to Helen . . *E. A. Poe* 373
Poet Welcomes Death, A . *Hallam, Lord Tennyson* 332
Pope's affection for his mother . *Alexander Pope* 91
Portrait of Cobbett, A . . . *W. Hazlitt* 310
Priceless Possession of Laughter, The . *Sully* 285
Priest of Aricia, The . . . *J. G. Frazer* 141
Pulse like a Cannon, A . . *R. W. Emerson* 28

Ready for Either Fate . . *William de Morgan* 288
Real and nominal Creeds . *Herbert Spencer* 147
Real Golden Moments, The . *G. E. Montague* 276
Real Problem in Education, The *Sir R. Livingstone* 413
Recipes for Old Age . . . — 399
Renan and Sabatier . . . *H. A. L. Fisher* 138
Renan Desires a Calm and Sudden Death *E. Renan* 293
Renan Exhorts Nature to Persevere . *E. Renan* 270
Revisiting the Old School . . *I. Walton* 267
Ripeness and Fulness of Age, The . *L. P. Smith* 285
Rose and the Lark, The . *Jeremy Taylor* 219

Saint at Whitehall, A . . . *John Evelyn* 87
Sala and his Critics . . . *G. A. Sala* 324
Saloop . . . . . *C. Lamb* 352
Sarah Bernhardt to Victorien Sardou *S. Bernhardt* 380
Sceptic on "Artificial Theology", A *Lord Bolingbroke* 126
Scholar's Devotion to his Books, A *Mrs. Pattison* 319
Second Sir Roger, A . . . *R. Cumberland* 153
Seek God within thy own Soul . *John Smith* 122
"Shall it be a Succession?" . . *J. Amory* 395
Sharp Spikes where Flowers were . *G. Meredith* 290
Shelley's Funeral Pyre . . *Leigh Hunt* 305
Shepherd of the Wiltshire Downs, A *W. H. Hudson* 221
Shewing the Family Portraits . *Sir R. Steele* 415
Slipping into Accidie . . *Francis Paget* 136
Sole Survivor of an Army . . *J. Kaye* 75

INDEX OF SUBJECTS

Some Rules of Life . . . *M. Aurelius* 291
Sir C. Grandison begs "An Early Day"
          S. Richardson 383
Sir Gervase Clifton . . . *Dr. Thoroton* 151
Sir Pitt Crawley Proposes to Becky . *Thackeray* 387
Sir Ralph Abercromby . . . *John Brown* 64
Sir Richard Burton's odd Foibles . *Lady Burton* 326
Sir Tatton Sykes of Sledmere . *H. H. Dixon* 167
Spirit of a Faith, The . . . *Lord Acton* 131
Stars Proclaim Mankind's Deliverance, The
          W. S. Churchill 39
Stonewall Jackson . . . *Col. Henderson* 76
Story of a Blind old Pauper, A . *H. H. Dixon* 193
Strict Limits of Drinking, The . *Sir T. Browne* 432
Survival by Merit . . . *J. A. Froude* 426
Swinburne Recites Poetry . . *W. H. Mallock* 322
System or the Individual, The . *Lord Halifax* 280

Table Pleasures . . . . — 433
"Tell me you love me" . . *Laura Lyttelton* 108
Thackeray's Religious Feeling . *John Brown* 132
"That old Mahometan Blackguard" *C. E. Norton* 315
"Then fare thee well, Fanny"
          Frances Williams Wynne 99
Theological "Preamble", A . *Cardinal Newman* 146
"There is Death in that Hand" . *S. T. Coleridge* 302
Third and Last Marquis of Hastings, The
          H. H. Dixon 190
Thurlow retorts on the Duke of Grafton
          Lord Campbell 156
Time to Drink Port, The . . *M. Healy* 431
Tired Scientist cannot Concentrate, A *M. Faraday* 373
To avenge their dead Admiral . *S. Pepys* 59
To the last man and the last guinea *Sir W. Scott* 27
Told at the Cottage Door . . *W. H. Hudson* 222
Treasure Hunting in the Abbey . *W. Lilly* 338
Tumulus on the Downs, The . *R. Jefferies* 441

INDEX OF SUBJECTS

Two Naked Alternatives	.	.	*Lord Lothian*	35
Two Sisters, The	.	.	*Charlotte Brontë*	104
Two Wild Geese	.	.	*W. H. Hudson*	228
Under a Despotism	.	.	*W. S. Landor*	28
Up to their ankles in cards	.	*Fraser's Magazine*	409
Value of the Study of History, The	*Dr. Creighton*	279
Victorian Sportsman, A	.	.	*Francis Lawley*	165
Walpole's Dislike of Johnson	.	*H. Walpole*	306
Wanted, a Native Civilisation	.	.	*Dean Inge*	283
When Free Peoples Crouch	.	.	*Lord Bolingbroke*	21
When Religion is our Ruling Temper	*William Law*	125
Whirlpool at Old London Bridge, The	*G. Borrow*	360
Wise Bishop's Aphorisms, A	.	*Dr. Creighton*	277
Woman in White, A	.	*From "The Spectator"*	113
Women Storm the House of Lords				
		Lady Mary Wortley-Montagu	92
Words fail Roderick Random	.	*T. Smollett*	384
Written as with a Sunbeam	.	*Lord Acton*	32
"You are always new"	.	.	*J. Keats*	371
Youthful Burns, The	.	.	*R. Burns*	311

Index of First Lines

Ah Ben! Say how, or when . .	*Herrick*	300
An acre of land between the shore and the hills		
	Thomas	214
And she forgot the stars, the moon, and sun	*Keats*	248
And slowly answered Arthur from the barge		
	Tennyson	254
Around, around, flew each sweet sound	*Coleridge*	249
As some lone bird, without a mate .	*Shelley*	247
As the bee through the garden ranges	*Emerson*	119
At Runnymede, at Runnymede .	*R. Kipling*	33
At secret daybreak they had met .	*W. de la Mare*	206
At the last, tenderly . .	*W. Whitman*	250
Before the beginning of years .	*Swinburne*	278
Be great in act as you have been in thought		
	Shakespeare	20
Below lies one whose name was traced in sand		
	D. Gray	298
Britain belted by the sea . .	*C. A. W.*	30
Christmas Eve, and twelve of the clock .	*Hardy*	261
Close up the casement, draw the blind .	*Hardy*	244
Cruel, but composed and bland .	*M. Arnold*	422
Deep silence round us spreading . .	*Anon*	253
Dost thou remember, soldier, old and hoary		
	Macleod	67
Every night and every morn .	*Blake*	243

Garlands upon his grave . . . *Longfellow* 169
Glory be to God for dappled things . *Hopkins* 204

Had'st thou but lived, though stripped of power
Sir Walter Scott 26
Here at the fountain's sliding foot . . *Marvel* 203
Here lies a Dove, and was the same . *Anon* 245
Here lie the bones of Robert Lowe . *Anon* 173
Here they went with smock and crook . *Blunden* 215
He that loves a rosy cheek . . *Carew* 237
How oft do they their silver bowers leave *Spenser* 83

I am the ancient Apple Queen . . *W. Morris* 215
I dreamed that, as I wandered by the way *Shelley* 201
If this be pride in one of ancient birth *Macnaughten* 174
I have been here before . . *D. G. Rossetti* 242
I have a life with Christ to live . . *Shairp* 121
I know a little garden close . . *W. Morris* 202
I know my soul hath power to know all things
Sir John Davies 233
I live, and yet methinks I do not breathe *Anon* 233
I look into my glass . . . *Hardy* 243
I love the fitful gust that shakes . *Clare* 207
I praised the earth, in beauty seen . *Heber* 117
Inland, within a hollow vale, I stood *Wordsworth* 36
Is the night chilly and dark? . . *Coleridge* 209
It is not Beauty I demand . . *Darley* 238
It must be so—Plato, thou reasonest well—
(from "Seneca.") . . *Dr. Bland* 297
I who the watcher of your ways have been
Mrs. Henry Cust 182

Like to the falling of a star . . *King* 234
London, thou art of townes . . *W. Dunbar* 336
Long night succeeds thy little day . *Peacock* 245
Love guards the roses of thy lips . *Lodge* 237

My friend, the things that do attain
                    H. Howard, Earl of Surrey   234
My heart is like a singing bird   .   . *C. Rossetti*   248
My soul, there is a country   .   .   *Vaughan*   116
My time, O ye Muses, was happily spent   *Byrom*   240
"Much may be said on both sides." Hark! I hear
                                        Canning   408
Music, when soft voices die   .   .   *Shelley*   249

No lovelier hills than thine have laid . *De la Mare* 200
Now I know that Spring will come again   *Thomas*   212

O Captain! my Captain! our fearful trip is done
                                    W. Whitman   164
Of all the birds that rove and sing   . *De la Mare* 205
Of those that died in Thermopylæ   . *A. Burrell*   51
    (from *Simonides*)
O my beloved Nymph! fair Dove .   .   *Cotton*   214
One feast, of holy days the crest .   . *Lowell*   120

Patting the crest of his well-managed steed
                                    "Pat-roclus"   351
Perhaps I may allow the Dean   .   .   *Swift*   300
Pitch thy behaviour low, thy projects high *Herbert* 266
Proud Maisie's in the wood .   .   .   *Scott*   257

Seated once by a brook, watching a child *E. Thomas* 211
Shall we, with temper spoiled   .   *M. Arnold*   273
So live that when thy summons comes to join
                                        Bryant   290
Stern daughter of the Voice of God   *Wordsworth*   251
Stop and consider! Life is but a day .   *Keats*   242
Strew on her roses, roses   .   .   *M. Arnold*   246

Tax not the royal saint with vain expense
                                    Wordsworth   253
The daffodils were fair to see   .   . *Ingelow*   205

The grateful heart for all things blesses . *Landor* 234
The lily has a smooth stalk . . *C. Rossetti* 204
The lowest trees have tops . . . *Anon* 266
The man was wild . . . . *Thomas* 218
The murmur of the mourning ghost . *S. Dobell* 258
There is a garden in her face . *H. Campion* 236
Therefore all seasons shall be sweet to thee
Coleridge 208
The sun descending in the west . . *Blake* 209
The wine of Love is music . . *J. Thomson* 247
The world's great age begins anew . *Shelley* 255
Those who were children yesterday *Herbert Asquith* 84
'Tis late and cold, stir up the fire . *Fletcher* 407
To dare boldly in a fair cause . . *Massinger* 58

Upon this leafy bush . . . *De la Mare* 206

Weary of myself and sick of asking *M. Arnold* 272
Well, people say this hollow track . *Barnes* 210
Were I as base as is the lowly plain . *Sylvester* 235
Were this impossible, I know full well *Leigh Hunt* 217
"What happened here?" said the Stranger
Herbert Asquith 259
What if some little pain the passage have
E. Spenser 286
When as the mildest month . . *Howell* 203
When one, whose nervous English verse
Lord Houghton 321
When to her lute Corinna sings . . *Campion* 236
When youthful faith hath fled . . *Lockhart* 250
Whoso hath felt the vision of the Highest
F. H. Myers 118
Why, who makes much of a miracle? *W. Whitman* 271

You that have faith to look with fearless eyes
Seaman 33